"John Schmid has be[en...] wisdom and connection with the Holy Spirit are nowhere more evident than in his writing."

- **John Carter Cash**

"As a songwriter, hearing from John Schmid that he had just used one of my songs at a prison concert and that the inmates were deeply moved by it is like winning a Grammy... only bigger! Annie and I initially met John Schmid several years ago through an Ohio prison inmate who recognized that we had much in common in regard to music. How grateful we are for that introduction! We have come to appreciate John's servant heart that is so well displayed in his devotion to his wife Lydia, to their family, and to his musical work that reaches out with compassion to all who hear, especially those who have lost their freedom. Now we are blessed that we get to learn even more about his life and ministry through his excellent book, *Encounters/In & Out of Prison with John Schmid*. We can promise that every chapter is a treasure trove of inspiration."

- **Steve & Annie Chapman**

"My friend John Schmid's *Encounters* takes you on a mesmerizing journey; the relationships and front line ministry stories are priceless. It would take 5 lifetimes for an ordinary man to accomplish the travels and experiences of Brother John, but this is a very special man of God who has been blessed, gifted, and anointed to do extraordinary work for the Lord. You will certainly enjoy Encounters; it's an exciting Kingdom Adventure!"

- **Jack "Murf the Surf" Murphy**
Director, Inmate Encounter Ministry
Ex-convict and Author of *Jewels for the Journey*

"Our friend and fellow musician John Schmid is a multi-talented man with a heart for the Lord and a heart for people. He faithfully uses his gifts to entertain and inspire crowds in all kinds of settings – prisons, churches, coffee shops, house concerts, and more. In his book *Encounters*, John tells stories of his life; stories of traveling the world, singing, and sharing the Gospel message of hope. We enjoyed reading Encounters and were thoroughly entertained, encouraged, and inspired! We were reminded that everyone can use their God-given gifts to be a good influence on others. Our friend John is making a difference in the world and we know you'll be blessed by his stories!"

- **Sharon White and Ricky Skaggs**

"I have known John Schmid for a long time and it is my great pleasure to highly recommend his book on his life's work of music and ministry. I've had the privilege over the years to do a number of his recordings; not only is he a great music entertainer, but he can leave you spellbound with his stories. It can be a family gathering, a business banquet, or a concert with hundreds; his message for Jesus Christ has never changed. He brings hope, laughter, and inspiration to hundreds of prison inmates as he shares his ministry in song. John's organization, Common Ground Ministries, has for years sponsored correspondence Bible studies for men and women in prison in the state of Ohio. What a great brother! You will find these stories very interesting and inspirational."

- **Marvin Beachy**
President of Gospel Echoes Team

"With wit and honesty, John Schmid provides story after poignant story of the people he ministers to in our nation's prisons. Some of the stories in *Encounters* are as warm as summer rain while others are as bracing as ice water. This is an exceptionally rich and varied collection that, besides the author's prison experiences, includes his friends and local acquaintances such as basketball star Freeman.

John Schmid understands and puts into practice Jesus' command, 'Inasmuch as ye have done it unto one of the least of these my brethren, ye have done it unto me.' I love this book."

- David Kline
Amish minister, farmer, author of *Scratching the Woodchuck* and *Great Possessions*

"John is a great storyteller and is a master at connecting with his audiences. From the man in the pew to the one who has never darkened the door of a church, John brings a relevant message. Drawing from history and current life/ministry events, this book gives you a front row seat to what God is doing through John and Common Ground Ministries."

- Glendon Bender
Serving with Gospel Echoes Team Prison Ministry since 1980

JOHN SCHMID

Encounters

IN & OUT OF PRISON WITH
JOHN SCHMID
2006 - 2016

JPV PRESS

Copyright © 2017 John Schmid

All rights reserved. No part of this publication may be reproduced, distributed, or transmitted in any form or by any means, including photocopying, recording, or other electronic or mechanical methods, without the prior written permission of the publisher, except in the case of brief quotations embodied in critical reviews and certain other noncommercial uses permitted by copyright law.

Printed in the United States of America

First Printing, 2017

ISBN 978-1-946389-03-9

JPV Press
2106 Main Street / PO Box 201
Winesburg, Ohio 44690

www.jpvpress.com

Dedication

This book is dedicated to Lydia, my faithful wife of 38 years, who endured (and even encouraged) my travels, notions, crazy ideas, and shares my love for Jesus and the desire to make Him known. Also to Adam, Amelia and Katie, my dear children, who were victims of all of the above and still love Jesus and me.

Table of Contents

FOREWORD
By: Steve Wingfield 15

Preface 19

2006
Time 23
Alcatraz 25
A Trip to Germany 27
He is Risen! 29
Israel 31
Ireland 34
Happiness and Security 36
What is Important? 38
Family Advice From Willie Nelson 40
Variety; the Spice of Life 42
As We Forgive... 44
Silent Night 46

2007
2006 in Review 49
The Power of a Song 53
Watoto Children's Ministry 56
Take-Away Value 58
It Happened in Nashville 60
New England Grad Trip 62
To the Third and Fourth Generation 64
I've Been to... Ireland 66
Message in a Bottle 68
One Person Can Make a Difference 70

2008

Happy New Year!	75
Bushnell, Florida	77
Don't Ask	79
Benjamin	81
April	84
Graduation Speech (and book?)	85
Thoughts on Freedom	87
CC's Gone	90
London Prison Freedom Rally	92
Bantry Christian Fellowship	93
Nicaragua	96
Merry Christmas!	99

2009

Happy New Year!	103
January, February, March	105
Africa, Florida (again), & Alabama	107
Angels, Success, Standards...	109
A Witness	112
Church on a Boat	114
Croquet, Motorcycles, Ricky Scaggs, Pat Boone, and Prison	116
Funerals and Small Stuff	118
Empty Nest	121
They're Listening	123
The Most Interesting Person in 20 Years?	126
Christmas 2009	128

2010

A Reunion	133
Prison Crusade	135
The Gates of Hell	137
A Fresh Look at Jesus	139
In His Service	143
Diversity	144
A Lesson From Alaska	146
Family Reunions	148
September	151
Pennyslvania Deutscher	153
The American Dream	155
Home For Christmas	157

2011

Happy New Year! 2011! ... 161
(Another) Divine Appointment ... 164
"...there were also other boats with Him..." ... 166
The Carter Fold! ... 168
Lorain Fisher Schmid ... 171
The World Didn't End ... 173
Give 'em Hope ... 175
Children in Prison ... 178
Parents of Prisoners ... 181
Parents of Good Kids ... 184
"News" Letter ... 187
Grapevine Faith Academy vs. Gainesville State Prison ... 189

2012

I Was in Prison ... 195
The Best Laid Plans ... 198
Cruise Control ... 201
Thoughts About Work ... 203
The Boundary Lines Have Fallen ... 205
Communication ... 207
Christmas in May? ... 209
A Wasted Life? ... 211
Prison Song ... 214
Finish Strong ... 216
God on the Mountain ... 219
Angels We Have Heard on High ... 221

2013

Another Year... ... 225
The Little Girl in the Picture ... 228
Of All the Things I've Lost... ... 231
Only One Life... ... 233
Fame and Greatness ... 236
A Song Will Jog a Memory ... 238
Biking for Bibles ... 241
God's Timing ... 244
The Big Ride ... 246
Show Up ... 248
Merry Christmas! ... 251

2014

January	253
Ice, Ice Baby!	256
Timothy's Gift	258
Pavoncito Prison, Guatemala	261
The Power of a Cookie	263
Generosity	265
Bicycle Tour!	268
More on Dr. Freeman Miller	271
Every Day is a Gift	273
A Song Can (begin to) Change a Heart	276
My Word... Shall Not Return to Me Void	279
Seeds That Grow	281

2015

2014 Summary	285
The Acts of an Apostle	287
Homer Schmid	290
April News	292
Here I Stand, I Can Do No Other	294
Spring Gleaning	297
Story of a Faithful Chaplain	300
A Firm Foundation	303
God's Timing is Perfect	306
We'll Understand it All By and By	309
Old Friends	311
Christmas 2015	314

2016

Happy New Year!	317
A Letter of...	319
Thoughts on Community	323
Thoughts on Education	326
A Redeemed Life	328
The Power of Prayer	330
Howard Gray	333
A Totally Committed Life	336
Little Boy Blue	339
I Come From a Long Line of Dead People	342
Good Tidings of Great Joy	345

ENCOUNTERS

Foreword

"I first met John Schmid in 1972 in Berlin, OH, at Berlin Mennonite Church; that's where our friendship began. John and Lydia had returned home from the mission field and Common Ground Ministries was born. He also started serving as a prison evangelist for Wingfield Ministries. John and I have had the privilege of ministering in many places, not only here in America, but around the world. I have so many fond memories of being with John that it would take another book to tell all those stories. I am sure a few of them will be included in this book.

I always enjoy receiving John's newsletter. Not only does it help me know how to pray for him and his ministry, but I always enjoy his stories. John is a great storyteller. I think he learned from the greatest storyteller that ever lived, Jesus. People can argue about lots of things, but they can't argue about your story because it's yours. I know each of the stories will not only be enjoyable to read, but they will bring encouragement and hope to your life, and each of the stories will honor our Savior.

Evangelists are a rare breed; maybe that's why I like John so much. We're both a little crazy, but I hope and believe we are both crazy in love with Jesus. Our hearts' desire is to see other people come to know Him and experience the joy that we have in following our Lord and Savior Jesus Christ.

So grab a cup of coffee or tea, find a comfortable chair, and enjoy this book. I hope you all enjoy it so much that you will buy copies and give them to your friends. As you read it, remember that there are other stories to be written. I hope you will be motivated to pray for and support my friend John Schmid. He's going where many people can't go, won't go, or are afraid to go, and God is using him to rescue the perishing and care for the dying."

"God has not lost his enthusiasm for the great commission."
- Theologian Carl FH Henry

Written by: Steve Wingfield
CEO and Evangelist of the Steve Wingfield Evangelistic Association & Victory Weekend

ENCOUNTERS

Preface

Country Music legend George Hamilton IV once approached Willie Nelson from behind, put his hands on Willie's shoulders, and began singing,

"I want a girl..."

and Willie finished the line,

> *"... just like the girl that married dear old dad."*

George said, "No, not that one! The one you wrote for me:

'I want a girl, whose heart has been broken by a love that has passed her by...' "

Willie turned around with eyebrows raised and an inquisitive look on his face. "Did I write that?!"

As I read through these monthly stories that I supposedly wrote, I find myself asking, "Did I write that?!" Some of the stories jog my memory, some take me right back to the place and time they happened, some I tell often from on stage or behind the pulpit (or at the coffee shop), and some I have to ask, "Did that really happen?" I'm rumored to have a good memory, but I'm beginning to wonder...

These stories remind me that maybe my life did make a difference. Isn't that what we want? To make a difference (for good) in someone's life? I think I started writing *stories* instead of *monthly reports* after reading the weekly blogs by good friend – and now New York Times bestseller – Ira Wagler. His stuff is easy to read. Why? They are real life stories. They really happened. And he wrote them well. And because of Ira, I now try to do that.

I hope you enjoy these true to life stories. That really happened. (That's another thing I learned from Ira. Incomplete sentences. Just like we talk.) They were written to inform, inspire, educate, spur, and help "our people" to not forget the work of Common Ground Ministries. We go to prisons, churches, camps, living rooms... wherever we are invited to sing and share. May God bless you as you read.

ENCOUNTERS

Time...

1949, 1967, 1980, 1985, 1987, 1989, 2005, 2006!

In December, we think about winter and Christmas and the end of the year. In January, we think about... *time*. The Bible tells me that I was allotted a certain amount of time the day I was born, and when that time is up, I will go home, where "time is no more." We are also admonished in the Bible to redeem the time, make good use of it, because the days are evil (Eph. 5:16). The modern seminars tell us to schedule every minute, because time is money and each of us has the same amount – 24 hours each day.

In the year 2005, and especially these last six weeks, I was reminded again of the brevity and uncertainty of life and how quickly things can change. On Nov. 20, my 26-year-old nephew was killed in a car accident, and two weeks later, my 90-year-old friend Ed Maxwell died. One was tragic and one was "normal," or at least Ed had lived "threescore and ten" years and then some. But even 90 years can seem like a short time when viewed from the perspective of eternity. On Christmas Day, my 81-year-old dad pulled up to our door to unload some presents, and then was going to pull back down the hill while it was still light. He didn't want to back down the hill in the dark. I did it for him, and then backed the car up the hill so he could leave in the dark going forward, but it made me think, how time changes! It seems like not long ago he was showing me how to drive a tractor, and then a car, and he was always the one in control – and now I am helping him. Two years ago my son Adam and I went for a jog and for the first time I not only didn't have to slow the pace for him, but I couldn't keep up. Time changes, roles reverse, and how quickly life moves on. It won't be long before Adam will move my car for me so I can leave in the dark. I learned several years ago that I wasn't bulletproof, and slowly I am realizing that I am no longer young. I am more and more grateful for good health, and more grateful for each day of life. I want to redeem the time, make every day count; to look back on each day and be able to say, "I did my best." If God blows the whistle today, I don't want to have to say, "Oh, if only I had done such and such yet..."

I am writing this the week between Christmas and New Year's and am hoping to use this time to review 2005 and evaluate my life and work. I then want to plan and visualize 2006 and see what I can do make my life and ministry count. And yes, I am even going to make some resolutions (plans). Dr. Dennis Kinlaw reminds us that we can look back at 2005 and see the undeserved goodness of God, and we can look forward with joyous anticipation because He is faithful! Friends, life is short and uncertain, time flies... Make every day count. Until the next *time*...

January - 2006

Alcatraz

In its day, no word was more feared among prisoners than the word, "Alcatraz." A mile and a half from San Francisco in the cold, swirling waters of the San Francisco Bay, it was a fortress prison known as "The Rock." It was usually cold and damp. The cells were never warm. It was America's first super-max prison. Escape was almost impossible. Not only was it an impenetrable physical structure, but also the tough warden and guards had never heard of prison reform. Infractions were dealt with by beatings, isolation, starvation, and extra-hard labor. Many men, including America's most famous criminal, Al Capone, went crazy there. Very little news ever got to the press from Alcatraz. These were America's incorrigibles, and the system would keep them safely away from the public. On top of all that, the view of San Francisco from The Rock was fantastic. Cars and trolleys could be seen moving in the streets, and if the wind and weather were just right, the prisoners could hear the voices and singing of people in the city, so there was a constant reminder of what their crimes had deprived them. That was almost as hard to bear as the beatings, according to several ex-cons.

Lydia and I had the privilege of visiting America's most famous prison. It's been closed since 1963. As we walked the corridors of the cell blocks on a self-guided walking tour, we viewed the cells of America's most wanted: Al Capone, Machine Gun Kelly, Robert Stroud (The Bird Man of Alcatraz), and Frank Morris, who escaped with two others through the ventilator and was never heard of again. From 1934 to 1963 Alcatraz housed the criminals who couldn't follow the rules elsewhere and were subjected to regimen meant to control their rebellious ways and crush their resistance. I was reminded that crime is not a modern phenomenon. Men schemed and plotted and killed and cut corners in the 1930's and '40s, just like they do today. Every society throughout history has had to deal with people who did not follow the rules. A sad commentary on the human race is that the first murder in history was committed by the first man ever born on planet earth. (Genesis 4:8)

Looking at it from a theological point of view, mankind has a major problem: sin. There is only one solution: Jesus. On earth we have prisons; in eternity there is a horrible place that the Bible calls Hell. As far as I'm concerned, a prison is a taste of hell, but even at a place like Alcatraz (some called it Hellcatraz), there was still hope, at least for the next life. I am more convinced and committed to bring the message of the gospel of Jesus to the least, the last, and the lost in prison (and anywhere else I am invited to sing or speak). If you are reading this, you are a part of this ministry. Thank you. (And if you get a chance, visit Alcatraz.)

SAN QUENTIN...ALMOST

One of the reasons we are in California is the opportunity I had to be a part of a chapel program at the famous San Quentin Prison. Everything was approved – for the wrong date! I called the chaplain and he was working on changing it when two days before the chapel service, a prisoner stabbed a guard and the whole prison went on lockdown – no movement, no outsiders, no nothing! Service cancelled. Even if he had scheduled the correct date from the beginning, it would have been cancelled. Ironically, I got the word from the chaplain while I was touring Alcatraz. Sometimes you're the windshield; sometimes you're the bug. (P.S. This whole trip is being paid for by Smucker's Harness Shop, Narvon, PA.)

February - 2006

A Trip To Germany

We visited daughter Amy at Bodenseehof Bible School in Friedrichshafen, Germany. I was favorably impressed with the spirit and the teaching of the school, which is also known as "Fackeltragers," or, Torchbearers. It is a British system of lectures and lots of reading. We attended a few lectures with Amy, took a few day trips (Salzburg, Austria; Neuschwanstein Castle), and also a five-day trip to visit friends I had met when I was there with the USO in the late '70's.

I discovered that my recording, *In Dutch,* is making the rounds in linguistic circles there, and also among musicians who are trying to preserve the Palatinate dialect. They are very interested in the fact that a group of people still speak a German dialect in America. I was invited to Dr. Michael Werner's house in Mainz (he is the editor of a Pennsylvania Dutch newspaper, *Hiwwa wie Driwwa*), to talk about Dutch songs and sing with Palatinate musicians Paul Reinig and Peter Braun. We stayed up way past my bedtime, singing and playing music. Their Pfalz dialect is very similar to Pennsylvania Dutch, so we understood each other very well.

I was interested in looking up my roots, but since I don't know the village where great-great grandfather Adam Schmid came from, it was like looking for a needle in a haystack, especially since Schmid (with its various spellings) is one of the three most common names in Germany. His obituary says he was born in Carbunda, Baden, Germany. The problem is, no one has ever heard of such a town. However, we did know where some of Lydia's ancestors came from, so we went to Langendorf and saw the ancestral home of her great-great-great Grandfather, Daniel Bender. The lady who showed us around invited us to stay at her home, the oldest house in town, built in 1632! We thanked her, but instead, we headed for Mengeringhausen, the village where the Gingerich ancestors were living when they left for America in 1833. Although we didn't know which house was theirs, we saw the mill where they worked and we also visited the Waldeck castle (nearby) where the Gingerichs and two Swartzentruber families farmed the Prince's royal farm until 1833.

The apostle Paul talks about "endless genealogies" and how futile they are, so I want to be careful not to go overboard on the subject. I am, however, grateful for the chance to see the land of my forefathers and to appreciate what they went through and the risk they took in crossing the ocean, back when 20% of the passengers died enroute. (Would you travel with an airline that advertised: "80% guarantee of arriving alive!"?) Many of our ancestors came here with only what they could carry, and some even less than that: some were sold as indentured servants (slaves) for seven years to pay their passage! What freedom and opportunity I have because of their dreams and courage! God has given me a "goodly heritage" and I want to honor Him by being faithful. We had a great trip! We saw several ancestors and one descendant.

UPDATE: I have learned that Adam Schmid came from Konigsbach, near Karlsruhe.

March - 2006

He is Risen!
HE IS RISEN INDEED!

April 16 is Easter. For the last several prison services in March, I have been ending with an Easter song and some comments about the resurrection of Jesus. The resurrection is undoubtedly the most significant event that ever happened on planet Earth! The Word became flesh and dwelt among us! Because Christ died in my place, I can have my sins forgiven. Because

He rose from the dead, I can have eternal life. I tell prisoners that because Jesus lived, died, and rose again from the dead, I have the audacity to come to a prison (or the First Church downtown, or a company banquet...) and confidently proclaim that Jesus Christ can change your life.

If the resurrection were not true, I would be pretty stupid to go to prison chapels when I could be home with my family and friends. In March, I missed my high school's appearance at the state basketball finals because of a chapel service, and because I was in prison, I couldn't go to the airport with my wife to pick up my daughter who was coming home after seven months in Germany. I have missed other events at home because of being in prison. I'm not complaining. I could have scheduled differently if I had been more alert. I could have canceled when the schedule at home changed. What I am trying to say is: because Jesus rose from the dead, and because He called me to do what I'm am doing, I can look the prisoners in the eye and tell them, "I'd rather be here than anywhere else in the world." The only thing I love more than going to prison chapels is... *leaving the prison!* I love to *leave* prisons! I love freedom, especially the freedom that comes through Jesus Christ. I will tell you the same thing I tell prisoners: because the Bible is true, and because Jesus is alive, I can say to anyone who reads this letter – "Jesus Christ can change your life!" He is risen! He is risen indeed!

PRAYER OF JABEZ AUTHOR AT KIDRON

Last week I had the privilege to be on the platform with Bruce Wilkinson, author of *The Prayer of Jabez*, at the P. Graham Dunn Dealer's Show. And even more significant for me, he is the founder of *Walk Through The Bible Ministries*. WTB is a two-day conference on the Bible. After I had graduated from seminary, I had the chance to be a part of a Walk Through The Bible weekend, and I couldn't believe how it made the Bible come alive for me; it put everything together! I had studied theology, philosophy, and homiletics, etc., for three years and I thought I had a pretty good grip on the scriptures, but Wilkinson's simple and fun memory method gave me a new handle on God's overall plan as outlined in the Bible. Last week he challenged us to be open to God's blessing. What a privilege and inspiration to get to know this servant of God and to sit under his teaching! Oh yes, and I also got to be with Peter and LeAnne Dunn, who left the next day for Bodenseehof, Germany, to visit his daughter – the one who talked our Amy into attending.

April - 2006

Israel

My daughter Amy and I were in Jerusalem last week when you should have been reading this newsletter, but I didn't get it written because I was in Jerusalem ☺. What a trip! We walked where Jesus walked. (Well, sometimes we ran where Jesus walked!)

Of all the amazing places and things that we saw, let me share a lesson I learned from the Western Wall and its builder, Herod the Great. It used to be called the "Wailing Wall" because Jews from all over the world would come to pray here at the only original part of the temple that survived the destruction of Jerusalem by Titus in AD 70. In their prayers, they would mourn the fact that Jerusalem fell and Israel was gone. Bystanders who heard their wails began to call it the Wailing Wall, but in 1948, when Israel became a country again after 1,878 years, the Jews began to call it the Western Wall. No more wailing.

Our group was able to enter and walk through the tunnel that was dug along the wall to the north. Archeologists were trying to see just how long the original wall was and how deep it went. They found that it is almost 1/4 mile long! I was fascinated. The foundation stones upon which the wall rests are 45 feet long, 11 feet high and 11 feet wide. Solid stone! Hundreds of them, each one larger than a Greyhound bus and weighing 628 tons! By comparison, the largest stone in the pyramids of Egypt weighs 50 tons. A shaft was dug to see how far down the base of this wall is, and it went down 70 feet before it hit bedrock! Herod the Great built this wall 60 feet high with these huge stones, somehow lifting them up and putting them in place without modern cranes and mechanical equipment! We saw a short movie that tried to explain how the stones were quarried and moved, but experts are still baffled as to how it was done.

The lesson I wanted to share is about two builders. Our guide pointed out that Herod the Great built at least six palaces, several fortresses, 9 Olympic sized swimming pools, roads, aqueducts, cities... He built the city of Caesarea on the Mediterranean, but it had no harbor, so he created a 40-acre harbor by making breakwater walls of cement, poured in water close to 100 feet deep! And this was 40 BC! There is evidence of his buildings all over Israel. We visited his amazing palace and the fortress of Masada near the Dead Sea, which was so formidable that 70 years after his death, about 1,000 Jewish zealots were able to hold off the powerful Roman 10th Legion (20,000 soldiers) for over 1-1/2 years before they fell.

Herod the Great was the greatest builder the Middle East has ever known. But as powerful and great as Herod was in his day, Ray Vander Laan asks: What do you remember about Herod? Answer: He killed the babies. He was cruel and ruthless. He murdered two of his own sons and two of his wives. A Roman emperor said it was better to be Herod's pig than his son.

By contrast, Jesus of Nazareth never built a physical structure. He never wrote a book. He died a criminal's death. And yet He is the one known as the Rock. Those who build their lives on Him are promised stability, joy, security, and eternal life. In fact, the Bible calls those who don't build their lives on Him, "fools."

I am still amazed at Herod's buildings. I can't believe how huge those stones are. I thought we knew something about building, because here in Amish country we can start building an 80' by 40' timber frame barn in the morning and be milking cows in it by 5:30 PM. But Herod's accomplishments blow me away.

But where is Herod today? Just 3 miles from his most elaborate palace in Herodium was a cave (stable) where a peasant family had a baby named Jesus. He challenged the people to follow Him. In Luke 21, even the disciples were smitten by the majesty of the building that Herod built. Jesus said, *"Follow Me."*

Here's the lesson: build your life on the Rock. Not the amazing rocks of this world (Herod, this world, job, fame, fortune...) but on Jesus. In AD 4000, if tourists are looking at the ruins of our society, they will be amazed, but the culture will be gone. Where will you be? If you built your life on things of this world, you will be where Herod is, but if Jesus is your Rock, you will be with Him. Forever! Life without end, Amen!

Build your life on Jesus!

May - 2006

Ireland

I am writing this from Belfast, Northern Ireland (June 8, 2006). We (daughter Katie and I) just returned from Dunfanaghy, County Donegal, which is in the North of the Republic of Ireland, and we are now in Northern Ireland. (It took a while for me to realize that Northern Ireland and Ireland are two different countries.) Ten of us were in the village of Dunfanaghy with missionaries Alan and Rosemary Armstrong, helping them to establish Bible studies in neighboring villages. On day one we walked through selected areas, distributing invitations for people to receive the Jesus film, the most viewed film in history. (Over 800 million people have viewed it.) The next day we went to the same houses to actually give them the film. They could view it over the weekend and we would be back on Monday to pick it up and ask what they thought of it. It was a way of making contacts for Alan and Rosemary. I didn't think we had much success (most people thought we were Jehovah Witnesses or some other cult), but last night (6/7/06) when we got home, we discovered that someone had left a phone message for the Armstrongs; "Thank you for the literature you left in my mail slot. I would like to talk to you about my spiritual life... " This was the first such call the Armstrongs have received in two years. Maybe something did happen.

The other method to make our presence known was through concerts. In the eight days we were there, I had seven concerts in various places – concert halls, community centers, churches, and a hotel. Tom and Noirin DeLasa, local residents and friends of the Armstrongs, helped to arrange several of the concerts. I discovered that knowing a lot of Johnny Cash songs is a free ticket to winning the hearts of the Irish people in this area. These were advertised as "Country Gospel" concerts, so I sang country songs and I soon learned that if I sing Cash songs, I can say whatever I want to about the gospel and they will listen. Larry Skrant was with us and each night after I sang a few prison songs and explained that I am a prison minister, he would give his testimony of being transformed from being a three-time convicted felon to an ordained minister and the founder of Changed Life Ministries. Hearts were touched as he gave credence to the message of the songs. The local missionaries were thrilled with the response and the contacts that were made. There was so much positive feedback that this morning when we filled up with gas (whoops! I mean "petrol") before we left Dunfanaghy, the owner of the station came out and wanted to tell me how much he enjoyed the concert last week. This is an area of beautiful people; an area that is religious but in need of an understanding of the true gospel. We already have an invitation to come back, with the promise that the concerts will be even fuller because of all the positive buzz. Pray for Donegal and the Armstrongs.

June - 2006

Happiness and Security

During the Wingfield Encounter Festival in Martinsburg, PA, last week, Power Team Member Jonathan Caldwell told us about the time he was a bodyguard for a famous rapper (singer). He was on the singer's private jet as they flew from his mansion on the East Coast to one of his mansions on the West Coast. During the flight, when the singer realized that Jonathon did not even know who he was, he let down his guard and turned to him to speak. He had several gold necklaces around his neck and a Rolex watch on his wrist. The value of the jewelry he had on was worth more than my house. He sighed as he looked at bodyguard Jonathon and said, "There's got to be more than this…"

Several years ago at a Bill Glass prison weekend, I had the privilege to be on stage with heavyweight boxer Ernie Shavers. He lost the Heavyweight Championship fight to Mohammad Ali, but Ali said that Shavers hit him so hard that it "shook me back to my ancestors in Africa." Ernie said that with all the friends, money, fame, and the physical fitness of a professional boxer, he of all people should have been secure, but he wasn't. He felt more insecure and fearful than he did when he was young and poor. It wasn't until he committed his life to Jesus Christ that he began to sleep all night and not worry about losing his possessions. "Now I am secure," he said.

I remember talking to a prisoner at Mansfield Prison who was holding a coffee cup as he told me of his privileged upbringing with maids and chauffeurs and possessions. He held up his coffee cup and said; "Now all I own is this coffee cup and the things in my foot locker, but for the first time in my life I am happy. I have shamed my family and lost my freedom and all of my possessions, but now I have Jesus. I'd rather have Jesus and nothing else than all the wealth and privilege without Him."

I think what I am trying to say is that as necessary as money and possessions are, they are limited in their ability to bring happiness and fulfillment. The world and its possessions can be very alluring. In fact, even in my own life, every time I think I have this in perspective I see that bumper sticker that says, "Lord, help me prove that winning the lottery wouldn't ruin me." It's just hard for someone in my economic position to believe that the *large life* is as empty as they say it is, but the truth is that only Jesus satisfies. There is no security in this world. Living is hazardous to your health. Life is risky. Our only security is Jesus. Ask the rapper, or Ernie Shavers, or the once-wealthy prisoner. They've been there, done that. Anne Graham Lotz says it best; "Just give me Jesus."

July - 2006

What is Important?

I had coffee last week with a school friend whom I hadn't seen in over thirty years. After telling each other that we hadn't changed a bit (right!) and how good we each looked, we talked about families and careers and what have you done in the last thirty years? When I asked why he wasn't a football coach like he wanted to be when we were young, he said, "Well, I guess I sold my soul to the company I was with. I have worked 10 to 12 hours a day ever since 1971." I asked him, "Did it pay?" I figured a man who worked that hard for so long would be rewarded by being financially secure. He answered, almost expressionless, "No, not at all. It didn't pay." Whether he meant it didn't pay financially or family-wise (he was divorced), or that it had derailed his original plans for his life, I don't know. He had a far-away look in his eyes which gave me the feeling that if he could do it over, he would be a teacher and a coach, which is what he really wanted to do.

FOUR DAYS LATER: I talked to a friend that I hadn't seen for 25 years. He had contacted me after hearing one of my CDs and was complimenting the songs and their message. He is a successful lawyer in a Midwest city, and after comparing notes on each of our families and our financial situations, one of his comments was, "All I do is sue people. What you are doing is helping them in an eternal way." He then went on to say that maybe some of the career choices he made when he was young were based on his youth, ambition, inexperience. and the times (Vietnam, late 60's, etc.). If he could do it over, maybe he would realize that what he used to think was important was not so important after all. His pursuit of success had cost him his family and I got the feeling that this friend, whom I had thought was so successful, was reevaluating what was really important in life.

Two friends – out of the blue – within four days of each other, made comments that made me ask myself again, "What is really important?" In our task-oriented society, we can get *"worried and upset about many things..."* But as Jesus went on to tell Martha in Luke 10, *"...only one thing is [important]. Mary has chosen what is better..."* Steve Wingfield boiled it down to Faith, Family, and Friends. One of his goals is to live in such a way that there will be at least 12 friends at his funeral who don't look at their watches. Rev. Dwight Mason summarized it as the difference between "...making a living and making a life." Jesus said, *"Seek ye first the Kingdom of God and His righteousness and all these things [the necessities of life] will be given to you as well."* (Matt 6:33)

If you want to live a life without regrets and "what ifs," I have some 3,000-year-old advice from a wise king: *"Trust in the Lord with all your heart and lean not on your own understanding; in all your ways acknowledge Him, and He will direct your paths."* (Prov. 3:5, 6)

I have been encouraged to continue to sing and speak about Jesus and not worry about "many things" (I confess, now and then I worry about "things"). Allow me to rephrase Prov. 3:5,6 – "Instead of allowing our culture to guide you, seek godly advice and pray about every decision and God will keep you from making decisions that you will regret."

August - 2006

Family Advice From Willie Nelson

"MAMAS, DON'T LET YOUR BABIES GROW UP TO BE COWBOYS..."

Adam and I just returned from a ten day trip to Wapiti, WY, to see where he worked as a wrangler the last two years, and just to spend some time together before he heads for college. And yes, Adam's mama let him grow up to be a cowboy! Willie Nelson would say, "I tried to tell you..." After two seasons (a total of about six months) of saddling and unsaddling five to ten horses a day for the hunters, and "wrangling" (rounding up) about 30 others on free range, I noticed that Adam really knows how to handle horses. He is a cowboy. (What a funny language – a man who handles horses is a "cow" boy and a person who works with cows is a dairyman or a milkmaid.)

We rode the 24 miles back to Ron Dube's Mountain Creek Camp, which is in the Shoshone National Forest and is southwest of Cody, just a few miles east of the southeast corner of Yellowstone National Park. (Did you follow that?) It is a designated wilderness area, so no chainsaws or motorized devices are allowed. We cleared the trails of fallen trees (there was a forest fire in 1988) so that when hunting season begins on Sept. 1, the guides can get their horses and hunters to the good hunting spots. We used an axe and a crosscut saw. I remember a crosscut saw hanging in our barn when I was young, but we moved before I was old enough to use it much. But even so, cutting downed trees and firewood at the camp with a crosscut brought back memories of a farm house back a long lane where I was raised until I was 11 years old.

Loren Neuenschwander is the camp cook and his son Nick is a guide. They left the camp on Sunday and Adam and I stayed until Tuesday because a camp cannot be left unattended overnight in a wilderness area. The next morning, as I was praying and walking around the beautiful meadow area with mountains and forest all around (with my hand near my bear spray, like a quick draw artist), I began to pray for prisoners that I could remember. As I looked around at the majestic Glacier Pass and over to the Bull Range Peak and all the other mountain peaks that Adam could call by name, it dawned on me: *What could be more opposite of a prison than where I am right now?* Even with bear tracks and the sounds of coyotes and wolves at night. I was looking at everything that represented freedom to me: wide open spaces, a million acres of forest, mountains (we rode up to those places in the two days we were alone), no schedule or pressure... A prison is a confined space with bells that ring before your cell door opens and bells to tell you when to eat, when to sleep, when to go to recreation, when to clear the yard...

And then another thought occurred to me – you don't have to be in prison to be in prison. What I just described is what many working people experience every day! If I remember correctly between naps in my psychology class, the greatest human need after security is freedom. In America, the cowboy symbolizes freedom, among other things. As a student of the Bible, I know that true freedom only comes through a relationship with God through Jesus Christ. *"Ye shall know the truth*

[Jesus] and the truth shall set you free." (John 8:32) So after one of the most fun, hardest, *free-est* trips I have ever taken, let me contradict Willie Nelson: "Mamas, make sure your babies grow up to be cowboys (free)."

September - 2006

Variety; The Spice of Life

One of the more interesting aspects of the type of ministry God has called me to is the amazing variety of situations in which I find myself. After starting the month of September singing on the square in Berlin, OH, I was asked to help an Amish employer host a wedding reception for one of his Mexican workers. There were about 100 in attendance. It was the first time I ever sang the Dutch song, "Maydly Vit du Hayara?" with a Spanish translation (Me Hija, quieres casarse?). I gave a meditation in Spanish without translation because my Amish friend said he wanted to know what a non-Amish visitor felt like at his church. (Amish services are in German.) I think he now has a feel for it. ☺

In the afternoon of that same day, I was getting ready to sing at the Fredericksburg Homecoming when I got a call from Perry Chupp. "I bought two tickets to be at Beachfest in Long Beach, MS, tomorrow. Do you want to go?" In other words, your name is on one of the tickets and in this terrorist era, you can't change it. So the day after the Amish/Spanish program and the Fredericksburg Homecoming, I was on stage with Randy Travis in Mississippi! I didn't sing with him, but, hey! I was on the same stage! Beachfest was a three-day evangelistic event put on by the Steve Wingfield team for the hard-hit victims of Hurricane Katrina.

After two days in a row at Trumbull Correctional near Youngstown, OH, I found myself at Diamondback Prison in Watonga, OK, at the invitation of Darwin Hartman, pastor of Pleasant View Mennonite Church in Hydro, OK. I performed two concerts at his church as well as participating on Sunday morning, and then we went to Great Plains Prison in Hinton, OK, where every one of the prisoners at the chapel service was from Hawaii! There is not enough prison space in Hawaii, so they come to Oklahoma.

On the 15th of September I sang at the Gospel Echoes/Common Ground Freedom Rally at London Prison. I left the prison early to be a part of a benefit concert at the Helmuth farm in Plain City and then drove to Cleveland that night to leave the next day for a Transport for Christ Retreat in Muskegon, MI. From there I flew to Denver, CO, where I met up with Lydia, and we attended a Ministry/Marriage retreat at Sonscape Retreats in Divide, CO. As I write this, I still have concerts at the Amish Farm in Berlin, the Amish Flea Market in Walnut Creek, and the Methodist Church in West Lebanon. In the month of September, we ministered in ten concerts, four churches, six prisons, and various meetings (breakfasts, lunches, church meetings, etc.) in six different states. We were told at the retreat in Colorado that we probably need to slow down, so we are looking into that.

October - 2006

As We Forgive...

We were all shocked at the tragic news of a school shooting in an Amish school in Nickel Mines, PA, on Oct. 2. Of all the places and of all the people to choose, this cowardly pervert chose an elementary school of defenseless Amish children, ages 6-14, to terrorize and then murder. This act of terror would be shocking no matter whom the victims would be, but to target a group of people who would not resist because of age, isolation, and because of their belief system makes this monster seem even more despicable. And to make matters even worse, consider that this was a man that many of the children knew and trusted. In the Amish community, one of the most trusted outsiders is the milkman. He is on their farm every other day. He brings the news. He becomes a friend and a confidant. And this "trusted" one came to rape, rob, and pillage. So now on top of the physical and emotional scars and nightmares that will haunt these children (and the adults) the rest of their lives, they have to deal with the fact that one of their most trusted "friends" became a demon. Can they ever trust anyone again?

As unbelievable and horrible as this act was, even more amazing is the Christ-like manner in which the Amish community has dealt with it. Their forgiveness of the murderer and their lack of malice toward his family has baffled the world and convicted the church. The Amish leaders refused to set up a fund from all the generous donations that poured in from around the world unless the killer's widow was also included. (Can you imagine what this man did to his own wife and children?)

I wrote a sympathy card to the families. After expressing my sympathy to the families, I said, *"You have represented your church well. You have represented the Christian faith well. You made Jesus look good to the world. The news reporters are speechless, and the world is taking notice. May God bless you."*

It's not easy to forgive such an atrocious act, but through Christ, it's not impossible. I know of another tragic case where a girl was murdered. Her devastated family has filed lawsuits and blamed this person and that department. There have been articles in the paper about their grief and bitterness. They simply cannot get over it. Frankly, I would have felt the same way. But this Amish community has given me a new look at an old truth. *"If you forgive men when they sin against you, your heavenly Father will also forgive you. But if you do not forgive men their sins, your Father will not forgive your sins."* (Matt. 6:14, 15)

In other words, if we want freedom, if we want relief, if we want forgiveness for ourselves, if we want *eternal life*, we must follow the way of Jesus. He came to forgive. The most innocent victim in all of world history looked down at His perpetrators from the instrument of torture and death and said, "Father, forgive them. They don't know what they're doing."

Pray for the Amish community at Nickel Mines. Their reaction to this horrible tragedy has made the world (and the church) take notice and say, "Now, that's Christianity!" They still need our support. Thank them for reminding us that no matter what happens in our lives, God is in control. Thank them for showing us how Christ would have reacted. Thank them for representing us well.

November - 2006

Silent Night

It's that time of the year again! We had a wonderful Thanksgiving! All the children were home (Adam from EMU, Amy from Rosedale, and Katie all the way from Hiland), I went deer hunting (no deer), we ate turkey with friends and relatives, went to my Mom and Dad's place, the Ohio State Buckeyes are #1... What more could a person ask? And now we look to the season when we celebrate the birth of our Savior, Jesus Christ.

Christmas is a favorite time of the year for me. I love snow (until mid-February – then spring becomes my favorite time of the year). I enjoy the family traditions and gatherings. I love the Christmas carols. This time of year I get to be at many company Christmas banquets, and this is the easiest time of the year for a singer/performer to bring up the subject of Jesus in a concert setting.

In February, while visiting our daughter Amy in Germany, Lydia and I had the privilege to be in Oberndorf, Austria, where in 1818 at the St Nikolas Church, Franz Gruber first sang "Silent Night" (Stille Nacht). The organ had broken down (mice in the bellows) and it was Christmas Eve, one of the most important days of the church year. In Europe, the big Christmas celebration is not Christmas morning, but the night before. The annual Christmas Eve service held in the Catholic Church is called the "Christ Mass," which is where we get our English word, "Christmas." With not much time until the service and nothing open on Christmas Eve, Franz Gruber brought out his new poem and Joseph Mohr put it to music.

Gruber wanted a simple tune so the whole congregation could sing it without much rehearsal (actually, without any rehearsal). As the simple song was sung at that Christ Mass service with Joseph Mohr accompanying with his guitar (a very undignified instrument, especially for a church), people seemed to sense already that this was a special song. It has probably become the most beloved Christmas Carol of all time, and crosses many cultures. And it was written and sung because of a crisis. The organ is broke, time is limited, it's Christmas Eve... what are we going to do? As a performer, I know the feeling of last minute panic when things don't go right, and the people are already gathering for the event

Many times during a concert, "Silent Night" is the song that I sing to transition from fun, secular songs to begin to tell the real meaning of Christmas. I have never seen a frowning face in the crowd while singing that beloved carol (although I have seen tears).

This Christmas, may we be reminded that in the rush and hustle of shopping and planning, and amidst the uncertainty of world events, and in the crisis of daily living, we can sing, *"All is calm, all is bright..."* because *"Jesus, Lord at thy birth"* is in our hearts. I can *"sleep in Heavenly peace"* in the midst of the storm.

Merry Christmas!

December - 2006

2007

2006 in Review

AD, Anno Domini, *The Year of Our Lord* – approximately 2006 years since Jesus was born...

The first day of the year AD 2006 found me in Spencer, OH, at the Baptist Church where fellow prison minister Larry Skrant attends, and the last day of the year I was at a New Year's Eve Concert at Troyer's Dutch Heritage Restaurant in Sarasota, FL, with prison minister Nelson Coblentz. So the year started and ended with ministries that focus on prisons. In between was a year filled with prisons, travel, concerts, chapel services, banquets... what a blast!

Here are a few of the highlights:

- A three-week trip to San Fran and Los Angeles with harness maker Mose Smucker of Pennsylvania, who gave seminars on fitting horses with a harness. My scheduled service at San Quentin Prison was canceled when an inmate stabbed a guard, sparking riots in several California prisons.

- A trip to Germany, Austria, and Switzerland to visit our daughter Amy at Bodenseehof Bible School. While we were there, we visited the Gingerich and Bender family ancestral homes in Mengeringhausen and Langendorf, Germany, (Lydia's ancestors).

- In April, Amy and I were invited to go with Steve Wingfield to Israel where I was the song leader for the team of about 25 pilgrims.

- Katie and I went to Ireland with Larry Skrant, the Jerry Schlabach family, and Esther Frink. We went door to door in northern villages offering the Jesus film. We also performed ten concerts.

- After a Transport for Christ banquet in Michigan, I flew to Colorado to attend a ministry/marriage seminar with Lydia. She flew home from there, and I flew to Nashville to attend the Christian Country Music Convention. While there I had the privilege to have separate lunches with Steve Chapman (Steve and Annie), Lee Domann (who wrote Howard Gray), Lance Dary (guitarist for Randy Travis), Bobby G. Rice (old time country singer – "Sugar Shack," "Pick Me Up On Your Way Down"), and many other friends. I connected with Rick Hendrix who is going to send out my rendition of "I Will Sing of My Redeemer" on a radio compilation this year.

- I took two trips that were purely (OK, mostly) for recreation: in August, I went with son Adam to Cody, WY, to help set up the hunting camp where he worked for the last 2 elk seasons. It was 24 miles back in by horseback! In November, I hiked down the Grand Canyon with my childhood friend Bob Weaver. While we were in Arizona, I had several church services in Phoenix.

- In between trips I went to Ohio prisons – 55 services in all – and tried to keep up with the family and all the correspondence and office work here at the International Headquarters in greater downtown Benton, OH. There were over 300 decisions for Christ in the prison services and many more in the other ministries I was privileged to be a part of: Wingfield Festivals, Gospel Echoes Freedom Rallies, Bill Glass weekends, Gospel Express events...

It was a great year! God is good! On top of the ministry news, my family is doing well.

HAPPY NEAR YEAR! May your troubles in 2007 be as short as your New Year's resolutions.

SIMON BYLER 1944-2006
My good friend and brother-in-law Simon Byler died suddenly on Dec. 5 while doing a remodel job for our friends Jim and Ruby Neuenschwander. Simon had just answered Ruby's question, and as she went into the kitchen, she heard a thud.

She turned around and saw him lying on the floor, and although EMTs were there in a matter of minutes, the doctors think he was gone before he hit the floor. Simon went out about the same way he lived his life: simply, quietly, without much fanfare.

I first met Simon in Florida in 1967, even though we lived just ten miles apart in Wayne Co. The next summer we played fast pitch softball together in the Kidron league. Simon and I were on a mission trip to Costa Rica in 1978 when he received word of his dad's sudden death. He moved back home to help his mother, and that's when I got to know his sister, Lydia, who is now my wife. Throughout the years, we remained close friends. He came to visit us several times while we lived in Costa Rica and he organized the first short term work team in 1985 to come and help us in construction projects there.

Although he never accumulated much of this world's goods, he put away treasures in Heaven. Since he lived alone, we feared that something might happen and no one would find out. We are glad that friends were there when God chose to take him and that everything was done to revive him so that we are confident that this was God's doing and not some mistake that could have been avoided. Simon's work was finished, and he was called Home. His death was not tragic, even though we miss him. May I also live my life so that when I am called Home, it will not be considered tragic, but God's timing. Good-bye, Simon, my faithful friend.

January - 2007

The Power of a Song

I love stories of how a song can change a situation, or in this case, even a life. I am especially touched that I had the privilege to be a part of the story. A friend told me about a man who was suffering from depression and was helped by a recording. I asked him if he would put that story in writing. Here are parts of his letter:

> This is a true story of how John Schmid's In Dutch recording literally saved a young man from destruction. Ben was born in an Amish home of 12 brothers and sisters. His father was hospitalized with mental illness (for years!), and the children became desperately hungry. Many times there was no food in the house. He became so desperate that he ran away from home and began breaking and entering into grocery stores as a means of survival. He lived in a barn for seven months and wore the same clothes for the whole time. Ben was not criminally minded; he was just hungry. Eventually, he got caught and put in a detention center. It was at this time that we went to the court of the county where the crime was committed and made a plea to have Ben sentenced to our home, and we would be totally responsible for him and give regular progress reports to the court. The court agreed, and Ben came to live in our home.
>
> Ben was one of the sweetest and most sunny-tempered 12-year-olds that we had ever met. He registered in school as a 7th grader only because we had no idea

what schooling he had actually had. He loved school and did well in academics and sports. We made sure he had every opportunity to participate. He still holds athletic records at this high school. He said he never played to win, but just because it was fun.

He went to college in another state, and there he met the sweetest girl. They both graduated from college, got married, and they eventually had two children. They had good jobs and felt the call of God on their lives to go to the former Soviet Union to teach English. But then Ben's wife became pregnant, and after several check-ups, they discovered that the baby to be born had severe health issues. They were advised to abort the baby. They ignored that advice. The baby was born with severe problems. He was nervous, cried or screamed most of the time and Ben and his wife were so worn out that their marriage was beginning to crack right down the middle. Ben was in depression and ready just to give up.

We (Ben's parents by choice) went to one of Johnny Schmid's concerts and heard that he had just made a recording in Dutch – the language of the Amish. We bought that CD, thinking that Ben could possibly relate to something in Dutch before he completely gave up. We called Ben and asked if we could hand deliver something that we thought he would enjoy. In a defeated sound he said, "I guess so... "

We jumped in the car and drove 1,500 miles and ran into the house and turned on the Dutch music. We were so excited about having some music in Ben's native language that we couldn't wait to start the player. Ben sat straight up in bed. He began to laugh and laugh and then laugh some more. Soon he was up on his feet dancing. He said, "I can understand that language!" and he laughed some more. "I have not had any relationship with my Amish relatives since I left home." He later said. "This CD activated in my heart a whole new joy." He came alive with that wonderful music, renewed his walk with the Lord, went back to work again and his family and marriage was saved. We thanked God over and over for that CD in Dutch!

Today, the child who was so ill and needed so much care is in a special needs Christian school. Several months ago we saw Ben and his family and his son quoted the first five chapters of the book of John from memory! Tears were streaming down our faces and Ben's son looked at us and said, "Don't cry, it will be alright." After he quoted those verses he began to sing one of those Dutch songs from Johnny's CD. We all laughed till the tears fell.

Bill Gaither said in a recording session, "I want you to remember something. There's no higher honor than to know that when you do what you do, someone is moved by your voice. All this works together, and people love to listen to it. It can change their lives."

February - 2007

Watoto Children's Ministry

UGANDA, AFRICA

In February I went to the city of Kampala in the country of Uganda, Africa, with Tom Miller and a team from Dayspring Mennonite Church in Berlin to help build two houses for Watoto Child Care Ministries. We actually went to build one house, but with 23 hard-working Holmes County young folks (ok, a couple of us were old), we were able to leave the project with two houses finished! When I say "finished," I mean up to the top course of brick. From there, the local builders pour a concrete crown beam on the last course of brick and then build truss rafters and put on the steel roof. Each house will have eight children (four boys and four girls) and a housemother. There are two bedrooms for the children and one for the housemother, a kitchen, a bathroom, and a living room. The house is basic by American standards, but it is luxurious compared to where the children came from.

Watoto is a children's ministry created to help deal with the tragic crisis of street children and orphans in Uganda, the result of war and the highest number of AIDS deaths in the world. The poverty and disorder were overwhelming, even for me, and I lived in a third world country for seven years! We finished houses number 84 and 88 in the Bbira Village, one of five such villages in the Watoto organization. There are close to 1,000 children being raised by this ministry in a Christian environment with all their basic needs (food, clothing, shelter, and school) being met. Watoto's slogan is, "Raising Leaders to Change Uganda." The first children who were accepted in the mid-'90's have now graduated; some of them have come back to work with Watoto as employees, and one graduate is in the Ugandan Parliament! I was impressed by the organization.

Again, I was a little embarrassed that I ever complained about anything here in the U.S. I still believe that the best way to eliminate complaining and dissatisfaction here in the U.S. is to go *anywhere* else in the world and see how nice we have it here. That is not to say that we don't have problems here and that we don't need to improve, but what a reminder that I am blessed simply by virtue of where I was born.

Also, if you would like to be a part of helping an orphan in Uganda by supporting him financially, visit www.watoto.com. You could be a part of helping to change this country that has been impoverished by war, AIDS, Idi Amin, tribal conflict, colonization... Each child needs six sponsors, and each house-mother needs four.

Thank you, Tom Miller and United Dayspring Mennonite for taking me to Uganda!

March - 2007

Take-Away Value

The highlight of the month of March for me was a "Spring Celebration" sponsored by P. Graham Dunn. I was one of the guest singers, and Jerry Jenkins was the special speaker. He is the author or co-author of 120(!) books, including the Left Behind series with Tim LaHaye. His topic was "Stellar Lives." *(Stellar adj. 1. of or relating to stars. 2. A star performer.)* He told of some of the stellar lives he has had the privilege of interviewing as a biographer, including NFL players Walter Payton and Mike Singletary, strong man Paul Anderson, and home run king Hank Aaron.

The highlight of his career, however, was the thirteen months he spent with Billy Graham as he worked on Graham's biography, *Just As I Am*. Jenkins always tries to think, "What is the 'take-away' value of a book or a story? What can I gain from this that will impact my life or the lives of those reading this?" Of the many stories he shared about being with and interviewing Billy Graham, the one that had take-away value for me was the answer to a question he asked Graham about his "secret" of spiritual depth and consistency. "How do you keep your deep relationship with God?" It took him several tries to ask the question correctly, and finally Graham said, "It's really no secret. It's right there in the Bible. Search the scriptures. And pray without ceasing."

Jerry said, "Yes, but, 'pray without ceasing' is just symbolic, isn't it? Surely you can't pray all the time..." Billy replied, "No, it's not symbolic. I pray all the time – without ceasing. I'm praying right now, as we speak."

Jenkins thought, "Oh, no. It's not symbolic! I've never 'prayed without ceasing.' "

Billy Graham went on to say, "I search the scriptures. I read the Bible every day. Then I leave the Bible open where I will see it during the day. As I walk by it, I will pick it up and read a verse or two... or a chapter or two... or an hour or two..." As Billy spoke, Jenkins could see his open Bible on the desk behind them.

Jerry then asked him, "When you miss a day or two, how do you catch up?"

Graham said, "I don't know. I have never missed a day."

"Never?" asked Jenkins.

"Never. Since the day I was saved I have read the Bible every day and have prayed without ceasing."

Jerry reminded us that Billy Graham is not the best preacher in the world. His sermons are plain and simple. But when he preaches, there is power. God has used him more than any man in our generation. Can you now understand why God has used this man so greatly? He has communed with God every hour since the day he was saved! That story was my take-away.

Here's a take-away for you this month. Search the scriptures. Pray without ceasing.

April - 2007

It Happened in Nashville

Last month I wrote about Billy Graham's statement to Jerry Jenkins that the "secret" to a powerful life is to (1.) *search the scriptures* and (2.) *pray without ceasing.* Although I have been trying to implement that simple imperative into my life, instead of *praying without ceasing* I find myself *thinking without logic*: what should I be doing, where are my shoes, how could the Yankees score six runs with two outs in the ninth, why did that knucklehead in the Cadillac cut in front of me?... you know – real important issues!

Is it actually possible to pray without ceasing? I trust Billy Graham, and if he says he practices it, then I believe it's possible. So, I keep trying.

Here's a story that encourages me:

Last month I was in a Nashville studio recording a new CD. These musicians are professionals. They do studio work six hours a day, five days a week, and they are good. They have played for the best. (The bass player tours with Ricky Skaggs, the guitarist tours with Dolly Parton... get the picture?) I have performed in front of enough people to be able to tell when they are impressed. These studio musicians were friendly, fun, personable – and totally unimpressed with my singing. They were just doing their jobs. After each song, the drummer would leave first and head for the coffee, followed by the bass player and myself. The guitarist was the head musician, and he would stay in his booth and go over the song one more time to correct mistakes and add some licks while the rest of us drank coffee and joked around in the kitchen.

After the fourth song, the drummer left first as usual, and I was right behind him. "Boy, is that song the truth!" he said, even before he had his coffee poured. I was a little surprised that he had even been listening to the words. The song was, "He Believes In Lost Causes" by Phillips, Craig & Dean, and it reminds us that in God's eyes there are no lost causes. It's a great prison song.

"My son is homeless," he said. "We have tried for years to get him to go to drug rehab and get his life straightened out, but he has just wasted his life. He's 45 years old and homeless!" I made a few sympathetic comments, and I began to think about this man's son. I didn't "pray without ceasing," but I did pray without moving my lips. I don't even remember what I prayed. "Lord, help this poor son and give relief to his dad and the rest of his family," or some thought like that.

As we began the next song, I watched this professional keeping time with his drums, and I prayed for him. When the song was over, instead of heading out the door, he came right over to my booth and opened the door. "My son's going to rehab! I just talked to my wife, and she said our son just called and he is sick of his life and wants to change!" He was smiling so big that he could have eaten a banana sideways! "Has he been to rehab before?" I asked. "Never! We've been after him for years, and now he's finally going to try to do something!"

I was amazed! Twenty minutes after a song opened the door for him to tell me about his son who had been on drugs for

20 years, he came over to me to report the good news. He didn't go to his musician friends first, or the engineer or the producer, even though he knew them well. He came to the guy who sang the song (and sort of prayed). I have a hard time believing that my prayer could have been answered so soon so powerfully, but I also can't believe it was just coincidence. I am encouraged, however, to, (1.) keep singing and, (2.) pray without ceasing. Pray for Buddy in rehab.

May - 2007

New England Grad Trip

Katie and I departed for our New England Graduation Trip on May 29. We got to the Boston area late that night. The next day we visited Martha's Vineyard, and that night we went to Fenway Park to see the Red Sox play the Cleveland Indians. We paid $25(!) to park, and then we couldn't get in because they were sold out! Not even scalpers on the street had tickets, so we went to a fancy restaurant under the stadium and watched the innings on the big screen TVs. (The Indians won.)

We spent two weeks together, traveling to all six New England states. Can you name them? Hint: Massachusetts, Connecticut, Vermont, New Hampshire, Maine, and Rhode Island. Here is a summary and some highlights of our trip:

- Fenway Park *(even if we couldn't get in)*

- Freedom Trail in Boston *(a two-mile walk to see historic sites)*
- Paul Revere's house
- USS Constitution *(Old Ironsides)* Battle record: 40-0
- John Greenleaf Whittier *(poet)* birthplace, Haverhill, MA
- Norman Rockwell Museum, Rutland, VT
- President Calvin Coolidge, birthplace, VT
- Von Trapp Lodge, Stowe, VT
- We worked on a lobster boat in Friendship, ME *(Katie's highlight)*
- Visited several lighthouses in Maine
- Concert at Monson, ME, Evangelical Free Church with Daryl Witmer
- Services at Advent Churches in Friendship and Port Clyde, ME
- We stayed with friends, Mike and Martha Henderson, Friendship, ME

SOME INTERESTING FACTS:
- Maine has more coastline than all the rest of the United States put together. *(5,300 miles! – because it is so "jagged" – coves and bays)*
- Years ago, before good roads and quick transportation, lobster was considered "poor man's food."

- Maine passed a law stating that the Maine State Prison could only serve lobster to the prisoners three times a week because it was considered cruel and unusual punishment to serve it more often.

- When I crossed the state line going into Maine, I visited my 49th state.

- This is my last graduation trip.

On the way home, we stopped at Greenwood, DE, and participated in a Steve Wingfield banquet at the Sam Yoder farm. We arrived home on June 12, two weeks after we left. It was a great father/daughter time. Katie is now ready to take on the world. Well, at least she's excited about going to Portantorchas Bible School in San Jose, Costa Rica, this fall.

July - 2007

To the Third and Fourth Generation...

In the 1940's, a church-going man was known to be unfaithful to his wife. This man's daughter picked up on this lifestyle and had a baby out of wedlock. That baby grew up and followed these generational sins and is now in prison. I see him several times a year.

I'm sure that this prisoner's grandfather figured, "It's my life, and I'll live it the way I want to. It won't affect anyone else."

He was wrong; it affected his relationship with his wife, who felt betrayed and could never trust him again. It affected the behavior of his daughter and helped to ruin her chances for a happy, healthy marriage. It affected the child who was born to this single mother who was not ready for the responsibility of raising a child. It affected the son who grew up angry and bitter. It affected several families who lost loved ones due to the crimes of this son. And now it affects every taxpayer in Ohio as we are paying the $30,000 a year it costs to keep him in prison.

King David thought he was above the law of God when he summoned another man's wife (Bathsheba) to his palace and committed adultery with her. I suppose he thought, "I am the king. I can get away with this." But his sin was then covered up by other sins: lying, deceit, and murder. Even after he was confronted, confessed his sin, and was forgiven, the sin still had its effect. This sin caused adultery, murder (Uriah), son Amnon raped Tamar, brother Absalom was so angry that he killed Amnon, and there was enmity between David and Absalom. Absalom was killed in a battle against his own father after rebelling publicly with the king's concubines. Son Solomon had 300 wives and 700 concubines and didn't know how to raise children. Solomon's son, King Rehoboam, made it so hard on his subjects that the kingdom of Israel was split. I don't think it's too far of a stretch to say that the fall of the nation of Israel can be traced back to one night when a man thought he could break God's law and get away with it!

Sin will take you farther than you want to go, it will keep you longer than you want to stay, and it will cost you more than you want to pay. Sin never affects only me. It always spreads like cancer (or as in the Old Testament, like leprosy).

The prisoner in this sad story is responsible for his actions. His mother is responsible for her behavior. They cannot blame their immoral, cheating grandfather. But oh, how much easier it would have been for them with a godly example at home. I thank God for my parents who celebrated 62 years of marriage on July 1 and for their example of faithfulness at home. I am responsible for my actions, but they made it easy for me.

August - 2007

I've Been to... Ireland

I've been to Dublin, Dundalk, Dingle, Donegal, Limerick, Leitrim, Lisburn, Fingal, Waterford, Swinford, Longford, Newcastle, Sligo, Wicklow, Carlow Clare, Cashel, Glenveagh, Galway, Coleraine, County Kerry, Letterkenny, Kilkenny, Gortahork, Tipperary...! I've Been Everywhere, Man! I've Been Everywhere, Man...!

I added that Irish verse to Hank Snow's hit song, "I've Been Everywhere," and it won the hearts of the audiences in County Donegal in the northern part of the Republic of Ireland. I followed that song with an Irish folk song, "The Fields of Athenry." At our last concert in the village of Gortahork, I started, "By a lonely prison wall...," the audience began to sing along, and then they took over! I quit singing and just played guitar for them. It sounded like a huge choir! Then I introduced

Larry Skrant who was in Ireland with Changed Lives Ministries, and he gave a short testimony of his journey from prison inmate to president of a ministry. Then he sat down, and I began to sing gospel songs. We had won their attention and earned the right to be heard and for the next hour (they have long concerts in Ireland!) we gave directions on how to get to Heaven through songs and stories.

One man said, "Best ten euros (dollars) I ever spent!" Another man said, "The best night I've had in the last thirty years!" I thought, Wow! Either this was a great night or that poor man doesn't get out much. Either way, the people were excited and wondered when we are coming back.

The local missionaries were also elated. They had planned this event not only as a Christian outreach, but also to help build a youth facility in the village of Gortahork with the proceeds of the concert. Their standing in the community took a hit when they became Protestants, but this event was a definite step forward in re-establishing them as normal. (When you leave the Catholic Church in these small villages, you are not normal.) Over $2,500 was raised for the Youth Facility building fund!

After the concert part of our tour was over, we left for Dublin by bus and rented a car to drive to Waterford (on the wrong side of the road) to visit friends and maybe do some genealogy study. My mother's grandmother came from Waterford. We visited the local genealogy office, but no luck. Great-grandma left Ireland during the potato famine and never looked back. Lydia's family left Europe for religious freedom; my ancestors left because they were starving. Either way, they were just so thankful to be in America! Me too! (Although my real citizenship is in Heaven! By the way, have you applied for citizenship there, or are you an illegal?)

As always, after seeing so many beautiful sights and meeting so many wonderful people, the highlight of our trip was the sight of our own front yard.

September - 2007

Message in a Bottle
(OR, ANOTHER DIVINE ENCOUNTER)

Eileen is one of our new friends from Ireland. One of the amazing stories we heard while we were in Ireland both this year and last year was how Eileen became a believer. She came to several of our concerts last year and helped to organize the Gortahork concert this year (2007). She runs a bed and breakfast near Tom and Noireen DeLasa's home in Falcarrah. Noireen befriended Eileen and during their morning walks along the beach on the northern coast of Ireland, Noireen would tell her the gospel story and how God sent His Son to redeem us from our sin. Eileen was friendly but unresponsive.

One morning when Noireen was sick, Eileen went walking by herself. She spied a bottle that had washed up on the beach. All her life she had wanted to find a message in a bottle, so she always checked all the bottles that she saw near the water. Although she had lived on the coast all her life and had found many bottles, she had never found one with a message. This particular morning she picked up the bottle, and to her joy and amazement, she saw that it had a note in it! She opened it with excitement and anticipation. Did it come from Africa? New York? Australia? She fished the note out of the bottle and to her utter disappointment and almost anger, she read the note: "Have you been born again?" What a letdown! And it was from Belfast – just down the coast, a couple of hundred miles away!

She couldn't believe it! All her life she had wanted to find a message in a bottle and when she finally does, it is from some religious fanatic! But as she continued her walk, she remembered that Noireen had told her that she was going to pray that God would speak to her in a way that she would know that it's from Him. Maybe this was God speaking to her. The more she thought about it, the more she began to realize that this was no coincidence. By the time she finished her walk that morning she had prayed a sinner's prayer, and later, with Noireen's help, she became a disciple of Jesus!

One of our team members stayed in Eileen's bed and breakfast (for free), and when we stopped to pick him up, I asked Eileen if this was a true story. She said it sure is and then she went and got her Bible and showed me the note: "Have you been born again?" She said, "I keep it in my Bible to remind me that God still speaks today!"

God promised that if we seek Him, we will find Him if we seek Him with all our heart.

October - 2007

WATCH EILEEN'S STORY AT: https://m.youtube.com/watch?feature=youtu.be&v=RYLrX27s8Gw

One Person Can Make a Difference

From "The Whistling Ploughboy of Ecclefechan" by: Derrick Bingham:

In 1815, John D'Estere was killed in a duel in Dublin, Ireland. His beautiful and vivacious widow, Jane, was devastated. Only 18 years old with two small children, she was faced with the added horror of bailiffs arriving at her home and seizing all of her husband's goods. As they left, they threatened to return the next day and sell her husband's body to the hospital mortuary if there was nothing else to sell.

That night, with a few friends, she stole her husband's body out of the city and buried it in an unmarked grave by the lantern light, and later fled to the village of Ecclefechan, Scotland. It was pitiful thing to see such a vivacious person so low. Jane was a gifted musician. Her father was the leader of George III's Court Band, and was of the most outstanding solo players in all of England.

One day, the destitute Jane sat by a river and contemplated suicide. Life seemed absolutely pointless. Suddenly, the noise of movement across the river caused Jane to lift her head. A young boy about her own age was entering a field behind a horse and plow and, with obvious skill, enthusiasm, and determination, began plowing. He was known for whistling

Christian hymns while he worked. Jane became absorbed in watching him work happily, with attention to detail. On the edge of death, Jane was challenged by the young boy's spirit and excitement for life in his work, in what was considered a low position in her society. If the young plowboy was dedicated to his responsibilities, why should she not return to Dublin and face her problems? After all, she had two small children who were completely dependent on her.

She returned to Ireland and, some weeks later, attended St. George's Church in Dublin, where she came to faith in Jesus Christ after hearing a sermon on John 3:16. Fourteen years later she married Captain John Guinness, son of Arthur Guinness, founder of the famous Dublin brewery. Jane did a fascinating thing the rest of her life. She prayed frequently for twelve generations of her family. She prayed for her children, her grandchildren, her great-grandchildren, her great-great-grandchildren, and so on... She asked God that He would bring out a continuing Christian witness in her family through those coming twelve generations. There is no question that God answered her prayer. Her son Grattan gave away his fortune and became a minister. He preached to literally thousands outside the brewery. He was greatly used of God in the 1859 Irish Revival when 100,000 people came to personal faith in Christ in one year. The largest buildings available for his use failed to accommodate the numbers of people who thronged to hear him. To follow the story of what is known as "The Grattan Line" is just fascinating. It is full of dedicated servants of Jesus Christ who traveled the world with the good news of the Gospel. The ministers, missionaries, humanitarians, professors, doctors, and Christian workers who came from the line number in the hundreds.

Derrick Bingham was recently at a Trinity Forum in Europe attended by "movers and shakers" from the worlds of finance, media, sport, academia, and politics, as Dr. Os Guinness helped deal with modern-day issues in the context of Christ-centered teaching. Dr. Guinness was born to missionary parents in China. His mother was a surgeon. The man Bingham was hearing was, in fact, the great-great grandson of the lady who had watched the whistling plowboy of Ecclefechan on that seemingly uneventful day in 1815. Jane, who turned from suicide to Christ at the inspiration of a plowboy who whistled while he worked.

Do you suppose the plowboy ever knew the significance of the "work" he did that day? Did he have any idea of the effect it had on a suicidal girl on the other side of the river, on a family's destiny, and on the destiny of untold thousands who were touched by that family's Christian witness down through subsequent generations? As far as we know, that boy didn't know anyone was near on that day. He had no idea that simply doing his work with joy and enthusiasm would change a girl's mind, save a family, and change the influence of generations of a family that is better known for beer and the Guinness' Book of World Records than it is for Christian service.

I wonder if when that boy got to Heaven, he was absolutely amazed that he would get credit for thousands of changed lives simply because he whistled while he worked. Are you in a situation where you think you have no influence? I have a suggestion: whistle while you work. *"...whatever you do, do it all in the name of the Lord Jesus..."* (Col. 3:17). You never know who is watching. It may change a life, a family, a country... You can make a difference!

EXTRACTS TAKEN FROM THE BOOKLET "THE WHISTLING PLOUGHBOY" WRITTEN BY: DERICK BINGHAM. USED BY PERMISSION FROM TBF & KL THOMPSON TRUST.

November - 2007

## Happy New Year!

2007 is history, 2008 is a mystery, and I am looking forward to a great year! We have just finished a wonderful Christmas with all the children home and most of the extended family here. The children were appalled that I got my dear wife, Lydia, a chainsaw for Christmas, but even more baffled that she was genuinely excited about it! They weren't sure if she qualifies as a cowgirl, a redneck woman, or a practical Pennsylvania Dutch girl who does most of the yard work around the estate. The children got me a John Deere lunch box, even though I eat lunch at a restaurant most of the time. The younger generation isn't always practical.

The year of our Lord 2007 started out for us at a New Year's Eve concert in Sarasota, FL, and ended with a get-together at Lydia's cousin's house in Berlin, OH. In between times, I (we) made trips to Pennsylvania, Virginia, Wisconsin, Delaware, Tennessee, Indiana, South Carolina, Ireland, Uganda, Africa... and many places in Ohio. There were prisons, concerts, camps, revival meetings, and banquets. The month of December was filled with local company Christmas banquets where I had the privilege to sing, entertain, and tell the story of Christmas. It was a month filled with fun, food, financial benefits for the ministry, and the freedom to speak about the Hope of the world who came as a baby and died as a Savior for us. A great way to end the year!

January is always a time to reflect, readjust, and set goals (make resolutions) for the coming year. I am one who makes attempts at planning the coming year during the time between Christmas and New Year's. One of my annual goals is to read through the Bible each year. In 2007 I finished reading through the Bible the day before Thanksgiving. I recommend this goal to everyone who claims the name of Christ. God's Word not only gives us instructions on how to live, but it gives us inspiration to live for Him. It teaches, rebukes, corrects, and trains us in righteousness; it equips us for every good work.

2008 could be the year that Jesus returns to gather His elect; it could be the year that The Great Revival begins and sweeps across the United States like it did several times in the 18th and 19th centuries. (Sadly, there were no great revivals in the 20th century.)

We don't know what will happen in 2008, but we do know that every day with Jesus is sweeter than the day before, and today we are closer to His return than we were yesterday. I plan to work while it is day because night is coming when no one can work. I thank God that I can do this work by singing, speaking, and actually make my living by doing so. I thank God for your generosity to fund what we are doing. Have a great year!

January - 2008

Bushnell, Florida
LIFE WITHOUT PAROLE - AT AGE 14!

I left Sarasota at 5:00 AM to join the Gospel Echoes at Sumter Prison in Bushnell, FL. After the first chapel service, an inmate asked me what I was doing in Sarasota. When I told him I had sung at Bahia Vista Mennonite Church, he lit up. "Yes! That is the church that is going to help me when I get out!" As the story unfolded, I learned that this inmate, Tim, was 14 years old when he went with some older boys who robbed a house and then brutally murdered the couple they robbed. Although Tim was hiding under the table in fear, he was tried as an adult and charged with first-degree murder; life in prison – at age fourteen! About 12 years ago his story was on NBC Dateline. Nashville executive Ron Miller was so touched by the tragic story that he contacted NBC, got Tim's address, began to write to him, and is now working with lawyers to see if his sentence could be commuted.

BIRMINGHAM, ALABAMA - SET FREE!

I was five years old when my father died. My mother tried to care for us, but we were too much for her, and she had a nervous breakdown. The state came in and put us in foster homes. They put us boys in one home and my sisters in another. I was lonely and scared, and I would often just start crying. My foster parent's reaction to my crying was to beat me. I began to resent authority. I hated policemen, schoolteachers, anyone who would try to tell me what to do. I got into all kinds of trouble, and that's why I'm here [a prison near Birmingham, AL]. I was bitter and resentful of everything and everyone. But last night at the We Care service I gave my resentments and my bitterness and my life to Jesus Christ. For the first time since I was five years old, I feel free!

CLEVELAND, OHIO
17 YEARS IN PRISON FOR COVERUP

This morning I went to the Gospel House Church near Cleveland for a meeting of prison ministries from all over Northern Ohio. One of the chaplains looked familiar. He greeted me by name and reminded me that we had met at Trumbull Correctional when he was an inmate there. He gave me his story in tract form, and it is one more sad story of bad choices and being in the wrong place at the wrong time. He drove to Pennsylvania to answer his brother's desperate plea for help. His brother had stolen some stereo equipment, and his partner had just been arrested. He was sure the police would soon be here to get him. What should he do? While they were wondering, his partner showed up, they got in a fight, and his brother killed the partner! Now what? In a quick, foolish decision, my chaplain friend covered for his brother, lied to the police, and when the truth was finally discovered, he went to prison for 17 years for obstruction of justice.

These stories are not unusual. Many men are in prison not because they are criminally minded, but because they made bad choices in friends, loyalties, places... Some are victims of bad circumstances, dysfunctional families, etc. But the bottom line is that we are all responsible for our choices. For those who have made bad choices, we have an advocate (lawyer, παρακλητον," for you Greek scholars) who will represent us before the Father.

February - 2008

Don't Ask

One of the cardinal rules of prison ministry is, don't ever ask an inmate what he did to get in prison. I have never broken that rule in 19 years of prison ministry. Except once.

Sometimes a prisoner will voluntarily let you know what his crime was. That's fine. We're just not supposed to ask. I suppose it's a breach of etiquette or an embarrassment to the inmate. But I found out that it's not just to protect the privacy of the inmate. I learned that it's also to protect the minister.

Several years ago there was a series of articles in the local paper about a woman who had been physically and cruelly attacked by her husband. The number of surgeries and therapy that she endured was unbelievable, and she is still scarred and disfigured for life. Her last name was common in our area, even though she was not from here.

I was welcoming the inmates into the chapel at a northern Ohio prison when I happened to see an inmate's name stenciled on his shirt. It was the same name as the woman in the newspaper articles. Before I thought, I asked the next inmate to come through the door, "What's that guy in here for?" "Oh, he [attacked his wife]." The way he answered, I knew it was this woman's husband (ex). I looked at him in disbelief. "That's the guy!"

During the service, I noticed that this man looked like any other inmate. He sat near the front. He sang the hymns, joined in prayer, laughed when I said something funny, nodded when I made a good point... he didn't look evil. But I knew what he had done; I had read the newspaper articles of the horror and suffering that he had put his wife through. As I looked at him and proclaimed the power of the blood and the forgiving gospel of Jesus Christ, deep down I was thinking, "You dirty rat... you destroyed your wife... how can God forgive a sinner like you... look what you did!" and even worse thoughts. When the invitation was given, no one responded.

I have probably been in well over 1,000 prison chapel services since 1990 when Common Ground Ministries was started. Some are memorable because of the movement of the Spirit of God, and some are just "normal" prison services, but always there is some response – a raised hand, someone wanting prayer, a recommitment... In over 1,000 services, I had never been part of a prison service where there was no response. Until now.

Now I know why you never ask. God can handle the hideous sins that these men have committed. I can't. I wanted to take that man out and beat the daylights out of him (in love, of course). I wanted to make him listen to the screams of his wife and know the torment that she is going through, even now, because of his actions. I wanted him to suffer.

Folks, sin is horrible. It kills. It causes suffering. It put Jesus on the cross. It takes you farther than you want to go, keeps you longer than you want to stay, costs you more than you want to pay, and it separates you from God. I think I got a glimpse of the horribleness of sin. I couldn't handle it. God can. I think I got a glimpse of the awesomeness of the power of the gospel I proclaim. What a mighty God we serve! I am more inspired to proclaim the mighty gospel to the captives. It is powerful. But I won't ask again why a man is in prison. It doesn't help at all.

March - 2008

Benjamin

"I have no greater joy than to hear that my children are living according to the truth." (3 John 4)

Because a work team to Costa Rica didn't develop this year, Lydia and I went by ourselves. I performed concerts, we visited former churches and work sites, scouted future work projects, and – oh yes, visited our daughter, Katie, who is studying at Portantorchas Bible School near San Jose.

My several concerts were for the students at Katie's Bible School, an English-speaking church, and a Spanish Bible study conducted by a friend who used to attend our youth group meetings when Lydia and I were in charge of the English-speaking youth group in the early 1980's. The leader of this group is a Costa Rican named Benjamin who married one of the English-speaking girls from our youth group.

Benjamin was a student who became a Christian through his contact with our youth group. Although he was from a prominent business family in San Jose, he went to Columbia Bible College in South Carolina before returning to start his computer business. After several years, he returned to Columbia, SC, for more training and eventually sold his business and is now full time in Christian ministry, leading Bible studies across San Jose.

The study that I attended was for the very upper class of youth. Costa Rica has a very wealthy class, what some would call the "up-and-outers." They are hard to reach for Christ because they have everything they need materially (sound familiar?) and besides, Protestant Christianity is really for the lower classes. They even have a derogatory name for Christians: "panderetas" – tambourine shakers. But since Benjamin's family is from this same upper class, he is able to gain an audience with them. His last name is recognized throughout the city. He is not a pandereta.

We met in a huge, modern, warehouse-style building that

houses an advertising agency owned by a friend of Benjamin. He, incidentally, also attended our English-speaking youth group, but never made a serious commitment to Christ until just a year ago. (Some 25 years later! You never know when a seed may sprout!) The warehouse is offered to Benjamin free of charge.

March 11 was their third meeting. Benjamin was nervous because tonight he was going to be more evangelistic. Were they ready for this? Was it too soon? After I had sung, Benjamin began his high tech talk on love. There were scenes of movies flashed on the screen as he talked, lyrics from well known love songs, news clips, quotes from famous people, and scripture. When he finished, it was very plain that the true love that we're all looking for comes only from Jesus Christ. When Benjamin gave an invitation to follow Christ, he was almost shocked. Of the 47 wealthy young adults there, 25 raised their hand indicating that they wanted to get serious with God. He started over. Maybe they didn't understand. When he asked again, the same hands went up. Their faces were saying, "I want this love. I want to know more about Jesus!"

Benjamin had done his homework. He had eight people ready to start weekly Bible studies in their homes. Everyone who raised a hand was assigned a Bible study, depending on which night was best. Right now, one month later, there are at least 25 new students of the Bible in San Jose. These are students who will be in positions of influence. Pray for them. Pray for Benjamin. With John, I say, *"There is no greater joy..."*

April - 2008

April

April was a busy month for the entire staff here at the International Headquarters of Common Ground Ministries. In case you're wondering whom that includes, let me remind you that CGM has a staff of one.

I was finishing up a four-day revival at the Methodist Church in Louisville, OH, as the month started. As I preached, I was hoping to see a stream of people wanting to rededicate their lives or make first time commitments; I was hoping to see the town drunk stagger in and be struck by the power of the gospel and have a life changing experience. I left, not sure if anything had happened. But according to Webster, "revival" is: *1. anew presentation. 2. renewed interest in religion. 3. a meeting, or series of meetings in order to awaken religious faith, often marked by impassioned evangelism and public professions of faith.* If you put it that way, we did have a revival. There was new presentation, renewed interest, impassioned evangelism, and public professions of faith. So, even though it was not dramatic, God moved in that church and I believe will continue to move through their Godly pastor.

April also included two concerts at the Blue Gate Theatre in Shipshewana, IN, a fundraising banquet for CGM in Hartville, four prison services, a Gospel Echoes fundraising auction in Goshen, a Bill Glass Kickoff Banquet in Findlay, a men's retreat in Florida, and son Adam's graduation in Harrisonburg, VA!

BUS - SOLD!

In 2001, Sam Yoder from Greenwood, DE, donated 75% of the

money for a bus for this ministry. It was a 1984 Greyhound with a new conversion. It was a dream! After almost seven years, well over 1,000 services and concerts and 100,000 miles, we have sold the bus to another prison ministry in Indiana. We would like to thank Sam Yoder and all of the local donors who made this wonderful gift possible. It made travel so much easier for the family.

Thank you again! Your investment made our work so much easier and more enjoyable!

May - 2008

Graduation Speech (and book?)

THE POWER OF A SONG

I had the privilege of being the graduation speaker at the Sharp Run School near Berlin on May 31. What a contrast to son Adam's graduation at Eastern Mennonite University one month earlier! First of all, at EMU there were over 300 graduates. I knew five. Check that – I knew one of the graduates, and I knew the parents of several others. Sharp Run had five graduates, and although I didn't know them, I knew the families of four of them, and by the time I left the graduation ceremonies, I knew the parents of all of them. Presenting the diplomas at EMU took well over an hour (yawn). At Sharp Run, it took two minutes. The graduation speaker at EMU droned on and on; at Sharp Run, the speaker was fascinating! (Just kidding on that last one.)

I was instructed not to lecture the students, just tell some of the stories of my ministry. Boy, was that an easy assignment! I had been to Ireland with Jerry Schlabach, a teacher at Sharp Run, so the students had heard one of the stories of how a song, "The Fields of Athenry," had changed the whole atmosphere of a concert crowd in the north of Ireland. Could I tell that story?

I decided to let the parents in on a little secret: I'm going to write a book, and the title is going to be "The Power of a Song." And then I proceeded to tell several stories of how a song sung at a certain time had changed everything. Some are personal stories, and some are from church history, WWI, prisons, scripture... there are many examples. And since I was telling them all of the stories, they could save $14.95 by not having to buy the book!

The most powerful story happened in 1978 when I was singing at an Army base in Heidelberg, Germany, for the 8th Army Division. They were discouraged and angry because they were forced to attend our 'stupid' Christmas program, but when I sang "Silent Night," a whole new attitude descended on the crowd. The angry faces began to glisten with tears of homesickness and nostalgia, and they began to sing along, and the crowd changed from hostile to hospitable.

Another time I was in a crowded restaurant in Dallas, TX. The customers were grouchy. The waitresses were grouchy. The cashier was frowning. Suddenly, from one of the tables in the back corner, we heard singing:

"Dear waitress don't worry, we're in no hurry, relax and don't get uptight.

We'll sit here and wait, we don't have a date, everything will turn out all right..."

The whole atmosphere of that restaurant changed from grouchy to grateful in about 10 seconds. I was embarrassed that I had been so impatient. A song had changed everything.

I gave several other examples: the singing of "Silent Night" during WWI, Leroy Beachy's account of an Amish bishop singing for one of Napoleon's magistrates that resulted in exemption from war for his church, and of course, the singing of "Athenrey" in Ireland in 2006.

I have been involved in several aspects of the church: missions, youth work, preaching, singing... I feel that when I speak, people listen. But when I sing, there is power. I'm going to put ten stories together about the power of a song and call it a book. This is your first warning. A song can be powerful!

June - 2008

Thoughts on Freedom

By the time you read this, July 4 will have passed. It's the day we celebrate our freedom and independence from England. Every country has a "Fourth of July." In Costa Rica, it was "Quince de Setiembre" (September 15). In France, it is July

14. I know the French day well because I had a one-day stop in Paris in 1977 and it happened to be July 14. Nothing was open. I wandered around Paris and saw the Eifel Tower and the Louvre and Notre Dame – all the famous landmarks – from the outside. I couldn't go in. Everything was closed. Even the restrooms! I had the notion of starting a revolution!

Last week we visited colonial Williamsburg, VA, and Jamestown, the first permanent English settlement in America. We walked around Jamestown and heard stories of the hardships and adventures of the first settlers. Disease, starvation, attacks, discord... Pocahontas and John Smith. (By the way, no matter how dutchy or German I pronounce my name, people still always ask me, "Where's Pocahontas?")

We walked around the restored city of Williamsburg, which, along with Boston and Philadelphia, was one of the big three cities in colonial America. Patrick Henry, Thomas Jefferson, and George Washington all hung out there. The seeds of the Revolution were sown there. We couldn't absorb all the history in the day and a half we were there.

I was reminded of the thoughts I had when we visited our daughter Amy in Germany. We saw ancestral family homes and heard the stories of risk and sacrifice that our ancestors endured to come to this land of freedom and opportunity. I came back to the U.S. with this thought: "I cherish my German heritage. But I am so glad that I was born over here!" Even today, as modern and wonderful as Europe is, I'll take America.

And even though many things in our land and culture are

going south right now, those people who say, "It's never been this bad," simply don't know their history. Without condoning the direction our nation is going, I believe if the average person from any era or any culture in history could be transplanted to my house in Holmes County for the next two weeks, I believe they would exclaim, "It's never been this good!" We have food, clothing, shelter, and transportation (a car for every family member!) As Russian immigrant comedian Jakov Smirnoff says, "What a Country!"

The freedom and opportunity we have enjoyed for the last 200 years is actually an aberration in history. As our nation drifts away from the Christian heritage that our forefathers instilled in the founding documents, our culture will become more normal. Chaos and fear will reign. The only time I have ever locked the doors of my house was when I lived in Central America, which does not share what Francis Schaffer calls a "Reformation-based" Christianity. Even people in Jerusalem, the Holy City, lived behind walls; they closed the gates at night and took turns doing guard duty. (The "fourth watch" in Matt. 14:25 was from 3-6 AM. There were four "watches" during the night.)

Having said all that, one more thought: I am grateful to be a citizen of the U.S. I am even more grateful to be a citizen of Heaven. Citizens of Heaven do not have an Independence Day. We recognize "Dependence Day," the day we gave up control of our lives and turned the reins over to Jesus. If you love independence, you are a great American. If you are an "Independent Christian," you are a man without a country. Don't get the kingdoms mixed up. Let freedom ring!

July - 2008

CC's Gone

(Note: I have made it a policy to avoid talking about money in this newsletter. This month is an exception.)

CC Sabathia is no longer a Cleveland Indian. If you're a baseball fan, I don't have to explain, but just in case you don't know what I'm talking about, the Indian's ace pitcher has been traded to the Milwaukee Brewers. If you're an Indians fan, it's one more heartbreaking loss of a player we grew to love and admire. I for one was a great fan of CC. Until July 8, 2008.

The day after he was traded, I was thinking this whole thing over. Something is out of balance. It doesn't add up. CC said he wanted to stay in Cleveland, the club he started with as a 17-year-old who, according to the pitching coach Carl Willis, didn't know how to grip a baseball or how to stand correctly on the pitching rubber. As an Indian, he developed into a premiere pitcher in the Major Leagues and last year won the highest award for a pitcher, the Cy Young Award.

Why did the Cleveland Indians Baseball Company trade him? Why didn't they offer him enough money to stay? He wanted to stay. That's what I was asking myself on Tuesday morning as I was packing for a trip. Then I got to thinking. They did offer him a lot of money to stay. Seventy-four million dollars for four years, to be exact. I got to thinking some more. $74,000,000.00!!! 18 million dollars a year ($18,000,000.00!) to play a game that most of us would play for free. If he starts 40 games a year as a pitcher, that's $450,000.00 per game (as in almost a half a million dollars! Per game!) If he throws 100 pitches per game, which would be about average, the Indians offered him $4,500.00 for every pitch he would make. It doesn't matter if the pitch is a ball, a strike, over the center field fence, or over the backstop! $4,500.00! The average fan that brings his family to the ballpark pays about a day's wages to watch a game. Day's wages for CC: $49,315.07 (based on $18,000,000.00 divided by 365 days).

He was offered enough to pay off my house every inning he pitched for the next four years! He could buy 500 houses like mine! My mortgage is set up to be paid off in 30 years (10,950 days). CC could pay it off in the first inning before the third batter even comes to the plate; about fifteen minutes of "work." He says he wanted to stay in Cleveland. But he broke off contract talks before the start of the season because they didn't offer him enough money, and he let it be known that he would not talk about it until the end of the season when he becomes a free agent.

General manager Mark Shapiro told the media that CC wanted to "test the free agency market." Mark, that's the kindest way I've ever heard of calling this what it is: greed, money hungry, selfishness, avarice, _____, _____, (you can fill in the blanks).

I still love baseball, but I'm sad to see what money and notoriety can do to a man who would have given everything he had for the privilege to play in the big leagues, and now he won't do it for a million dollars. Or 74 million dollars. Something doesn't add up.

The baseball players say we don't understand. They're right.

I Timothy 6:10

August - 2008

London Prison Freedom Rally

"Pray for my three-year-old son. He has spinal meningitis, and the doctors only give him two weeks to live. I get out in 16 days. Please pray that he lives until I can get out to see him before he dies." My heart went out to this heartbroken man.

I said, "At least he's with his mother."

"No," he said. "She's in prison, too..."

I heard this and many other sad, twisted, messed up stories this weekend.

Approximately 150 volunteers went into London Correctional for two days to barbecue 5,000 hamburgers and hotdogs for the 2,400 inmates there, which went well with the potato salad donated by Der Dutchmen Restaurant and the whoopie pies made by local ladies. They also presented three concerts and sermons during the two-day event, which was sponsored jointly by The Gospel Echoes Team and Common Ground Ministries. (O.K. – The Echoes did most of the work and Common Ground just showed up, but hey...)

We saw many smiling faces on men who don't usually smile. I heard many comments from inmates that not only was the food extra good, but just the fact that somebody would come in and do all this was heart warming. One man said, "We seldom hear an encouraging word in here, and just to see all of you outsiders who care enough to come in and cook for us..." his voice trailed off. He was overcome with emotion. "We will definitely be at the concert tonight!"

Every two years for the past six years we have gone into London Prison for a weekend cookout and concert. Jake Yoder was waiting for us at the main entrance. He had just wheeled Jimmy Garver up the handicap ramp when the mother and sister of an inmate came out from the visiting area. She said to Jimmy and Jake, "Thank you, folks, for coming in! You don't know what this does for the inmates! My son has been looking forward to this for weeks!" And we hadn't even been in yet!

What good does it do? From a spiritual point of view, we trust that many inmates will be in Heaven because of decisions made during these meetings. But not only that, we hope they will be better citizens here on earth after they get released from prison. Ninety-five percent of them will be released. Will they be bitter and angry, or better able to function as productive citizens of the society they once violated? Also, the chaplains tell us that for a period of time after an event like this, the whole atmosphere of the prison is better. There are fewer incidents of violence and rebellion. The officers don't write up as many inmates for misconduct. The proclamation of the gospel in Satan's territory actually makes a noticeable difference! It was a great time!

September - 2008

Bantry Christian Fellowship

I went to Ireland at the invitation of the Bantry Christian Fellowship of Bantry, County Cork, to sing and speak for their church and to reach out to the community with concerts. Pastor David Ross kept me busy with 21 concerts in 12 days! I almost got tired!

My daughter Katie and I started in Bantry and sang in a variety of venues, including schools, hospitals, nursing homes, and community halls in villages such as Drimoleague, Schull, Glengarriff, Skibbereen, Dunmanway, Youghal, Waterford, Dungarvan, and Dunmore East. Irish people love Johnny Cash, so when I told them that my great-grandmother came from Ireland (therefore making me "Irish") and then sang Cash songs, the audiences would light up.

The local paper in Youghal (pronounced "Y'all") had the following article about our concert:

> John Schmid from Ohio was on a two-week tour of Cork and Waterford and included a couple of days in Youghal at the invitation of the local Baptist community. He did a full-length concert in the Mall Arts Centre on Saturday, October 4.
>
> In cooperation with Anne Fitzgerald from the Music department in the Pobalscoil, he spoke and sang to around 60 students on Monday afternoon, October 6. In the first 20 minutes, he treated the students as if they were inmates in a prison in Ohio, and his mixture of real life stories and Johnny Cash songs went down really well. Throughout the rest of the time, he sang from a wide repertoire of songs including the "Auctioneer's Song," other funny songs, and a song especially for Chemistry students. You could have

heard a pin drop as he sang "Howard Gray," a song based on a true story about one man's regret for taking part in bullying another pupil in his school. John received warm applause from the students for his time with them, and they made a presentation to him of a piece of Waterford Crystal. (This was very fitting, because during his stay in Waterford he had managed to trace his Great-Grandmother's roots to a Townland between Tramore and Dunmore East.) Mervyn Scott from the Baptist community hopes that John Schmid will be able to return to Youghal in the near future.

Comment in the Youghal Times by Kay Donnelly on October 5, 2008:

I went to hear John Schmid on Saturday night last, and his performance was both entertaining and uplifting. In the style of Johnny Cash, he wove a story of prison life, inmates, characters, and the difference it made when a prisoner accepted Jesus into his life as his Saviour. Starting off with "Forty Shades of Green" and "The Fields of Athenry," John Schmid interspersed his songs with anecdotes and personal experiences, which kept the audience entertained for nearly two hours. The audience loved him as he warmed to the task and shared many jokes and life experiences with them. It was interesting to hear him speak about the Amish community in Dunmore East and his connection with them.

John Schmid showed that music can transcend race

and creed and that it can be a very effective way of communication with young and old.

Kay Donnelly

In other words, it was a successful tour. Lives were touched, and the Bantry Christian Fellowship was able to make many new contacts in their community and across Southern Ireland.

October - 2008

Nicaragua

If all goes according to our plans, we are in Nicaragua while you read this. We are on a work team that is helping to build a church in a village called Rio Blanco, about four hours from Managua (by car, I assume). About sixteen of us will be working with Rosedale Missions missionaries Duane & Karen Schlabach. This will be their last work team before they return to Ohio to continue Duane's plumbing business near Kidron, OH. I have been to Nicaragua, but only in the airport, so this will be my first trip to actually mingle with the people and the culture. When I used to stop in Managua on my way to Costa Rica, it was not safe for an American to be in that war-torn country, but times have changed, and here we go! I will tell you about it when I get back.

THANKSGIVING

One of the by-products of a trip to Central America (or anywhere else in the world, for that matter) is to realize how blessed I am to have been born in America, and to have what I have: health, wealth, happiness, family, freedom, possessions, a future.... Nowhere else in the world could I have had the opportunity that I was given here. When I came home from Costa Rica in 1987 after seven years in that beautiful place, I didn't see a hill, a bad road, or a poor person for a year. Not that they weren't here. It's just that (by comparison) what we call hills here, they would think was just "not quite level." Our "bad roads" would be super highways there. And what we call "poor?" They would say, "Let me show you what poor is... no food, no work, no chance, no welfare system, no one who cares..." I'm not saying we don't have problems here. I'm saying that after a two-week work trip to what used to be called a third world country, I am embarrassed at what I often complain about here. Compared to some of my friends in Central America, I don't have any problems.

Which brings me to *Thanksgiving!* We enjoy the turkey, pumpkin pie, mashed potatoes, family, football, deer hunting... but most of all, we need to pause and recognize from whence come all these blessings. Dr. Dennis Kinlaw once said, "A man can be thankful without being a Christian, but you can't be a Christian and not be thankful." Rather than explain the origins of our national holiday, I found a copy of the original proclamation. This is how our government used to think:

BY THE UNITED STATES IN CONGRESS ASSEMBLED. 1782

PROCLAMATION.

IT being the indispensable duty of all Nations, not

*only to offer up their supplications to **ALMIGHTY GOD**, the giver of all good, for his gracious assistance in a time of distress, but also in a solemn and public manner to give him praise for his goodness in general, and especially for great and signal interpositions of his providence in their behalf: Therefore the United States in Congress assembled, taking into their consideration the many instances of divine goodness to these States, in the course of the important conflict in which they have been so long engaged; the present happy and promising state of public affairs; and the events of the war, in the course of the year now drawing to a close; particularly the harmony of the public Councils, which is so necessary to the success of the public cause; the perfect union and good understanding which has hitherto subsisted between them and their Allies, notwithstanding the artful and unwearied attempts of the common enemy to divide them; the success of the arms of the United States, and those of their Allies, and the acknowledgment of their independence by another European power, whose friendship and commerce must be of great and lasting advantage to these States:— Do hereby recommend to the inhabitants of these States in general, to observe, and request the several States to interpose their authority in appointing and commanding the observation of **THURSDAY** the twenty-eight day of **NOVEMBER** next, as a day of solemn **THANKSGIVING** to **GOD** for all his mercies: and they do further recommend to all ranks, to testify to their gratitude to GOD for his* *goodness, by a cheerful obedience of his laws, and by promoting, each in his and by his influence, the practice of true and undefiled religion, which is the great foundation of public prosperity and national happiness. Done in Congress, at Philadelphia, the eleventh day of October, in the year of our LORD one thousand seven hundred and eighty-two, and of our Sovereignty and Independence, the seventh.*

JOHN HANSON, President

Charles Thomson, Secretary.

November - 2008

Merry Christmas!

"And it came to pass... " Those are the first few words of the beautiful Christmas story from Luke 2. They are also becoming the theme of my life. It seems like everything is "coming to pass," and quicker than it used to.

We started November in Nicaragua with a team of 18 people. We built trusses and put the roof on a new building for the Mennonite Church in Rio Blanco, a village about 7 hours by bus from the capital city of Managua. Our team also held daily Bible school for the children and the ladies had classes for the women of the village, teaching crafts and sewing and having Bible studies.

I got home on Nov. 11 and went to five prisons in the next

seven days, as well as a concert in Shipshewana and a church service in Smithville. Then a Christmas banquet and a Johnny Cash tribute concert in Berlin. (Now, that was a blast!) *"...it came to pass..."*

For the past ten years or so, we have had a Thanksgiving prison service at London Correctional on the evening before Thanksgiving, then I lead Christmas carols at "Christmas in Berlin" the evening after. Sandwiched in between those two events this year was a wonderful Thanksgiving Day with all of our family (our children and my parents) and several friends. I am always thankful for what God has given me, but this year, after just returning from Nicaragua with its poverty, lack of basics, and families missing loved ones because of war, I am extra grateful to the Lord for the way He has blessed us.

As this Christmas season approaches, I want to thank you for your prayers and financial support. We give gifts at Christmas to symbolize that God gave us the greatest gift ever given on planet earth: His Son. Your financial gifts let us know that you believe in giving this gift of His Son to prisoners (as well as others) through this ministry, which means you also believe in this ministry. Thank you!

We put lights on our houses and trees to symbolize that Jesus is the Light of the world. We go to family gatherings because Christmas symbolizes families. We spend money like crazy to symbolize that we are not too smart and we need a Savior. OK, just kidding. But be smart this Christmas. We need a Savior, not because we are not smart, but because we are sinners.

This Christmas will come to pass, as well as another year in our lives. The older I get, the more I believe the old couplet: *"Only one life and soon 'tis past. Only what's done for Christ will last. "*

May God bless you this Christmas season! Even in the midst of financial crisis and turmoil, may you have a blessed Christmas. May we "do things for Christ" during this one life we have.

"Glory to God in the highest, and on earth peace, goodwill toward men!" Luke 2:14

MERRY CHRISTMAS!

December - 2008

2009

Happy New Year!

Another year has come and gone. It doesn't seem that long ago that I was typing a letter for the 2008 New Year's newsletter. There is a reason for that – it wasn't that long ago.

At this time of the year we think about time. Many of the new calendars I get have little bits of wisdom about time:

"Take care of the minutes, for the hours will take care of themselves." – Lord Chesterfield

"Does't thou love life? Then do not squander time, for that is the stuff life is made of " – Ben Franklin

"We should all be concerned about the future because we will have to spend the rest of our lives there." – Charles F. Kettering

Get the point? If we don't watch ourselves, we end up squandering the most important thing in the world – time. No wonder we try to reform on January 1 and make resolutions and commitments to change our ways and do better in the coming year. Deep down we all know that we could use our time better. I have had a very busy year. But was it productive? Did I "redeem the time," as Paul admonished us to do in his letter to the Ephesians? *"Be careful then, how you live, not as unwise, but as wise, making the most of every opportunity* ('redeem the time' in KJV) *because the days are evil"* (Eph. 5:15-16). Or, as Ernest Hemingway said: *"Never confuse motion with action."*

OK, so what did Common Ground Ministries do in 2008? (This is called reflection.) I started out the year in Cleveland with a Cavs game and a rescue mission service and then headed to Florida for our annual concert with The Inspirations. Then: Alabama prison crusade, Oklahoma church meetings, Costa Rica to visit our daughter Katie, back home for banquets, prisons, reunions, revivals, camps, (and even a wagon train), and a bicycle trip of 360 miles to EMU in Harrisonburg, VA, with our son Adam for his last semester of school. After the Apple Festival in Nappanee, IN, Katie and I went to Ireland on a concert tour (22 concerts in 14 days). Back home for several prisons, concerts, our annual Fall Banquet, then off to Rio Blanco, Nicaragua, with a work/mission team for 12 days. After nine prisons and several churches in November came the Christmas banquet season – 16 company banquets in December! As I write this, we have just had our Christmas Eve Schmid Christmas, our Christmas Day Byler gathering, and another bunch of family this coming Sunday! What a busy, fun, family time! It was a great year! Every day is a gift.

In 2009 I am planning on getting better, more efficient, closer to family, closer to God, more faithful in prayer, deeper in scripture, kinder, lose weight, read more books....

HAPPY NEW YEAR!
I hope 2009 is your best year yet!
"The best is yet to be." – Robert Coleman

January - 2009

January, February, March...

For the last thirteen Januarys (minus one) I have been part of a Haiti Mission benefit concert with The Inspirations Quartet at Bahia Vista Mennonite Church in Sarasota, FL. The funds generated by this concert help Christian Fellowship Mission with their monthly trips to Haiti to oversee and support an orphanage and a conference of churches. All expenses for the concert are covered by local businesses so that 100% of the offering goes to help alleviate the physical and spiritual poverty in Haiti. They also lead short-term work teams there throughout the year (hint, hint).

What a great way to raise funds, meet friends, and praise the Lord in song! What a great way to start the year! And in the process, I have become good friends with some of God's finest servants. After the Friday night concert, I usually sing the next morning at the Bahia Vista Estates monthly coffee hour, or I participate in a chapel service at Sumter Prison near Bushnell, FL (similar crowds?). And then Saturday evening for the last several years I have had a concert at the Pinecraft Park with the Marc Schlabach family. This year the weather was beautiful and so was the crowd. Great time!

At the end of January is the We Care Prison Crusade, centered in Atmore, AL, where 300 volunteers and 20 some preachers and music groups will blitz 17 different prisons with chapel services and friendship evangelism. February is a short-term mission trip (this year I will be in Uganda as you read this), and in March we start gearing up to visit as many Ohio prisons as we can in 2009.

So that's how the first three months of Common Ground Ministries has been shaping up for the last ten years or so, and one reason for this monthly letter is to inform you and thank you for your support. You are the ones who keep us going with your prayers, your encouragement, and your finances, even during this turbulent economy. Thank you!

The schedule for the next three months, April, May, and June, isn't quite as cut and dried, but I'll try to summarize it in a future letter. (That may even help me to get organized.)

YOU ATE WITH US...

Speaking of Sumter Prison... I didn't go this year because the date was changed, but two things stick out in my memory from my visit there with the Gospel Echoes last year. One is that I met Tim Kane, a 32-year-old prisoner who was sentenced to life in prison when he was 14 years old because he was with the wrong 'friends' at the wrong place at the wrong time. Nashville executive Ron Miller is working to get Tim's sentence commuted. If you're interested in a sad story that could have a good ending, visit Ron's website, www.friendsoftimkane.com. The other incident I remember is speaking with an inmate who approached me. He wasn't very talkative, but after a couple of minutes, I asked him if we had met before. He said, "You were here several years ago. You ate with us. I never forgot that." The simple act of eating with the inmates had made such an impression on this man that he went out of his way to talk to me and then he came to the chapel service. You never know what a simple act of kindness may produce.

February - 2009

Africa, Florida (again), & Alabama

AFRICA

January & February were slim months for prisons here at Common Ground Ministries. That is not unusual for this time of the year. We had four prison services in Alabama with We Care Ministries, and then it was off to Uganda, Africa, on a work/mission trip to help build a house for the Watoto Child

Care Ministries. We also did some singing and speaking at various places around the Watoto Villages of Bbira and Suubie. There were twenty of us from the Holmes County area on the team! By the time we left for a safari in western Uganda, we had built 1/4 of a fourplex apartment for teachers. The theory is that if they provide decent housing for teachers, they will attract decent teachers for their children.

FLORIDA (AGAIN)

We made our second trip to Florida in February. Along with other concerts and church services, we attempted our first (annual?) Common Ground Ministries Banquet in Sarasota. It turned out to be successful, except the facilities were too small. The meal and the service were excellent, but we had to turn people away. We are looking at bigger facilities for next year, and the date is already set – Feb. 22, 2010! Come on down! I promise there will be room for everyone this time.

ALABAMA

Speaking of We Care Prison Ministries (in Atmore, AL), I was reminded of an incident that took place at St. Clair Correctional near Birmingham this last trip. I have been going to the We Care annual prison crusade for about 15 years. I don't always go into the same prisons because as a "platform guest," I get shipped to four or five different prisons each time, but over time, I get back to the same prisons many times. As soon as I pulled into the parking lot of St. Clair, I remembered it: a long tunnel from the front desk, then an elevator, then a long walk across the yard to the gym where chapel was held. As I got off of the elevator at the last gate, the inmate 'trustees' were waiting to help carry the sound equipment to the chapel.

"Hey! Johnny Cash!" one of them yelled. "Good to see you again! Where you been?" "Hey, great to see you again! How you been?" I said. It was true that it was great to see him, so I let him believe that I remembered him (which I didn't). As we chatted on the way across the yard, he was telling me about the last time I was here several years ago and how the singing had impacted him. "I started playing guitar after I heard you. I've written a few songs." As we set up the equipment in the empty gym, he ran to his cell and got his guitar and sang one of his songs for me. The guard came over and listened, and I thought there might be trouble, but when the inmate finished the song, he said, "Hey Jim! Let's sing our song!" He and the officer then began a beautiful harmony about the love of Jesus. It's unusual (and in some states forbidden) for a guard to get too close to a prisoner. But this inmate, who will never get out of prison, has become a light in this dark place because of a volunteer coming in through We Care Prison Ministries and singing. Let me repeat one of my most worn out (and not totally accurate) proverbs about prison ministry: *80% of prison ministry is just showing up.* May I challenge you? Show up! You may inspire a lonely person.

March - 2009

Angels, Success, Standards,

Last night I texted singer Steve Chapman on my way to Lima: *"I'm going to Allen Correctional tonight. I'll tell James Alley hello for you."* He texted back: *"Yes... please do!!! Blessings on your time there! SC"*

It is because of my friendship with inmate James Alley and through a series of events that I was privileged to meet Steve and Annie Chapman. I was able to tell James in front of all of his peers in the chapel that Steve Chapman, Dove award-winning singer from Nashville, says hello. Some of the prisoners knew that Steve had recorded a song that was written by James. In a place where there is little individual recognition, it boosted James' self-confidence just a notch. His face lit up. It also gave me credibility in the prisoner's eyes because they realize I don't just come in and sing, but I think about them when I'm "outside."

On the way home I texted Steve: *"Service went well. Small crowd but James was encouraged to hear your greeting..."* Steve's answer: *"Thanks for passing on a howdy to James. Might have been a small group of men, but **did you count the angels?**"* (emphasis mine)

Did I count the angels? What a timely reminder! It is so easy for me to measure ministry 'success' by worldly standards. I was driving home wondering if my presence at the chapel had done any good.

Just last week I was talking to a farmer who told about trying to make his furrows straight as he plowed. Farmers in some areas (ahem... all areas) are judged by how straight they plow their furrows. The trick is to pick a fence post or a tree on the other end of the field and go straight for that immovable object. My friend chose a bush and kept the hood ornament of his John Deere tractor right in the middle of that bush. When he looked back towards the road, his plow furrow was curved – like a rainbow! He couldn't believe it! He looked back at his hood ornament squarely in the center of the bush and then he noticed that his 'bush' was a cow and she was walking slowly south as she grazed! He was following a standard that didn't stand.

Our standard is Jesus who is the same yesterday, today, and forever. One of the frustrations of ministry is that it's hard to measure success. When I built barns, I could see how much was accomplished at the end of each day. When I harvested wheat, we could count the bushels and acres each day. When I went to Allen Prison last night – well, I wasn't sure if anything 'happened.'

Every now and then someone will tell me, "Back in 1997 when you were at such-and-such a place you sang a certain song, and it spoke to me..." or "I gave my heart to Jesus when you came to my prison six years ago..." or "Because of that mission trip you lead I am a missionary today..." Success in ministry is not measured the same way it is in the world. Bill Bright said successful witnessing is sharing the gospel in the power of the Holy Spirit and leaving the results to God. Every now and then I take my eyes off of Jesus and follow some cow, thinking I am plowing a straight furrow. Last night a text message from a well-known singer helped me to *fix my eyes on Jesus*, realize that angels were in that prison chapel, and to keep singing and leave the results up to God.

No, Steve, I didn't count the angels last night, but they were there. Reminds me of what Steve Wingfield says: "If you reap having not sown, someone else did the sowing. Be humble. If you sow and do not reap, someone else will do the reaping. Be faithful."

Last night faithful Steve Chapman was one of the angels. I almost missed 'im.

April - 2009

A Witness

At a recent Weekend of Champions, Bill Glass was being driven from prison to prison by his long-time friend Bert Lyle. Listen to Bill's description of their conversation:

> *Bert began to tell me about his love and admiration for his wife, Susie. Bert confessed that before he was a Christian, he had little regard for his marriage vows and as a result, Susie prepared to take their children and leave him. Suddenly though, something happened. Susie came to Bert and admitted she had met another man. And because of that, she was not going to leave him! Then, she eagerly confessed that the other man was Jesus. Bert was dumbfounded. Despite his rejection of his marriage covenant, and of Jesus, Susie was loving to him. For two years she never pushed or nagged, but let her example be Bert's guide.*
>
> *Finally, Bert couldn't take it anymore. He saw in her the happiness and the direction which would make him complete. He surrendered and was born again*

because of Susie's life example. Bert went on to say that Susie was generally regarded as one of the finest Christian women in their community.

Imagine my surprise when, after our final program at the women's prison, she came to Bert and me in happy tears because she had led three female prisoners to Christ. She said that she had never before had the privilege of leading someone to Christ and she was overjoyed at her experience!

Susie is like so many wonderful Christians who do their best to live their faith every day but never have actually experienced the joy of leading someone to Christ. Now Susie knows that joy.

What a story! As believers in Jesus, it is our joy and privilege to share our faith with everyone, even the "least of these." One of the beauties of prison ministry is that it not only helps prisoners find a relationship with Jesus Christ, but it is a great place for wonderful Christians like Susie (and you?) to learn to share the faith verbally.

Statistics show that 95% of modern evangelical, Bible-believing Christians have never personally led someone to faith in Jesus. Yet the last command of Jesus just before He left planet earth was: *"...go...make disciples...teach them to obey..."* (Matt. 28:19a, 20a). If you think you can't do that, let me remind you of the very last sentence of our Lord according to Matthew: *"...and surely I will be with you always, to the very end of the age."* (Matt. 28:20b)

May - 2009

Church on a Boat

On Memorial Day Weekend we went to Goshen to attend Marv and Mary Beachy's wedding reception, a joyous occasion. On Sunday morning before the reception, we participated in a 'Boat-In.' It was a church service on a boat with loudspeakers on all sides to broadcast the singing and the preacher's words to the hundred or so boats that gathered around on the lake, and to the 175 people on the shore of Lake Wawasee in Syracuse, IN, about 25 miles south of Goshen.

What an experience! Every time I think I've been in just about every setting imaginable, I find myself in something like this: in the middle of a beautiful lake surrounded by boats on three sides and a yard full of people on the shore. I had been invited by Harlan Steffen, a 42-year resident of Syracuse, pastor of Wawasee Lakeside Chapel and native of Kidron, and former neighbor of my wife, Lydia. He has been doing the boat-in for 40 years. People who might not go to church will get in their boat and motor on over to the big gospel boat near the conference center and sit there and hear the word of God.

I think it's the first time I was ever in a church service where some people came in their swimming suits! Many of the boats had the family dog aboard. Harlan opened the service and asked the boats to let us know they were there. A hundred boat horns began to sound! What a call to worship! People for several miles around the town of Syracuse knew that the first boat-in of the season had begun!

I sang several songs, and a local pastor preached a short, plain (good) sermon. After I had sung a closing song, the "ushers" in small boats zigzagged in between all the boats with fishnets and took up the offering! Harlan told me that the average offering is between $1,000 and $3,000 per week. And then the boats that came close to our boat with their dogs got a dog biscuit. It was a beautiful day and a beautiful service of worship! God's word was proclaimed!

An interesting, if not ironic, twist to this 40th year of the boat-in is that the conference center where the people had been gathering and the boat had been docking for the past 40 years has been transferred to a denominational church. The church's lawyer advised them to not allow the boat-in because of liability, and they took his advice. The people of the lake got together: Catholics, Protestants, even nonbelievers, and said, "We can't let this boat-in not happen." So the owner of the local tavern offered his boat (a big double decker that can accommodate over a hundred people) so that the boat-in church could continue. It can anchor offshore, relieving the conference center of any liability. And it has a great sound system that can be heard for quite a distance, especially on the water!

Isn't that crazy? A church takes over the conference center, outlaws the only church service that some people will attend, and the local bar owner comes to the rescue! This has messed up my theology. I have to rethink a few of my prejudices and stereotypes. God will have His way, and He may even use a bartender!

I am reminded of Jesus' parable in Luke 16 where He says, *"...the people of this world are more shrewd... than are the people of light."*

June - 2009

Croquet, Motorcycles, Ricky Skaggs, Pat Boone, and Prison

In the last month, I have had the privilege to sing and speak in some very diverse places. On May 29 I sang at a croquet tournament in Harleysville, PA (pretty wild crowd!) and the very next night I was the singer/speaker at a weekend motorcycle rally in western Pennsylvania with seventy-some motorcycles lining the sanctuary of Pond Bank Mennonite Church (pretty wild tattoos). The week before that, I was part of a church service on a boat in the middle of Lake Wawasee in Indiana. After that were several Ohio prisons, a bookstore concert, a flea market, and a school reunion here in Holmes County. Last week I was in several Canadian prisons near the town of Kingston, Ontario, as part of the Steve Wingfield "Napanee Summerfest." (Yes, there is a Napanee in Ontario.)

More than 70 prisoners in the four prison chapel services made commitments to Christ, in addition to those who gave their lives to Christ at the main event, which was held at the local hockey arena in Napanee. On Friday of that week I had to privilege to open* for Ricky Skaggs, and on Sunday I opened* for Pat Boone! Can you believe that? I didn't even know Pat Boone was still around! He was the most popular singer in America in the '50's until Elvis Presley came on the scene. In fact, in 1955 Elvis opened for Pat Boone. Since I opened for Pat last week, now I can truthfully say, *I replaced Elvis!*

I got home on Monday, June 15, just in time to miss my

appointment at Hocking Hills Correctional. I thought that might happen, so I enlisted Joe Hochstetler to be prepared to go without me. He took two volunteers and drove the 125 miles to Nelsonville and conducted a non-singing chapel service. It went well. Maybe you don't need singing after all. A special aspect of that night was that a local man who is incarcerated there (for a good reason) came to the service and was able to sit with the volunteers who were old friends of his. He is in prison because he never had time for God when he was on the streets. Now he does. He was so glad to see hometown friends! He is a changed man!

However, about singing... Dennis Kinlaw reminds us that, "Song characterized the life of the people of God in the Old Testament. They sang when they worked, when they played, when they loved, and most of all when they worshiped. The adoration of God was difficult for them to conceive without a song. His presence quickened the impulse to sing... A Christian without a song is an anomaly." But singing (and song) is another subject that I might expand on in a future letter. Yes, it is possible to have a Christian service without singing, just as it is possible to have a major league baseball game without a crowd. "No greater mark of the difference between Christianity and other religions of the world can be found than that of a Bach choral piece, Handel's Messiah, or an ordinary hymn book in a Christian church." – Kinlaw

"I sing because I'm happy!" – Ethel Waters

From croquet to crooner! What a month! God is good!

*definition of "open" in concert terms: An unknown, usually not-too-good singer sings two or three songs to test the sound

system and alert the crowd that the real singer is almost ready. The real singer does not come out of his dressing room until the "opener" is already off stage and receiving congratulations from his mother and other family members. But the opener can now legally brag.

July - 2009

Funerals and Small Stuff

"Always go to other people's funerals, otherwise they won't come to yours." – Yogi Berra

"Don't sweat the small stuff. And it's all small stuff." - I can't remember who said this.

I knew better. Lydia's aunt Amanda died July 11, and Lydia and her sisters got tickets to fly down to Sarasota to the funeral. I would let her represent our family, and I would go to all the events on my schedule that week: an evangelistic meeting, two prisons, a board meeting, and the Mt Hope Sundown Sale. No use canceling all that.

However, on the way to Rehrersburg, PA, to be with Nelson Coblentz, I couldn't stop thinking about Aunt Amanda, and of her family planning a funeral. In prison work, 85% of ministry is just showing up. In the case of a funeral, it's 100%. There's nothing you can do to change the situation. Just show up. Be there. Hug people. Stand around. Listen much and say little.

A year from now I would wonder why I didn't just spend the money and change my plans and go. So I called my travel agency (about eight times) and finally hammered out a plan to fly from Harrisburg, PA, to Sarasota, attend the funeral, and then fly back to Harrisburg. I would then drive home to be there in time for the Friday evening Sundown Sale.

I spent the next hour or so calling prisons and board members and canceling stuff. Since it was a death, everyone was very understanding. I was within an hour of Rehrersburg, and I was all set. With all the modern bells and whistles of cell phones and credit cards, I had done two day's work in a couple of hours!

Just as I was thinking how amazing things are nowadays, I felt a thump, vibration, wobble, sway, and heard a loud noise. A flat tire. I stopped, got out and looked. The tire was not flat. But it was smoking. And it was leaning out like the wheels on the cars in cartoons. I can fix a flat tire, but I can't fix this! I called AAA, and then I called Nelson. AAA sent a wrecker, and Nelson sent Amos Raber. The van went to the Ford garage, and I went to Rehrersburg. I wasn't even late. The meeting went well. I flew to Florida and had a wonderful time with family, but when I called to see how the van was doing, I was told a part didn't come in. It won't be done until Friday morning (which you and I both know means: Friday afternoon or Monday). So I bought a new ticket (while I was at the graveyard!) to Akron/Canton so I wouldn't miss the big Sundown Sale on Friday. And guess what? My niece is arriving at Akron/Canton from Colorado the same time I am, and she has a car at the airport ☺! But guess again, my plane was delayed so

I called my daughters, and they came and got me at 1:00 AM!

The Sundown Sale was a blast and now all I have to do is get my van back from Harrisburg (six hours away). Nelson Coblentz called and reminded me that the Haiti Auction is in Lancaster, PA, this weekend and there would be Holmes County, OH, people there. I called around, found out who was there, got their phone number....

Long story short: Wayne Keims' swung by Harrisburg on their way home and brought my van home Saturday night! To quote Jakov Smirnoff: "What a country!"

Point of story: several things. First of all, I can honestly say that in all of these incidents I was not the least frustrated. In the case of the van wheel, which turned out to be a faulty ball joint (a mere $1,800!), I was thankful it happened while I was driving instead of Lydia. I was also thankful it happened when I had plenty of time to call a wrecker and still make it to my scheduled event. It happened when I had just planned to fly to Florida and wouldn't need the van for a couple of days. And it happened now and not next week when we'll be travelling on some desolate stretches of road in northern Ontario. AND the Lord gave me sense to pull off the road before the wheel fell off, which it was about to do! A wheel falling off at 70mph can mean bad things. $1,800 is nothing compared to no crashes, no injuries, and no hospitals. AND (because of many of you) we had the financial resources to cover this unplanned event.

What a blessing it was to be with Aunt Amanda's family! And I didn't sweat the small stuff! God is good!

August - 2009

Empty Nest

I remember the day Adam was born as if it were just last week. (I would say I remember it like it was yesterday, but I can't remember much about what happened yesterday.) We were in the hospital all night, and he was born at 9:00 AM. After four miscarriages, Adam was our miracle baby. He looked liked my grandmother, my dad, my mother, my wife, her brother, her nephew... it was amazing how many family features were in one tiny little baby. And people said he was so cute! And they said he looked like me! ☺

It was love at first sight. Actually, it was love before I ever saw him. It was the happiest day of my life: overshadowing the former happiest day of my life; our wedding. I thought nothing could ever make me this happy ever again. And then two years later Amy was born. It was the same thing all over again. It was the happiest day of my life; surpassing the former happiest day: Adam's birth. Nothing could make me happier. And then two years later Katie was born. Happiest day of my life! I think you get the picture.

Our children gave us great joy, and still do. So if you take that great joy and reverse it, maybe you can understand how we felt when we took Amy and Katie (and the dog) to Harrisonburg, VA. Amy is going to school, and Katie will live with her and get a job. They are all excited about having their own apartment and being on their own, even though we still help with school tuition.

I was happy for them and a little sad for myself. I found out later that my dear wife cried in the shower when we got home.

It will never be the same. Our little children used to run to the door squealing when I came home. At 10 or 12 years old they would look up and say, "Hello, Dad!" As teenagers, they would grunt and say, "Oh, were you gone?" But they were always there: evening family prayers, summer trips, the times when we traveled and sang as a family, hunting, ball games, high school events...

At Adam's ninth birthday party, I remember thinking, "If the next nine years go as fast as the last nine years went... I'd better pay attention!" Well, they not only went as fast, they went faster. Same with Amy and Katie. And now they're on their own, gone! They'll be back. But not as our little children; they are adults. The relationship is still precious, but it will be different.

It is not merely the end of formal parenting that has shaken my world today. I grieve for the human condition itself. When we left Amy and Katie and drove away, I comprehended anew the brevity of life and the temporary nature of all things. As I sat on the beds in my children's rooms, I heard not only their voices, but also the voice of Lydia's mother and her brother Simon, who laughed and loved in that place. Now they are gone. One day my parents, and then Lydia and I, will join them. First one and then another. We are just passing through this world. All of life boils down to a series of "hellos" and sad "goodbyes." Nothing is really permanent, not even the relationships that blossom in a healthy home. In time, we must release our grip on everything we hold dear. King David said it best, *"As for man, his days are as grass: as a flower of the field, so he flourishes. For the wind passes over it and it is gone; and the place thereof shall know it no more"* (Ps. 103:15-16). Yes, we have felt the chilly breeze of change blowing through our home the last few days.

James Dobson's dad once prayed: "Thank you, God, for what we have... which we know we cannot keep... we are keenly aware that the joy that is ours today is a temporal pleasure... change is inevitable, and it will come to us, too..."

I wish we could all capture the incredible concept. The only thing we can keep is that which we give to Christ: our hearts, our relationships, our lives. Only two things will last forever: the word of God, and those who know Jesus (the living Word of God).

The Empty Nest – A symbol of change. How temporary life is. How precious relationships are. I'm thinking of my children. My wife. My parents. Prisoners. You! Temporary and yet eternal.

September - 2009

They're Listening

"I've sat through a lot of chapel services, but I have to admit; this one was different! I've never heard it put together quite like that. That was something! Thank you."

Compliments like this are encouraging and feel good, and even though they give me energy and I appreciate them, I don't take them to the bank. If it's a written note, I will keep it and pull it out and read it now and then when I'm discouraged, but I try not to let these things make me think I'm something that I'm not.

This compliment was different. It occurred at a maximum-security prison here in Ohio. Prisoners often show their appreciation by gushing out stuff like that. Songs touch the emotions, and especially right after a chapel service where hearts were touched and men have made life-changing commitments, men will shake my hand with tears in their eyes and thank me profusely for coming and tell how something in the service spoke to them.

But this compliment was not from a prisoner. This was spoken by the tough-looking guard (officer) who sat in the back of the chapel with a watchful eye, feet up on a small table, looking for any kind of out-of-the-ordinary behavior among the inmates. He has probably sat through hundreds of chapel services: the Baptists, the Methodists, the Pentecostals, the Presbyterians, the Community Churches... all the different Christian volunteers who come to prison to serve.

When it was over, he walked up to the front after most of the inmates had filed out of the chapel. I didn't see tears in his eyes, but I did notice that up close he didn't look 'hard.' He looked grateful. Kind. He seemed glad that I had come. He looked me in the eyes. Some guards give me the feeling that they're rolling their eyes at our attempts to proclaim the gospel to a bunch of convicts who are only attending chapel so that it looks good on their record. "Jailhouse religion," they call it. And granted, some men attend for that reason. Guards get cynical and paranoid. But this officer was touched. God had spoken to him in this service.

The service that night was what I call the "Life of Christ" concert. I start in John 2 and tell about the wedding at Cana and then sing a song about it. Next, I talk about Nicodemus and I sing Larry Gatlin's song, "Help Me," and then on through the life of Jesus to the cross and resurrection. Lydia encouraged me to use this format, and that night it spoke to a guard whose assignment was to sit in the chapel service. I wonder if he thought he got the short end of the stick that night. Did his buddies grin as he left the lounge area and took up his post in the chapel?

A couple of thoughts:
1. You never know who is 'listening in' to our life. People are watching us. Steve Wingfield preaches about the other boats in Mark 4:36 who are watching how Jesus and His disciples are going to weather the storm. Other boats are watching us. How are we doing? A tough looking, bored officer was watching me (and actually listening)! God's word got through to him.

2. Even if you are in the right place for the wrong reason, God can speak to you. These officers are right; some men come to chapel for the wrong reasons. But God's word will not return void. Every now and then, one of these 'hypocrites' (or an officer) gets real and begins to follow Christ.

3. *"Your labor in the Lord is not in vain."* (I Cor. 15:58) Sometimes we think that our life here on earth is not making any difference. Don't be so sure! Those in the back are listening. Be faithful!

October - 2009

The Most Interesting Person in 20 Years?

Jack Murphy is probably the most amazing person I've met in 20 years of prison ministry. Murf the Surf – IQ of 160 (genius). Full ride tennis scholarship to the University of Pittsburg. A world class athlete. First chair violinist for the Pittsburgh Symphony Orchestra at age 17. High dive artist for the Barnum & Bailey Circus. Stuntman for MGM and Warner Bros. World Champion Hurricane Surfer. U.S. Surfer's Hall of Fame. Pulled off the biggest jewel robbery in American history. Incited a prison riot... and on and on. And then on death row in the Florida State Prison, he became a Christian. He now preaches in 500 prisons a year with Bill Glass Prison Ministries! What a character! The most amazing person I'd met in 20 years of prison ministry!

But that was before I met **Gary S. Paxton** in Branson, MO, last month! Gary S. Paxton is a music legend. I first heard his music in the '60s when he produced and sang the pop, million seller "Ally Oop." And then the "Monster Mash," "Cherish," "Sweet Pea," "Hurray for Hazel"... over 40 gold records in pop music! A legend and a millionaire who lost everything because of drugs and alcohol. And then he became a Christian.

That doesn't mean he became normal. He is still eccentric and a little crazy. In 1975, Paxton won the Best Inspirational Grammy for his album, *The Astonishing, Outrageous, Amazing, Incredible, Unbelievable, Different World of Gary S. Paxton*, which contained his oft-recorded gospel song, "He Was

There All the Time." The title of the album pretty much describes the man I met in Branson. We were there for a short vacation, and I accepted a ten-year-old invitation to visit him. We first met by telephone after I recorded his song, "Yuppies in the Sky." Later I recorded his "God Can Break Those Chains of Yesterday," and in a phone call to make sure I had all the information about paying royalties, securing the legal rights, etc., he took great interest in the fact that I went into prisons. "If you ever get to Branson, look me up!" So, I did.

In 1980 he was shot three times and left for dead by hit men hired by a disgruntled country artist. It put him out of music for eight years. When he got out of the hospital, he went to the prison and forgave the men who tried to kill him! For the first few years, Paxton said he still received threatening letters from the assailants until one of them became a Christian through a friend's prison ministry, and the other one got a life sentence for another crime.

Several months later, Gary came face to face with the man who hired the killers. The man crawled on his hands and knees across the room and started kissing Gary's feet. "He was begging me for forgiveness, and I told him that he had my forgiveness the night it happened, because God says if you don't forgive somebody, he won't heal you, and that is the reason I didn't die."

No wonder Gary was interested in someone who does prison ministry. While I was gazing at his wall covered with pictures of well-known singers and plaques of gold records, he was playing me songs that would minister to prisoners. "Here's one! Listen to this!" And then he would run down to his basement vault/museum and come up with another song. "You need to hear this!" We left his house (finally) with a dozen CDs (and lyrics) of songs that he had written or produced that he thought would fit my style and minister to prisoners.

Gary S. Paxton; crazy! Jack Murphy; wild! And I used to think that a life fully committed to Christ would by definition be boring. Folks, it has been an exciting adventure! Don't miss it! You meet the nicest (and craziest) people in the Kingdom of God.

November - 2009

Christmas 2009

"Without Christmas, Easter would be impossible. Without Easter, Christmas would be meaningless." - unknown author

Every season of the year is my favorite. I love living in an area that has four distinct seasons. Each one has its own flavor and specialties. Spring seems to remind us of new life. Then I'm ready for summer – carefree (& warm) life itself. Fall lets us know that there is beauty in growing old, and winter cold is offset by the beauty of snow. And Christmas! A favorite time of the year!

As much as I love winter, if it wouldn't be for Christmas, winter would be pretty long. C.S. Lewis talks about a desolate place in The Chronicles of Narnia, where it's "...always winter, but never Christmas." Wouldn't that be a hopeless place?

No Christmas? All winter?! Nothing to look forward to? Without Christmas, not only would winter be long and hopeless; the whole world would be a hopeless place.

But there is Christmas! *"Joy to the World, the Lord is come! Let earth receive her King."*

And if every heart would prepare Him room, Heaven and nature would surely sing!

And that just about sums up what Common Ground Ministries is all about. We sing (and preach) and try to convince people to prepare their hearts to receive the King. This past year several hundred people, mostly prisoners, have opened their hearts and invited the King to take up residence there. They are changed men. Now our prayer is that they will be able to face life with success and victory. In prison, and in society when they get out. This Christmas will have new meaning for them.

Christmas is a time of being home. The old Bing Crosby song says it well: *"I'll be home for Christmas, you can plan on me..."* We are fairly new 'empty nesters,' and only Amy came home for Thanksgiving, but all three are going to make an effort to make sure their work schedules allow them to be home for Christmas. Our house has a fireplace. We don't roast chestnuts, but we do have an open fire. And sometimes our family just sits together in silence and looks at the fire. It's just good to be home and be together. Especially at Christmas.

Of course, the ultimate meaning of Christmas is that at the end of our journey here on planet Earth, we will be able to go home. The place where family is; where we are somebody.

Where we are loved just as we are. Where we know our way around and remember stories and happenings from years gone by. Where we can be with our Father (and our family) forever.

In the midst of all the busyness and shopping and cooking and gift giving and holiday celebrations, our prayer is that you will not miss the real meaning of Christmas. Our Thanksgiving wasn't the same without Adam and Katie, but how much sadder it will be if some of our family is not able to make it to that ultimate banquet at our ultimate Home in the place that the Bible calls Heaven. Just as our children are planning their work schedules and making sure that their vehicles are in good shape for the six-hour trip home, I want to be sure that I am preparing every day for my final trip. And if my 'ride' shows up today, I want to be ready. Do you have your reservations made? You can't beat the price. And if you had to pay, you couldn't afford it! Jesus paid the price. MERRY CHRISTMAS! CHRIST THE SAVIOR IS BORN!

December - 2009

A Reunion

We received word on New Year's morning that Lydia's brother, Ed Byler, died suddenly and unexpectedly of an apparent heart attack during the morning hours in Waxhaw, NC, where he lived. So New Year's Day was spent making phone calls and notifying relatives scattered across the continent and overseas (some have no phone). On Saturday we traveled to Waxhaw for the memorial service and then back to Ohio for the funeral at the old Fairlawn Mennonite Church building where Ed was saved, baptized, and is now buried beside his brother, Simon. It was a time of grieving, rejoicing, reminiscing, and visiting with relatives and friends.

One of the comments that I heard several times was, "It's too bad we have to wait for a death to get together." I have thought that same thing myself. But at Ed's funeral I had a new thought; as Ed entered into the presence of the Lord, I imagine him lighting up and rejoicing as he walks (runs?) through the Pearly Gates and sees Jesus with open arms. Then there stand his Mom and Dad, and his brother, Simon. And his brother Andy, who died when Ed was just two years old. And then Grandma and Grandpa... and on and on. Friends and relatives from near and far from Ed's life of 63 years on earth, from the rest of the 20th century and then from millennia past. What a reunion! Meeting his great-great-great-great-etc. grandparents! Then Abraham! And Moses...!!!

I wonder if he isn't so busy hugging and shaking hands for the next hundred years that he won't even notice that he's gone until we get there and he has to run over and join the welcoming committee for us. Do you suppose St. Peter had to tap Tobe Byler on the shoulder to get his attention and get him to quit shaking hands with friends so he could say, "Hey Tobe! Look who's coming! You'd better get over there to the gate!"?

In other words, as Ed entered Heaven, it was (and will forever be) a **reunion**. As Ed exited this physical life, it was a reunion down here for us. We hugged and shook hands and told each other how old we looked. (Well, we thought it!) We laughed and cried and ate (and ate) and promised to stay in touch better, and not just wait for a sad occasion.

But the truth is, we are busy. And life happens. As pastor Jeremy Miller said in the funeral service, life is a struggle. Some relatives who wanted desperately to be there had to work.

Others couldn't come because of the weather. Others had family issues. They were in the middle of 'life.' And so, we won't see some of these relatives again until someone else in the family is called home. To a reunion. And then those of us who are left will get together to honor the life of the loved one and grieve and rejoice and reminisce...

So maybe death is not just separation. Maybe it's also a **Reunion!** In Heaven, and on earth. Yes, we miss Ed. But we grieve not as those who have no hope. There is a great reunion planned. Don't miss it!

(FOR MORE INFORMATION SEE JOHN 3:16)

January - 2010

Prison Crusade

I just got back from the 32nd annual We Care Prison Crusade. Over 400 volunteers from a dozen states came to Alabama at their own expense for a week of ministry in 20 prisons throughout southern Alabama and northern Florida. There were 21 music groups and 22 different speakers/preachers who sang and spoke to potentially over 20,000 prisoners! Every day, volunteers went into the prisons to roam the cell blocks and dorms and talk to prisoners, and each night the music groups and speakers came to a chapel service and presented the gospel to those who had been invited by the volunteers. I haven't heard any statistics, but I know that many prisoners were touched and changed by the singing and preaching of the Word.

I started out at Century Correctional in Century, FL, on Monday night, after a Sunday night concert at my college roommate's church in Niceville. (Two of my grade school classmates also showed up for the Niceville concert!). The rest of the week I was at two prisons near Montgomery and one near Troy, AL. Those four prisons have a combined population of 4,032!

"YOU ATE WITH US..."

I have been going to this event for around fifteen years, so anyone who has been in prison for a while may remember me. One prisoner came up to me and said, "I remember you. You ate with us." He looked me in the eye for a few seconds and then walked away. "You ate with us." That simple act (which may be simple, but it isn't always easy, depending on how the food is) touched this inmate, and he started to attend chapel. He didn't tell me where he was spiritually, just that he attended chapel. Because I ate with him. (I was hoping maybe he would say something about my singing. He didn't.)

I contend that 85% of prison ministry is simply showing up. Many of these prisoners don't get any visitors. I sang Randy Davenport's song that Gary Paxton gave me entitled, "Mail Call." It's the true story in song about an inmate in Missouri who went to mail call every day for 15 years and never got a single letter. After singing that sad song, I always hear similar testimonies: "I've been here for 15 years, and I've never gotten a letter..."

Prayer is important. Correspondence Bible Study courses are vital. Finances are needed. But the thing that catches the attention of a man in prison is... showing up. And if you eat with him, that's even better. And if something good happens spiritually... well, that's why we go to prisons.

February - 2010

The Gates of Hell

The day after our Common Ground Ministries Banquet in Sarasota, Lydia and I headed for Niceville, FL, to attend a mission conference at the Methodist Church pastored by my college roommate, Rurel Ausley. The speaker was one of our classmates, Jeannine Brabon.

Jeannine grew up in Medellin, Columbia, a city that was at one time known as the murder capital of the world. Along with teaching Hebrew at the OMS Seminary in Medellin, she works with Prison Fellowship at one of the most dangerous prisons in the world, Bellavista Prison.

Bellavista houses the most infamous and dangerous drug lords and hired killers in Columbia. It was built for 1,600 prisoners, but now has a population of 6,600! At one time, this prison averaged one murder per day! It was such an evil place that author David Miller tells of visitors watching the men play soccer in the yard with the head of a murdered inmate! Enemy drug cartels are housed together in the same prison, and the tension and hatred can be felt.

Into this atmosphere of evil, hatred, blood, and drugs entered Professor Jeannine Brabon to teach some newly converted killers and drug lords the truth of scripture. Here is a quote from the OMS website:

> Though few dared to visit Bellavista, Medellin's maximum-security prison noted for daily murders, Jeannine and a team of Colombian evangelists carried the Gospel inside. As a result, many lives have been transformed, and the murders have dissipated. In 1992 Jeannine began the Bellavista Prison Bible Institute. Through this discipleship program, over 400 prisoners have graduated and now minister to other inmates all across the nation in the penitentiaries where they are.

Jeannine is under constant death threats, false rumors, and pot shots, etc., but she continues to teach and disciple her class in prison. Every now and then a stranger will come to her and let her know that he was hired to kill her, so 'lay low.' Watch out. No way is he going to kill the beloved teacher, but be careful. She said every once and a while the Lord will nudge her and she will immediately drive to the airport, buy a ticket, and fly to the U.S. OMS has "strongly recommended" that she leave Columbia. She won't!

Every day she realizes that this might be her last day on earth. What does she do about that tension? Well, first of all, she says there is no tension. That's how we should live our lives anyway. And since this may be her last day on earth, she never misses an opportunity to tell anyone she meets about Jesus. She leads someone to Jesus every day!

I was challenged by her life. I told Pastor Rurel, "And I thought

I was in prison ministry!" He answered, "And I thought I was in ministry!" After hearing the life and death stories of Jeannine, we realized how easy we have it. I have never been threatened. I have never felt danger. But I am going to try to start living my life as if this is my last day on earth.

MORE ON JEANNINE:

In addition to her prison ministry, Jeannine is a professor of Biblical Hebrew at the OMS seminary in Medellin. She translated William LaSor's two-volume Hebrew grammar and lessons into Spanish. She is also involved in evangelism, discipleship, and training national church leadership. She currently serves in leadership with Prison Fellowship Colombia in the regional office of Antioquia.

March - 2010

A Fresh Look at Jesus

Taken from Power Source Magazine. December 2004 pg. 14.
(written by an anonymous grandpa)

Every year we attend a local church pageant at Christmas time, which tells the story of His birth through His resurrection. It is a spectacular event with live animals and hundreds of cast members in realistic costumes. The Magi enter the huge auditorium on llamas from the rear, descending the steps in pomp and majesty. Roman soldiers look huge and menacing in their costumes and makeup.

Of all the years we have attended, one stands out indelibly in my heart. It was the year we took our 3-year-old granddaughter, Bailey, who loves Jesus. She was mesmerized throughout the entire play, not just watching, but also involved as if she were there in history. She watched as Joseph and Mary traveled to the Inn and was thrilled when she saw the baby Jesus in His mother's arms. When Jesus, on a young donkey, descends the steps from the back of the auditorium, depicting His triumphal entry into Jerusalem, Bailey was ecstatic. As he neared our aisle, Bailey began jumping up and down, screaming, "Jesus, Jesus! There's Jesus!" She was not just saying the words but exclaiming them with every fiber of her being. She alternated between screaming his name and hugging us. "It's Jesus! Look!" I thought she might actually pass out. Tears filled my eyes as I looked at Jesus through the eyes of a child in love with Him, seeing Him for the first time. How much she was like the blind beggar screaming out in reckless abandon, "Jesus, Jesus!" – afraid he might miss Him, not caring what others thought (Mk. 10:46, 47). This was so much fun.

Then came the arrest scene. On stage, the soldiers shoved and slapped Jesus they moved Him from the Garden of Gethsemane to Pilate. Bailey responded as if she were in the crowd of women, with terror and anger. "Stop it!" she screamed. "Bad soldiers, stop it!" As I watched her reaction, I wished we had talked to her before the play.

"Bailey, it's okay. They are just pretending."

"They are hurting Jesus! Stop it!"

She stood in her seat, reacting to each and every move. People around us first smiled at her reaction, thinking, "How cute!" Then they quit smiling and began watching her watch Him. In a most powerful scene, the soldiers lead Jesus, carrying the cross, down the steps of the auditorium from the back. They were yelling, whipping, and cursing at Jesus who was bloodied and beaten. Bailey was now hysterical. "Stop it! Soldiers! Stop it!" she screamed. She must have been wondering why all these people did nothing. She then began to cry instead of scream, "Jesus, oh, Jesus!"

People all around us began to weep as we all watched this devoted little disciple see Jesus beaten and killed as those first-century disciples had. Going back and forth between her mother's lap and in need for comfort, she was distraught. I kept saying, "Bailey, it's okay. Jesus is going to be okay. These are just people pretending to be soldiers." She looked at me like I was crazy.

In my lap, we talked through the cross and burial. "Watch, Bailey, watch for Jesus!" The tomb began to tremble, and lightening flashed as the stone rolled away. A Super Bowl touchdown cheer couldn't come close to matching this little one's reaction to the resurrection. "Jesus! He's okay! Mommy, it's Jesus!"

I prayed that she wasn't going to be traumatized by

this event, but that she would remember it. I'll never forget it! I shall never forget seeing Jesus' suffering, crucifixion, and resurrection through the eyes of an innocent child.

Following the pageant, the actors all assembled in the foyer to be greeted by the audience. As we passed by some of the soldiers, Bailey screamed out, "Bad soldier, don't you hurt Jesus." The actor who portrayed Jesus was some distance away surrounded by well-wishers and friends. Bailey broke away from us and ran toward him, wrapping herself around his legs, holding on for dear life. He hugged her and said, "Jesus loves you." He patted her to go away. She wouldn't let go. She kept clinging to Him, laughing and calling His name. She wasn't about to let go of her Jesus.

I think God in Heaven stopped whatever was He doing on that day and made all the angels watch Bailey. "Now, look there! You see what I meant when I said, 'Of such is the kingdom of heaven?'" Bailey's reaction should be our reaction every day when we think of Him, who He is, what He did for us, and what He offers us.

How can we do anything less than worship Him?

April - 2010

In His Service

Five states,
  two countries,
    seven prisons,
      five churches,
        four funerals,
          two banquets,
            twelve concerts,
              ten lunch meetings with friends and supporters,
            four hours of mushroom hunting (found a few)...
      100 friends gained,
    20 lbs. Lost! (on purpose)

That was April in a nutshell. And that's not counting going to Columbus to meet with the head of Ohio Prison Chaplains to talk about a new ministry that may start in Holmes County. I came home from Thomas, OK, on March 29 and drove west and north through Detroit to join Nelson Coblentz in Leamington, Ontario, to travel with his Easter Tour through Ontario, New York, Pennsylvania, Maryland, and then back home. (It was a blast!) The month ended with a busy week of four prisons, two funerals, and two concerts.

One of the highlights of the month was our Annual Spring Banquet at Hartville. Our guests were Steve & Annie Chapman. I sing many of their songs about family and fathers in the prison chapels, and their sermon through song that night was inspiring as well as entertaining. And I not only had the privilege of being on the same program with them, I actually sang a couple of Steve's songs with Annie and him as my 'backup' singers! The evening was a blessing and a blast!

As we look forward to summer, we have an exciting and grueling schedule, including close to 20 prison services, a cruise to Alaska, Benton Days, a camp, several family reunions (one of them is our own family), two church conferences, the Holmes Co. Fair (Sat. night), a Wingfield Festival (tied in with the Mennonite Relief Sale in Kidron), and then ending the summer at Orrvilla Retirement Center (Orrville) on Aug. 28. (Just for the evening – we're not retiring!)

It is a privilege to serve God by doing what I love to do: sing, preach, travel, and be with people. And to know that my meager efforts sometimes result in a person's life being changed from death to life, from darkness to light, from despair to delight, from Hell to Heaven, makes it all worth it. And to know that many of you are on our side with your prayers, your presence, and your finances makes it even more enjoyable and endurable.

To quote a famous Norwegian from Minnesota: "Well, that's the news from Benton, OH. Where all the women are strong, all the men are good-looking, and all the children are above average."

May - 2010

Diversity

DIVERSITY adj. Latin. *diversus* < 1. unlike in kind: distinct. 2. Having diversity in form: varied.

We hear a lot about the word 'diversity' in our current

politically correct age. I have serious problems with the way it's being used and mandated in the political arena, but in our ministry, it helps to *"...become all things to all men so that by all possible means I might save some."* I Cor. 9:22

In the month of May I had the privilege to be a part of Wesleyan Camp Banquet, a Mennonite college graduation, a local park fundraiser, a new prison ministry starting up in Holmes County, a meeting in Nashville with singers and songwriters, two prison ministry banquets, eight prison chapel services, a guitar seminar in prison, an Amish school assembly, and an Amish funeral! Now, folks, that is "varied;" Diverse.

Several thoughts:

1. No matter what your background (or language, tongue, tribe, or nation), the Gospel that we proclaim *"...penetrates even to dividing soul and spirit, joints and marrow; it judges the thoughts and attitudes of the heart."* (Heb. 4:12)

2. With your help, we have been able to sing and speak in a wide variety of places and circumstances. The Gospel of Jesus Christ is for every human on planet Earth. *"He is not willing that **any** should perish, but **everyone** should come to repentance."* (2 Pet 3:9) (emphasis mine)

3. No matter what reaction a person has to the gospel, his heart is agreeing with God's Word. There is something in every person that recognizes the Truth. That is why we have the audacity to proclaim His word in prisons, overseas, places of higher learning... wherever we are invited.

"I love to tell the story, because I know it's true."

June - 2010

A Lesson From Alaska

After a prison and a motorcycle rally at Pond Bank Mennonite Church near Chambersburg, PA (with ex-con jewel thief "Murf the Surf" Jack Murphy), Lydia and I and 70 other friends headed for Seattle to board a ship for Alaska to be part of a Gospel Cruise with 8 different Gospel singing groups. We sailed up to Skagway and then down the Inside Passage. I had the privilege of being one of the singers. It was a great trip of ministry, relaxation, refreshment, and fellowship.

If all we would have had on the ship were the awesome scenery, the trip would have been worth it. If all we would have had were the fellowship, it would have been a great trip. If all we would have had was the singing... well, you get the point. It was a good time!

One of the amazing historical facts I learned was what took place in the late 1890s in Skagway, AK. Skagway is where the gold seekers departed from what little civilization there was and headed into the Yukon wilderness. The best and worst of humanity came out in the rush for wealth in what has become known as the Klondike Gold Rush. From what little history I gathered and a few books I bought, it seems that greed and the desire for gold possessed men so much that they lost all of their senses! They did brainless and heartless things.

On the other hand, the perseverance and determination of these men is unbelievable! Even admirable.

To get to the gold fields, they had to carry 2,000 lbs. of goods on their backs up a mountain path that was too steep for horses, and then down the other side. Canadian law would not allow any man to enter the Yukon unless he had a year's supply of goods (no WalMarts there). At the top of the mountain, the Canadian Mounties carefully weighed their supplies and stored them. Then back down to Skagway for another 50 lbs. Forty trips up and back, up and back, and then 40 trips down the other side and back until their year's supply was safely on the shores of Lake Bennett and ready for them to load onto a raft – which they would have to build. And then float another 400 miles north down the Yukon River to Dawson where the gold supposedly was!

These men walked 2,400 miles to get their ton of goods over the Chilkoot Trail to the other side – a distance of 33 miles! And 22,000 men actually did it! And the number of people who actually got rich (or even 'well off') in the gold rush is staggeringly small.

Part of me admires the stamina, the persistence, and the pure guts it took to complete the task. But part of me thinks, "What fools!" They played the lottery with their lives and with the lives of their families. Granted, it was the 'Gay Nineties,' the economy was bad, and life was tough. Some say they had nothing to lose. Others think that they just wanted adventure and an escape from the humdrum lives they were living.

At any rate, I was challenged. Challenged to spend my energy on something worthwhile. Try to steer from foolish endeavors. I only have so much time and energy left, and I want it to count. I am a risk-taker. But some risks are calculated risks, and some are foolhardy. You do have to leave the safety of first base if you ever want to make it to second base and eventually score. But it helps to evaluate the situation and at least know where the ball is and who has it, and how strong his arm is and how far away he is.

Life is uncertain. Ask those who had money in financial institutions that have failed. But God is the same yesterday, today, and forever. He is one 'risk' that is sure. No matter how bad things are down here, you can always depend on Him. He will never leave you or forsake you (Heb. 13:5). His law, His statutes, His precepts, and His commands *"...are more precious than gold, than much pure gold..."* (Ps. 19:10). We need gold (finances) to live. But even more important, we need God. I'm still learning. Even from a gold rush 100 years ago.

July - 2010

Family Reunions

FAMILY rt. 1. a fundamental social group in society consisting esp. of a man and woman and their offspring. 2. a group of people sharing common ancestry. 3. distinguished lineage. 4. all the members of a household living under one roof

REUNION n. 1. a gathering of members of a group who have been previously separated.

Reunions. We drove seven hundred miles to attend Lydia's family reunion in the Upper Peninsula of Michigan for our fourth family reunion this summer. The first three were not even our family. We attended those because I was asked to sing. Except one, I guess. Two years ago we were looking at the old pictures of this Hostetler family, and I noticed Lydia's grandmother in one of them. When I pointed it out to one of the family, he said, "Well, I guess we're cousins!" So, they invited us again. This time as singer/entertainer/preacher/... *and cousin!*

I'm beginning to disagree with legendary Ohio State coach Woody Hayes about Michigan. It is a beautiful state! Hayes wouldn't even pronounce the word, "Michigan." He referred to it as "That state up North." He once ran out of gas on the way home because he refused to buy gas in the state! :-) The Ohio State-Michigan rivalry is the greatest in all of sports. But even a Buckeye has to admit it's a beautiful state. Trees, woods, lakes, snowmobile trails... and in one little spot 250 miles west of the Mackinaw Bridge; Bylers!

Lydia's Byler family is big and diverse; everything from Old Order Amish to Arizona Rangers. They are scattered all over the place; New Hampshire to Idaho, Arizona to Sarasota, Central America to Romania.... If I counted right in the Byler book, Lydia is one of 76 Byler grandchildren. (And one of 99 Gingerich grandchildren! I had six first cousins. Talk about being outnumbered!)

The reunion was a blast! There were several hundred people, even though not even half of the clan showed up. We had an auction, a church service, sharing of family stories (some were true), and a weekend of catching up and just 'shooting the breeze' with people that are part of the family – not just the Byler family, but the family of God.

The few times my family went to reunions, I was not excited. Old people in wheelchairs, my dad talking to uncles and aunts that I had never seen before, not many kids my age... But now that I am one of those old people (no wheelchair, though, PTL), I would give a thousand dollars to be able to sit down with some of those old fogies and ask some questions about my family. (I'd borrow the money from Dad.) In fact, the older I get, the more I appreciate my family. On August 1 we celebrated Mom and Dad's 65th wedding anniversary! Their anniversary is July 1, but since we're all boys, nobody thought to celebrate until after the fact. Better late than never. Anyway, what a blessing to still have Mom & Dad. They are great-great-grandparents. And they are still healthy and still together!

Family. I hear talk that it takes a village to raise a child. But it takes a *home* to make a village. And it takes a family to make a home. The family is the basic unit of a nation. It takes a heritage like I saw at the Byler family reunion to make a legacy that is passed down through the generations so that our children carry on not just the family name, but a relationship with the living God through Jesus Christ. Lydia's dad, grandfather, and great-grandfather were preachers. Several uncles and a whole bunch of her cousins are in the ministry. Her immediate family is in the ministry. I want my family to pass a Godly heritage to my children and grandchildren, etc., and also to my neighbors (village) and to the world.

August - 2010

September

(AUTUMN, FALL, HARVEST)

I'm sitting on the front porch listening to the crickets and frogs and the sounds of summer. It's warm. Twilight is just about past, and it's getting dark. Last night I performed a 'A Tribute To Johnny Cash' concert at the John Streeter Garden Amphitheater at the Secrest Arboretum in Wooster. It was a perfect night, just like tonight. The amphitheater setting was almost as beautiful as the front yard I'm looking at now (OK, it was more beautiful, but I own this yard), and 400 plus people were there to listen. I had two good guitarists to help. All went well. What a great way to send off summer and bring in the fall.

"...summer's almost gone, and winter's coming on..." Remember that Bill Monroe song? *"I've been working on the chain gang too long..."* I haven't been working on the chain gang, but I have worked with them. Or at least with men who would be on the chain gang if Ohio had such a thing. In the last several years we have not had quite as many prison services during the summer. There are several reasons for that. One is the stage of our family. Our children are grown and gone. Another factor is the demand (opportunity) for other types of ministry: camps, revivals, concerts, and local events. And then there are factors in prison life: during nice summer nights, men are not as likely to attend a chapel service. And there are so many more 'outside' groups going into prisons that sometimes the chapel schedule is filled up for the summer.

So as the summer days grow shorter and cooler, I am reminded of how time just marches on. Did I get everything done I had planned? Is the harvest past, is summer over, and we are not saved (Jeremiah 8:20)? Have I done all I could do to prepare for winter? I still have some work to do in our yard. I still have several prison letters to answer. I have to prepare songs, sermons, and speeches for a singing and speaking tour to Ireland and Germany next month. (At least I won't be distracted by the Cleveland Indians this fall.)

Looking back, it was a great summer. Busy. Productive. Fun. About one prison service per week. A cruise to Alaska. About one concert per week. Several banquets, church services, five family reunions, the Mennonite Relief Sale in combination with a Wingfield Festival, a spiritual retreat in North Carolina, and two recording sessions at The Cash Cabin Studio in Hendersonville, TN. Visits from our children and trips to visit them.

If I would evaluate my life, I would have to say that summer is about past; I am entering the fall of my life. If I live to be 120 years old, I'm still in summer, but if God gives me three score and ten years, it's late fall for me. I feel great. I'm healthy. Happy. I have plans and goals and dreams. I guess what I'm trying to say is, every day is a gift. The passing of summer has made me think of how time passes – like what we think about on New Year's Eve. We have today. We have the promise of eternal life, but we don't have the promise of tomorrow. I want to live each day in the spirit of Martin Luther: "Live each day as if Christ was crucified yesterday, rose today, and is coming back tomorrow."

Have a great fall. Be ready for winter. I leave you with the words of Ravi Zacharias: "If you don't know Christ, turn to Him. If you do know Him, make Him known."

...summer's almost gone, winter's comin' on...

September - 2010

Pennsylvania Deutscher
COUNTRY-SÄNGER
JOHN SCHMID AUS BERLIN (OHIO)
GASTIERT IM AUSANDERLAND MUSEUM OBERALBEN

That's the headline of the Pfannenstiel, Germany, newspaper where I will be the featured speaker and singer at the German/Pennsylvania Dutch Association annual festival in a village near Mainz, Germany in October. They heard my "In Dutch" CD and figured I must be an expert, so they invited me to their festival! The headline translates: "Pennsylvania Dutch Country Singer, John Schmid, from Berlin (Ohio) is the guest at the Emigrant Museum of Oberalben."

We (Lydia, Katie, and I) plan to spend the first two weeks of October in Ireland where I have been invited to perform 'A Tribute to Johnny Cash' concerts in about a dozen Irish towns, including two concerts in the Northern Ireland city of Belfast. Katie is going to split off and visit her friends at the mission where she worked for close to a year in Galway, then she will meet up with us in Dublin to cross the English Channel into Germany. I am scheduled at three speaking and singing programs there, and we also plan to see if we can find out where my clan of Schmids came from. Last year we found my mother's grandmother's home farm in Waterford, Ireland, but my great-great-grandfather, Adam Schmid, didn't leave much of a trail when he left Germany in 1855. We have a few hints, so we'll be in some town halls and courthouses acting like Sherlock Holmes to see if we can pick up his scent.

Now, Paul told us not to devote ourselves to endless genealogies (My paraphrase of I Tim 1:4). All I can say in my defense is... they're not endless! We can't even figure out where they started! We just want to know what town in Germany grandpa Adam Schmid came from. By the way – believe it or not – his wife's name was Eve! I am the great-great-grandson of Adam & Eve!

The purpose of the trip, of course, is to plant seeds of the Gospel, as well as harvest. Since Ireland is generally a Catholic country and I am invited there by Protestants, the goal is to establish good will and trust between the two cultures as well as proclaim the way of salvation, no matter which church happens to be in the audience. This will be my second trip to County Cork in the south and my third time to County Donegal in the north, so even though they know that I am neither Irish nor Catholic, they seem to trust me, and I even get the feeling that they like me! And once the audience likes you, they will listen to your story. And on this 'A Tribute to Johnny Cash' concert tour, presenting the gospel will be as simple and inoffensive as singing Johnny Cash songs, telling his story and then singing some of the gospel songs that he wrote. I am excited about the potential that this trip has to proclaim Jesus! It's going to be fun! Pray for us.

October - 2010

The American Dream

"A chicken in every pot and a car in every garage."
– Herbert Hoover

My generation never knew anything less.

I thought of this as I stood on the pier at Bremerhaven, Germany, where my ancestor, Adam Schmid (not to be confused with my descendant, Adam T. Schmid), sailed away in 1855 from everything that was familiar to him and headed for the New World, looking for a better life. Although it would be 73 years before Hoover would utter that campaign slogan, I'm sure great-grandpa Schmid was already dreaming it. It didn't matter to him that cars weren't invented yet. Why else would someone leave his family, his home, what security there was, and get on a ship where the chances of arriving safely on the other shore were less than 90%? (Would you get on an airplane that had even a 98% record of safe flights?)

Even more desperate was the story of my mother's grandparents, who left Ireland sometime in the late 1800's. The potato famine had decimated and impoverished the country (i.e. – the people). They came over on unfit vessels that were called "famine ships." People were crammed in like sardines on the lower deck. And although the chances of the ship arriving safely were 90%, the staggering statistic is that when (if) the ship did arrive, 50% of the passengers had died en route! And one of my great-grandmothers friends, after risking everything and spending her last cent to get to NY, was coughing while standing in line at Ellis Island, so they put her back on the boat and shipped her back to Ireland.

There are some amazing immigrant success stories – the Carnegie's, the Kennedys, Levi Strauss, Henry Ford... immigrants who came to the New World looking for a better life and achieved success and accomplishment beyond their wildest dreams.

My family is one of those stories. Well, maybe not on the same scale as the aforementioned, but I have a chicken in every pot, several in the freezer, and a car in both of my garages! I'll bet Grandpa Schmid could never have imagined that a descendant would someday return to Germany to try to find his hometown and then write this newsletter about it on a computer while traveling home in a flying contraption at 600 MPH, 7 miles above the ocean! And make it from Frankfurt, Germany, to Benton, OH, in one day! (And then complain about the flight delays!)

The American Dream. I am living it. Never missed a meal. I own my own home. Several cars. My children went to college... etc.

The interesting thing is that I know some folks who have everything the American dream and the Hollywood advertisers say we should have to be happy – and they're not! In fact, some of them are miserable. Malcontents. Bitter. Like the rich young ruler in Matthew 19, they say, "I've done everything right (my paraphrase). "What do I still lack?" Jesus looked at the young man with love and basically said, (my paraphrase) "The best things in life are not **things**. Follow me."

Folks, I recommend the American Dream. But like the warning on cigarette packs, I must add: *"WARNING: The great physician wants you to know that following the American Dream will not bring contentment."* What do you still lack? Follow Him. Bill Bright once said, "If you want to bless your children, don't leave them a pile of money; leave them a Christian heritage."

Newsletter summary: We had a great trip. Genealogy side trips. I have a new perspective on the American Dream. Follow Jesus! HAPPY THANKSGIVING!

Oh! And I had 20 concerts in Ireland (in English) and 3 concerts in Germany (in Pennsylvania Dutch).

November - 2010

Home for Christmas

HOME n. 1. a place where one lives. 2. a dwelling place together with the family. 3. an environment affording security and happiness,

HEAVEN n. 2. the abode of God, the angels, and the souls of those granted salvation. 4. a condition or place of supreme happiness.

In 1943, Bing Crosby's recording of the song, "I'll Be Home For Christmas," shot to the top ten of the record charts that year and became a holiday musical tradition. One source says that the idea of being home for Christmas originated in World War I when soldiers at first thought that the war would be quick and they would return by Christmastime. This did not happen, hence the line in the song, *"...if only in my dreams."*

Who am I to argue with the experts? I don't doubt that the soldiers wanted to be home for Christmas, and I wasn't even born then, but I just don't believe that's where it started. The desire to be home for Christmas was in the heart of man long before WWI. I have always wanted to be home for Christmas, even before I knew there was a world war, or a song, "I'll Be Home for Christmas."

There is just something about Christmas. In 1976 I spent Christmas in Germany. I was also there in '77, '78 and '79. In 1980 I got married on Dec. 20 (same day as my wife). Our honeymoon was only three days long because we wanted to be *home for Christmas!* Then for the next seven years we were in Costa Rica for Christmas. So in that 14-year stretch, I was only 'home' for Christmas once. And even though Costa Rica was our home for seven years, it wasn't quite like being where my family was, where lifelong friends were, where every building and crossroad had a memory.

I will be home for Christmas this year, but now the question is: will all of our children be home? It doesn't look like it, since Adam has to work on Christmas Day every other year. He was here for Thanksgiving. The girls will be here, and we will probably call Adam that day as a poor consolation to his actually being here. There is just something about being home for Christmas!

I think Christmas is the greatest holiday of the year, even though I know that Easter is actually much more important theologically. Without the cross, Christmas would be meaningless. Of course, without Christmas, Easter would be impossible. But for some reason, our culture – and much of the world – has made a huge deal about Christmas. There is something about the lights, the decorations, the snow, and the spirit of things that seem to make it a special time.

Christmas: A time of joy, celebration, family, home... except in prison. There, it is a time of despair and depression. They can't go *home*. Everybody is celebrating and getting together at home, and they're... well, they are in prison. We long to be home.

I'll be home for Christmas! Family, fireplace, food, presents...

I think Christmas is symbolic of what it's going to be like when we really get 'home' - when we get to heaven. Family, warmth, nourishment, the presence of our Father... it don't get any better than that. And I guess that's what my goal in life is: to get home for Christmas. And to help as many as possible to get there, too. So just as December 25 is symbolic to help us remember the birth of Jesus Christ, may Christmas be symbolic to remind us to do all we can to make it home when all is said and done here on earth.

"Let every heart prepare Him room." "Sing, all ye citizens of Heaven above..."

MERRY CHRISTMAS! Home, sweet home...

December - 2010

Happy New Year! 2011!

The year in the rear view mirror...

The first day of 2010 we were awakened by a phone call to tell us that Lydia's brother Ed had died of a heart attack during the night. Our first week of the year was filled with a trip to Waxhaw, NC, and then back to Ohio to help with funeral arrangements (in both places). Ed was buried next to his brother Simon and near his parents at the Fairlawn Mennonite Cemetery, Apple Creek, OH.

January – Our years seem to be developing a pattern. In

January we went to Florida to be a part of The Inspirations benefit concert to benefit a mission in Haiti. This trip included a prison service at Bushnell, FL, with the Gospel Echoes, and then a variety of concerts in the Pinecraft area of Sarasota. Then to Atmore, AL, for the weeklong prison crusade (17 prisons!) with We Care Ministries. By the time you read this, we will doing the same thing... Florida concerts, prison, We Care... then back home.

In February we went back down to Florida (with a concert in Georgia on the way) for our Minister's Fellowship meetings and a few informal concerts and our first annual Common Ground Ministries Banquet, which turned out great!

Here are some highlights from the rest of the year: a Shipshewana concert, wild game night in Virginia, meeting with the state chaplain of Ohio about starting a ministry to mothers in prison with babies, and revival meetings in Plain City right during the girls state basketball tourney (Hiland – 2nd in state). Next, a series of meetings, prisons, and concerts in Hydro, OK, the Easter tour with Gospel Express through five states and Ontario, Canada, the EMU graduation (Adam's girlfriend, now fiancée), banquets in Hartville, OH, and Greenwood, DE, with prison services sprinkled all along the way.

Whew! Are you still with me? A motorcycle rally in Pennsylvania with Jack Murphy, five concerts on an Alaskan Cruise (life is rough), Benton Days, Doughty Valley Singing, a recording at the Cash Cabin Studio in Hendersonville, TN, Little Eden Camp, the Byler Reunion in the UP of Michigan, Conservative Mennonite Conference in Ohio, a retreat in North Carolina, a rest home in Plain City, the Nappanee Apple

Festival (Indiana), Freedom Rally-London Prison, a retreat in Harrisonburg, VA, and then...

Ireland! Twenty concerts in two weeks from County Cork in the south to County Donegal in the north. Then to Germany for the Deutsch-Pennsylvanisch Gemeinschaft Arbeitskreis and the Pfalzischer Mundartdichterwettstreit, which basically means, Pennsylvania Dutch dialect festivals. As soon as I got home (Oct 29), I took the new baby ministry committee (called 'Shelter an Angel') to Canyon City, CO, to visit New Horizons Ministries, the model for that type of prison baby care.

The week after Thanksgiving (everybody was home!), Adam announced his engagement to Katie Rodriquez of Grottos, VA. So we are all excited! Christmas was great (white) and now believe it or not, as we start a New Year all over again (or continue, depending on your perspective), I am making New Year's resolutions. Yes, I am resolved to be better, deeper, and closer to Jesus and His people and my family in 2011 than I was in 2010. I'm not guaranteed much more time, not even tomorrow, here on planet Earth, and I want my life to count. (Don't you?) So I make resolutions (plans). If I don't keep them, I am resolved to keep trying until I get it right. *"The noble man makes noble plans..."* (Isaiah 32:8)

HAPPY NEW YEAR! Thank you for your prayers, comments, support, friendship... I am so thankful for you, for this ministry, for health, for family, friends, faith, freedom, salvation... I'm out of room!

January - 2011

(Another) Divine Appointment

Carol Kent's son is serving a life sentence for murder. In her book, Between a Rock and a Grace Place, she tells about a woman, Tammy, who wrote to her after a women's conference.

In 1995, my mother was shot and killed by a boy named Matthew Ben Rodriquez. My mom was the most compassionate person anyone could ever meet. The last time we were together, she said something strange as she left for Florida: "If something ever happens to me, don't hate the person, only what he did." Two weeks later she was dead.

About a year after Mom died, I felt God tugging at my heart to forgive those who took her from me. I did not want to do it. But I wrote a letter to the man who pulled the trigger – Matthew Ben Rodriquez – telling him that I forgave him. I never mailed the letter.

I was so struck by your compassion for those who have lost loved ones as a result of crimes. I have forgiven Matt Rodriguez, though I must say it has been a struggle. I found out that your son, Jason, is in the same prison as Matt Rodriguez. Please know that... I will now pray for Jason and you as well...

Carol Kent sent this letter to her son, wondering if he happened to know Matt. She discovered that Matt Rodriguez is one of Jason's best friends in prison and is a dynamic Christian. The next time Jason saw Matt, he showed him the letter sent by his victim's daughter. Matt read it and began to weep. The next time Carol went to prison to visit her son, Matt saw her in the visiting room and came over and knelt down next to her. With tears in his eyes, told her that he had written a letter to Tammy but didn't know how to reach her. *"God has done so much in my life, and I want to be able to ask for forgiveness from the family..."* By this time, Jason was crying, and Carol could hardly control her emotions.

Long story short: Matt got in touch with Tammy, his murder victim's daughter. She wrote back. She forgave him. This story is not done, but in Carol's book, Tammy writes; *"Matthew and I are writing fairly often and are finding common safe ground."*

Carol quotes Johann Christoph Arnold: *"Forgiveness is power. It can heal both the forgiver and the forgiven. In fact, it could change the world if we allowed it to."*

It reminds me of the last paragraph in the book, *Forgiving the Dead Man Walking*. The victim, Debbie Morris, was asked after the perpetrator's execution if she believed in the death penalty: *"All I know is that justice never did a thing to help me recover. Forgiveness did."*

There is an addendum by Jesus after the Lord's Prayer that has been called the most frightening verse in all of scripture: **"...*if you do not forgive men their sins, your Father will not forgive your sins.*"** *(!)* (Matt. 6:15) (Emphasis and explanation point added.)

February - 2011

"...there were also other boats with him..."

You never know who is watching. Steve Wingfield points out that in the storm on the Sea of Galilee, *"...there were also other boats with him."* (Mark 4:36) They were watching how Jesus would deal with adversity. Do you realize that 'other boats' are watching you? And me? Read this letter a friend of mine received a couple of months ago from another boat:

> *Dear Joe [name changed],*
>
> *This is a letter I have been meaning to write for some time. Somehow the days and years have gone by, and I am just now sitting down and putting my words of gratitude on paper.*
>
> *If you didn't recognize my name on the return address, and I wouldn't expect that you would, I was the claims adjuster that handled the auto accident claim for your brother about 13 years ago. For the record, I no longer work for that Insurance Co. nor have I for over ten years. I am not writing this with any connection to the company or the terrible circumstances of that accident that caused us to meet. Rather, I am writing to you to express gratitude for a spark of connection I felt with you through our working together to resolve the claim.*
>
> *It's difficult for me to describe how our meeting affected me, so I apologize in advance if I stumble. This much I know - when I met you and the other families*

in the trauma waiting room, I saw and felt something I had never experienced before. As a "seasoned" claims adjuster, I had met many families in the aftermath of tragedies. Your family and situation was different. You may not recall, but you invited me into the room where not only was your family present, but also family members of the other people involved in the accident. You invited me to pray with all of you. Your prayer included my client who caused the accident. Having not been raised with any religious upbringing, this could have been a very awkward situation, and perhaps in some sense, it was. I do know that I felt there in that room my first inkling of God and the power of prayer. And for this I give thanks to you.

For me to work with you and see how you worked with integrity, fairness and kindness was a unique experience for me. For some reason, I felt this connection with you, and I hope you look back on the situation with similar regard and were satisfied with the resolution of the claim. Again though, my reason for contact with you is beyond the scope of that claim and of a deeper, more personal nature.

I really feel that our meeting was the beginning of my spiritual journey. Through your actions and those who also suffered as a result of the accident, I saw a different way of being. I have since tried many churches, read a lot of books, talked with a lot of people and of course life itself has been my greatest teacher.

ENCOUNTERS

I have been attending Community Mennonite Church of Lancaster for four years now. In preparation for joining the church I have been reflecting on my spiritual path, and I have to include you and the light that I saw in you. I hope that you are not uncomfortable with the intimate nature of my sharing. But letting my gratitude go unspoken seemed a sad alternative. I am grateful that our paths crossed and that the light of your spirit and God's spirit shone on my path.

With kindest Regards,

"LET YOUR LIGHT SHINE BEFORE MEN... That they may see your good deeds and praise your Father in Heaven." (Matt. 5:16) I have Joe's permission to reprint this letter. I'm sure that many of you who are reading this have – or should have – received a similar letter. But maybe we should be like this woman and write to those who have influenced us. You may help someone say what Joe said; "Best letter I ever received. It made my day!"

March - 2011

The Carter Fold!
SARASOTA... ARIZONA... WHAT A TRIP!

Our new CD, *The Church in the Wildwood; A Gospel Tribute to the Carter Family*, got us an invitation to The Carter Fold – home of the original Carter Family: A.P. Carter, his wife Sarah, and sister-in-law, Mother Maybelle (mother of June Carter

Cash). Starting in 1974, they have had a Saturday night singing at the old Carter barn in Maces Springs, VA, to honor the heritage of mountain music in general and the Carter Family music in particular. To be invited there is no big deal in the music industry, but for someone like me, it was an honor and a thrill (read: Big Deal).

So we left Ohio on Saturday, Feb. 19, on our way to Florida and Arizona and stopped at 'The Fold' on the way down. Flo Wolfe, A.P.'s granddaughter, welcomed us there and showed us the backstage music room. Mark Fain, the bass player for Ricky Skaggs and producer of our Carter CD, drove four hours from Nashville to play bass for me (!) and his uncle played the fiddle. We played a total of two songs! But, hey, we were there. And it was well received by the crowd of around 500.

The next day we attended the local Methodist Church and sang several songs. John Carter Cash's wife, Laura (who sang and played fiddle on our CD) was in the congregation and she very graciously accepted my invitation to sing with Lydia, Amy, and myself. We sang about the Star (Jesus) with a star (of Nashville)! I smiled all the way to Sarasota.

SARASOTA...

...which is 800 miles from Hiltons, VA. We arrive at 1:30 AM and we loafed, ate, visited, performed a concert or two, and held our Third Annual CGM Fund Raiser Banquet at Bahia Vista Mennonite. It was a great night! Lee Domann, the author of the song "Howard Gray," spoke and sang. David Howard, author, missionary, and brother of Elisabeth Elliot, spoke about how he grew up in a Christian home, knew and loved all the old hymns... but no song ever touched him like the song, "Howard Gray." Ron Miller, Nashville executive, founder of Timothy's Gift Ministries and native of Berlin, OH, introduced Timothy's Gift, a ministry of sharing Walk Through The Bible in prisons. His team member John Starnes sang. When I told Lee Domann that John Starnes was coming, Lee said, "John Starnes! He recorded one of my songs!" So part of Lee's introduction was John Starnes singing Lee's song, "Death Ain't No Big Deal." I could not have planned such a wonderful evening if I had tried! The Lord was (and is) faithful! Again, I smiled all the way to the Grand Canyon.

ARIZONA...

Did you know that Arizona is a long way from Sarasota? And Texas is big (and wide!)? After three days of (hard) driving, we arrived at Lydia's aunt's home in Black Canyon City, AZ. Our children flew in the next day, and after a day of four-wheeling all over Yavapai County with the Byler cousins, we headed for the Grand Canyon.

Wouldn't you know! It snowed the night before we got to the Grand Canyon and the trail was snowy and icy and treacherous. After a mile of slipping and sliding, the girls decided to turn back. Lydia went with them. Adam and I (BraveHeart types) went on down. After about two miles of small, cautious steps, the trail cleared and we hustled on down to Plateau Point, six miles from the top of South Rim. We could see the Colorado River! After lamenting the fact that we started late and now it was 5 PM and we couldn't hang around too long, we turned around and headed back up the hill. At 8 PM we arrived back up top in the pitch darkness and headed for the restaurant to join Lydia and the girls for a celebration meal.

A great trip! Concerts, ministry, family vacation... I'm rested and energized. Come on April! God is good!

April - 2011

Lorain Fisher Schmid
1924 - 2011

On Wednesday, April 20, I got a call from my brother. "Mom died." I was having breakfast at a restaurant, catching up with friends after being on the road for two weeks. I try not to answer my phone when I'm in a meeting, but my brother seldom calls at that time of the morning, so I answered. When I hung up, I nodded numbly to my friends, stood up in a daze, paid my bill, stumbled out the door and drove home. I called Lydia on the way.

I was in Wooster on Monday, April 11, just before the second leg of my two-week trip, so I stopped in to see Mom. She was sitting in her chair with her oxygen and a new bandage on her leg from a wound that had festered. She was feeling good. She and Dad were going out to eat that night, like they did most nights the last few years. She always carried her little oxygen bottle, and now she had to deal with a tube in her leg that drained the wound. But she ran around like nothing was wrong. I told her that Lydia and I would come in to go eat with them when I got back, like we did every week or so.

I got home on Monday the 18th and got ready for a 10 AM meeting the next day, and our annual Hartville Spring banquet that evening (Tues). I had prison services scheduled Wednesday and Thursday night, so I had decided in my mind that we would go eat with Mom & Dad on Good Friday. Brother Tim's call came Wednesday morning.

It's amazing how short 84 years can be! I remember when Mom worked at the Moreland General Store, and she told a customer, our neighbor Dan Weaver, that she was 29 years old. He said, "Me, too." I was six years old. I thought, "29! Wow! One foot in the grave and the other on a banana peel!" OK, maybe I didn't think that exact phrase, but I couldn't fathom so many years. Now, more than 50 years later, it seems like she left us too soon.

Mom was two years old when her dad died. Grandma remarried a man who did not love his stepchildren. On Mom's 18th birthday she was told that she's an adult now, so get out! My grandpa loved me. I had no idea how he treated my mother until years later. Mom married my dad and moved to his home area of Wayne County in 1945. She made sure that our home was different from hers. She constantly told us that she loved us. Right in front of our friends! And leave home at 18?! They didn't get rid of me until I was 24! Even though I thought our home was imperfect (it was) at the time, I realize now that we three boys grew up in an ideal setting. They could have filmed the TV show, "Leave it to Beaver" at our house, except we didn't live in town.

So, this letter is a tribute to my mom. She was my biggest fan (even though my brother Steve was her favorite). She sat on the front row of my concerts. Told everyone that she taught me everything I knew (partly true, greatly exaggerated). She loved my wife and the grandchildren. Married to Dad for 65+ years. A Wooster Hospital Auxiliary Volunteer for 39 years! She received the Wayne County Senior Citizen Hall of Fame Award in 2001 for volunteer service.

I had both of my parents for 62 years, sixty years more than either my mom or dad did! (Both of my parents were two years old when their fathers died.) I thank the Lord for such wonderful parents. For an old fashioned 'normal' family. For a godly mother. I am blessed.

May - 2011

The World Didn't End
(NEWS FLASH)

"Live your life like Jesus was crucified yesterday, rose from the dead today, and is coming back tomorrow." – Martin Luther

"Life is short. Death is quick. Hell is hot. Eternity is long."
– Paul Hummel

I am not a news addict, so I didn't even know the world was supposed to end on May 21 until just a week before the supposed event. (Nobody tells me anything!) But when I heard about it, I wasn't worried... for a couple of reasons. First of all, I didn't believe it. *"No one knows the day nor the hour, not even the angels in heaven, **nor the Son**)(!)..."* (Mark 13:32) (emphasis added). I reasoned that this man probably didn't know more than Jesus. And second, I'm ready... just in case this fool is correct. I don't use the word "fool" lightly, but according to the Bible, there are at least two ways to be a fool: (1.) Say there is no God. (2.) Predict the end of the world.

Think about it. This guy, Harold Camper, couldn't win. If his prediction proved correct and the world did end, so what? Are we all going to look at him on the way up and thank him? And if it doesn't end (which it didn't the first time he predicted this in 1994, either), he looks foolish. And for good reason.

One benefit of 'Chicken Little's' prediction is that it contains a grain of truth; someday the world is going to end (Matt. 13:40). And if it doesn't end in my lifetime, the fact remains that someday the world is going to end for me. My life on earth is short – three score and ten years – if I'm fortunate enough to live a 'biblical' length of life. Which in the scheme of eternal things is not very long.

Twenty-three years ago we were given 88 reasons why the Lord was coming back in 1988. I could have given one reason why He probably won't (see 1st paragraph above). But one thing that little booklet did for me was to remind me to make sure I'm ready. Jesus could come back today. The only thing holding Him back is His patience (2 Pet. 3:9). And even if He doesn't come today, this very day I could be called home to Him. In the last several years I have lost some friends and acquaintances who by all outside appearances were healthy, but for one medical reason or another, or an accident, they died. My mom was not the picture of health, but she died unexpectedly (at least to us) last month. Life is fragile. We are not guaranteed tomorrow.

So, here is my [totally unfoolish] prediction; the world is going to end! When? Sooner than you think. But *when?* I don't know. Even Jesus didn't know. So, what should we do? Get ready!

Oh, and there is another way to be a fool – by not being ready. According to Jesus in Matthew 25, the *foolish* virgins did not take any oil with them (they didn't get ready). Don't be a fool.

(1.) Don't deny the existence of God. (2.) Don't predict the end of the world. And (3.) be ready!

I can't tell WHEN He is coming back, but I can tell WHEN you should get ready:

NOW! TODAY is the day of salvation! (2 Cor. 6:2)

BE READY! HE IS COMING BACK!

"Therefore keep watch [be ready], because you do not know the day or the hour." – Jesus

June - 2011

Give 'em Hope

When I started this singing/prison ministry in 1990, Glendon Bender's (Gospel Echoes) advice was short and simple: "Give 'em hope."

As we entered London Correctional this month for at least the 50th time (three times a year x 21 years of ministry, minus a cancellation or two over the years = at least 50 times), I glanced up, as I always do, at the words written on the outside wall above the main entrance to the prison:

"HE WHO ENTERS HERE LEAVES NOT HOPE BEHIND."

We arrived early, so while we waited in the lobby, I wandered over to the huge bronze plaque on the lobby wall that I had passed at least a hundred times (50 times coming in and 50 times going out) in the last twenty-one years. As I was reading it carefully, Chaplain Cahill came out. He saw me reading it and told me the following story:

> *In Venice, Italy, the prison sits just across the river from the Judgment House (courthouse). When a man is sentenced to prison, he is shipped (literally) across the river to the prison. As he enters the prison, he passes under the following words above the door: "HE WHO ENTERS HERE LEAVES HOPE BEHIND." That was the European pessimism of the 19th and 20th century. A man doesn't change. Once a criminal, always a criminal. There is no redemption. No reform. Lock 'em up and throw the key away.*
>
> *In direct response to this European pessimism, London (Ohio) Correctional was built in an era of American optimism. The Reformation-based Christianity that helped found this nation held the optimistic Christian belief that anyone can change. In fact, prisons were not called "prisons." They were called 'reformatories' or 'penitentiaries,' from the word 'penance' or 'pen-*

sive,' 'to reform,' or 'to think.' Prisons were actually what we would call today, a 'time out.' Go think about what you did. Repent. Rethink. It was an alternative to the whippings and beatings of criminals, which began to be looked on as cruel and unusual punishment.

Here is what the huge eight-foot by four-foot bronze plaque in the London lobby says:

THIS BUILDING WAS COMPLETED IN NINETEEN HUNDRED TWENTY-FOUR UNDER THE ADMINISTRATION OF GOV. DONAHEY. IT IS THE NUCLEUS AROUND WHICH WE SHALL BUILD A GREAT INSTITUTION FOR THE SALVAGE OF MEN. ALWAYS LET THOSE WHO SHALL BE THE MERCIFUL ADMINISTRATORS OF THE GREAT TRUST THAT WE HAVE HERE REMEMBER: THAT THIS IS A PLACE OF FIRM BUT KIND RESTRAINT FOR THOSE WHOSE UNDEVELOPED MORAL FACULTIES HAVE LED INTO EVIL WAYS; THAT THE HIGH PURPOSE OF THIS HUMANE INSTITUTION IS A DETERRENT ONE; THAT IT SHALL BE THE WARNING LIGHTHOUSE OF THE BODY POLITIC BUILDED FOR THOSE WHOSE LIFE BARKS DRIFT TOWARD CRIMINAL SHOALS; THAT REFORM, EDUCATION AND REHABILITATION AS OBJECTIVES SHALL BE THE DOMINANT THOUGHT AND THE COMMAND TO ALL OF THOSE TO WHOM WE SHALL COMMIT THE KEEPING. AND WHEN THESE PURPOSES ARE

ATTAINED AND THE CONDITIONS MET, LET US SAY TO THE OFFENDERS IN THE LANGUAGE OF ONE WHO LOVED ALL MEN, 'GO AND SIN NO MORE.'

I can't imagine this kind of plaque being put in a prison lobby today. Imagine, quoting Jesus Christ in a state institution! But they had it right in 1924; a man can change! And if the change is to be real, it can only happen through the One who said, *"I came to give you life, and to give it more abundantly."* (John 10:10) Although our news media does not have an optimistic bone in its sick body, I believe the average American is still optimistic. I am optimistic enough to keep proclaiming Christ through song, sermon, and hopefully through my life. If I didn't believe a man could change, I would be pretty stupid to go into prisons and waste my time singing nice songs and telling Bible stories. Especially when the weather is beautiful like it was when we walked into London Prison. And the offering usually averages right close to zero!

But, I am optimistic! Read the last chapter! We win! Jesus is Lord! A man can change! *"Blessed is the man whose hope is in the Lord."* (Jer. 17:7) We have reason to "not leave hope behind!"

July - 2011

Children in Prison

"I met you when I was 13 years old!" a prisoner said after a chapel service last week.

Where had I met this 30-year-old man who was now dressed in orange?

Several times I have met prisoners who knew me because I had sung at their home church. Once I met a prisoner in Pennsylvania who said, "I saw you when you did a USO program for us while I was in the Army in Mannheim, Germany." Another time in a prison chapel I met a high school classmate! And I have actually seen former neighbors in prison!

But where had I met this young man when he was just 13 and who was now in prison? So I asked him.

"Where have we met?"

"At Indian River!" he said, with the excitement of a boy seeing an old friend.

Indian River! That is a youth facility (prison) near Massillon. This boy was in prison at age 13! I smiled and let him know how good it was to see him, but inside I wanted to cry. A thirteen-year-old child in prison! What in the world would an eighth grader do to end up in prison? He should be in school.

When a 13-year-old boy is in prison, something is terribly wrong. The system, his family, and our society have failed somewhere along the line. I asked him if he had been in prison since he was 13.

"No," he replied. "I got out a couple of times, but it never lasted long. I couldn't stay out of trouble. I'm back." Just matter of fact. That's life. He knows no other way. It seems he has accepted his lot in life.

I was thinking of the plague of prisons on our nation, and the fact that every one of them is overcrowded, and now this reminder that even children are not exempt. I had to think of Prov. 22:6, *"Train up a child in the way he should go, and when he is old he will not turn from it."* The Student Bible has this note: "An individual proverb should not be read as either an invariable rule or a binding promise from God... but this verse reinforces the importance of early training in forming a person's lifelong character. The general rule is this: good parents raise good children."

Although "spare the rod and spoil the child" may be the best-known verse about discipline, I think Prov. 29:15 may explain our current national situation better: *"The rod of correction imparts wisdom, but a child left to himself disgraces his mother"* *(!)* **(and ends up in prison!).** Since our society and many parents can't distinguish the difference between loving discipline and child abuse (there is a difference), let me share a few notes on the subject from *The Student Bible* (pg. 587): "The overwhelming emphasis of Proverbs is on verbal encouragement and teaching. The whole book is framed as a father's words to his son, teaching him those facts of life that have nothing to do with biology. Again and again, he pleads, 'Listen, my son...' Mother has equally important words. The parent-child conversation is a warm one, and Proverbs 17:6 bears out what the whole book implies: parents and children are not meant to be adversaries, but allies in life who are proud of each other."

I am thankful for loving parents who spared neither the rod (belt) nor the encouraging words. Many times my temptation to do wrong was checked by the fear of dad's belt, but also by my fear of disappointing him. My version of the 23rd Psalm might read: "Thy belt and thy encouraging words, they comfort me..." (and keep me out of prison).

I doubt that my inmate friend who met me at Indian River 17 years ago has ever been disciplined or encouraged by loving parents. But at least he came to chapel! The silver lining is that many men have had it worse than he has and they have done well. God can *"...restore the years the locust have eaten"* (Joel 2:25). That is my prayer. That is why we have the audacity to go to prisons and proclaim the Hope of Christ.

August - 2011

Parents of Prisoners

I was talking to a man whose son had been in prison. He told me what a parent goes through when a son is incarcerated: shock, disappointment, denial, hurt, anger, shame, embarrassment, tears, homesickness... As I listened to some of the emotion and history of this man's walk, I was reminded of what ex-con Frank Costantino's wife, Bunny, said in her book, *Lady In The Shadow:*

> When a man goes to prison, his whole family goes to prison. I had no income. I had to go on welfare. But that wasn't enough to make ends meet with four children, so I got a job to supplement my income. One day while I was at work, the social worker from welfare stopped by and asked my neighbor where I was.

> She told her I was working. That week I received a notice that I had to report my income to welfare so it could be deducted from my check, or quit working. I quit working.

Bunny goes on to tell of the hardships of driving 300 miles to prison every two weeks to visit her husband. That involved the expenses of gas, motel, food, and childcare. And when there was no money for a motel, she drove back home the same day; 600 miles, twelve hours of driving, for a two-hour visit. With four children, every two weeks. And in the meantime, no support from a husband.

My friend who was telling me about his son said that they had been well off financially, but that didn't make it any easier. Families visiting inmates are treated with disdain, at least at the facility where their son was. It took a whole day for a two-hour visit through a thick glass or across a table, with no privacy. And one forgotten document or the wrong type of clothing, either by the family or the inmate, and the visit is canceled. Come back in two weeks on your designated visit day. Then my friend said, "I spent my life's savings and all of my retirement in trying to help my son. I am now pretty much broke. But he is doing much better."

And then this amazing comment – without regret or even a hint of resentment, he said, "And I would do it again... "

The love of a father (& mother)! The foolishness of a son. This man's son was not one of the 80% of prisoners who never had a father at home. This boy messed up in spite of good parenting and Godly teaching. And what a cost! His mom and dad's savings and retirement! When they should be kicking back and relaxing, enjoying the fruits of years of labor, they are still scrambling to make ends meet. Why? Because of a bad economy? Laziness? Unwise investments? No. Because of a rebellious son.

I have heard many a rebellious son (including me) repeat the idiotic saying, "It's my life and I'll live it the way I want to. It's nobody else's business."

Wrong, my friend. It's your life alright. But to think that your actions don't affect hundreds, maybe even thousands of others is simply naive, shortsighted, selfish, and arrogant. (I'm running out of negative adjectives, but do you get the point?) Your life is a testimony, either for positive or for negative influence on people's lives. It IS somebody else's business.

When you succeed, your whole family succeeds. When you hurt, your whole family hurts. I wonder if this is what Paul had in mind when he told the Galatians (6:2,5) to *"carry each other's burdens,"* and in the same paragraph, *"each man should carry his own load."* If I don't carry my own load, it becomes someone else's burden. He told the Ephesians (4:28) to *"stop stealing... but work... with your own hands, that [you] may have something to share with those in need."* Paul is contrasting 'stealing' with 'work.' If you're not working, you're stealing! If you work, you have something to share.

But I digress. The point is that for each prisoner that I see in a prison chapel, there is a hurting father and mother, a hurting family and friends, hurting and shattered victims, hurting communities... Sin takes you farther than you want to go, it keeps you longer than you want to stay, and it costs you more than you want to pay. *"...the way of the unfaithful is hard..."* (Prov. 13:15). Suggestion: Follow Christ!

LADY IN THE SHADOW BY: CHERYL "BUNNY" COSTANTINO GREENWOOD
ACCLAIMED BOOKS. 1981. P. 155

September - 2011

Parents of Good Kids

OR, A TRIBUTE TO MY CHILDREN

Last month I wrote about "Parents of Prisoners." I received several responses from that, the most notable from an ex-convict:

> *Hi John: Just thought I would let you know I really enjoyed your newsletter. "Parents of Prisoners" was well written and very insightful. It really brought to mind my past, and it's very true that what we do has far-reaching consequences and hurts people in a way we can never truly make amends for. When I get to that point, I trust in God's forgiveness. If it wasn't for my reliance on His grace and mercy, the true magnitude of my sins would overwhelm me. Are you sure you never went to prison? :-)*

One ministry told me that my newsletter was read in their morning devotions. I figure as long as I'm on a roll, maybe I should say something about the other side of the fence: **Parents of Good Kids.**

As far as I know, I am in that category. I guess Lydia is, too. In fact, one reason I can claim to be in that category is because of my dear wife. Her heritage and work ethic have rubbed off on our children. Some of it has even rubbed off on me!

One reason I happen to be thinking about good kids is because of the reaction I got from the "Parents of Prisoners" letter, but also because this month we witnessed the joyous occasion of our son's wedding. Adam Schmid and Katie Rodriguez exchanged vows in the yard of a beautiful log cabin near Churchville, VA, on Sept. 18, 2011. It was every parent's dream; our son, who is a believer and has a good job (RN) marries a beautiful Christian girl in a Christian ceremony and seems to partially fulfill the prophecy of Jeremiah 29:11: *"...I have...plans to prosper you and not to harm you. Plans to give you hope and a future."* We have prayed for our children's spouses since before they were born and God seems to have answered our prayer for Adam. He has hope and a future!

We also have two daughters, and God is still working on their spouses (but neither God nor our daughters seem to be in a hurry). Our girls have also been a source of joy (and pride) for us. None of our children were stars in sports or academics, although they were good at both, but they have been stars to us because of their faithfulness and steadiness in life. They love to be at home, but they love to leave. They have travel in their blood. As I write this, Adam is in Italy (RNs take different types of honeymoons than their missionary parents did), Amy is in Northern Ireland as the official photographer on a six-country tour with Mennonite Mission Network, and Katie is planning to move to Florida in October where she just got accepted to work at Troyer's Dutch Heritage Restaurant in Sarasota. It would be nice to have them close to home, but as long as they are doing well and serving the Lord, I suppose it doesn't matter where they are.

It may sound like I am bragging, but if it does, let me again quote Jeremiah 9:24: *"...let him who boasts boast about this; that he understands and knows Me..."* I took that slightly out of context, but the point is, God has been good to us. Lydia reminded me of a quote: "If your children don't turn out right, you can't take all the blame. If they turn out well, you can't take all the credit." I can sure take all of the good feelings!

Every week in prisons across Ohio and the U.S., I see broken, abused, damaged lives because of family breakdown. Even here in our rural Amish & Mennonite community, not everything is perfect. There are messes even in some of the 'good' homes.

The bottom line is, I am bragging about God. He has blessed me with a wonderful family. I am a parent of good kids. Why? Because they chose to be who they are. We planted and watered, but each person is ultimately responsible for his own actions. Just as the son in my last newsletter chose to live in such a way that he ended up in prison, some choose to follow God. *"...choose for yourself this day whom you will serve..."* (Joshua 24:15). It's a choice!

So, this is a tribute to my children. Adam, Amy, and Katie, I am proud of you (in a humble way, of course).

October - 2011

"News" Letter

Sometimes a newsletter should have some news. I like to write about an event or some great thought that occurred during the month, but these last few days I have tried to think of something that would be of interest and I came up blank. So, I resort to simply reporting what we did since you last heard from us – a travelogue of sorts.

October started out in Shipshewana, IN, where I sang at a 'Crafter's Fair,' and I ended the month by being on the same platform with Christian apologist and nationally known lecturer Josh McDowell in Marlboro, OH. In between, there were eight concerts, four prisons, two auctions, one recording session, two banquets, one rest home, a funeral, and a wedding reception.

Merlin Yoder from Pigeon, MI, was killed in a farm accident, and although I knew his brother and sister much better than I knew him, his son was a good friend of my children. So when they all came home from Virginia to attend their friend's dad's funeral, I piled in the motorhome with them and we went to Pigeon. The funeral was as victorious as it was sad. Such a good husband, father, and community leader taken away before his time (at least that's what it looks like from this side of eternity). His life was a challenge to me; I wish I would have known him better.

We got home from the funeral in time to get ready for a reception here at our house for our son, Adam, and his new bride, Katie. (Not to be confused with our daughter, Katie Lorain, who we now call "K-Lo," and Adam's wife is known as

"K-Rod.") It was held on Saturday, October 29, and friends just dropped in to say hello and meet K-Rod. A great time! And our place looks good cleaned up!

In 1972 I went to Explo '72 in Dallas, Texas, a huge (over 100,000 people) Campus Crusade for Christ gathering which is where I committed my life to Christ. One of the many great speakers at this weeklong event was Josh McDowell, who had just written the book, *Evidence That Demands A Verdict,* probably the defining work on Christian apologetics in our time. I bought a copy that week and I have studied it and taught and preached from it many times. What a thrill, then, to be asked to team up with him for a "Josh McDowell Weekend" in Napanee, Ontario! I was pretty nervous to be with such a nationally know man, but I discovered that he is just a common guy. We had a blast! People committed their lives to Christ every time he spoke. And he liked my singing! When he learned that I don't live far from Marlboro, OH, where he was to be the next weekend, he requested that I be a part of the Sunday night service with him!

Other highlights of the month: a concert at The Carpenter's Cafe at Keim Lumber, Charm Days, which is always a great time and good crowd, our annual Fall CGM Fundraiser Banquet, a concert for Kyle Hostetler and all the residents at Walnut Hills to celebrate Kyle's birthday, and a concert at a deer hunt. (Yes, you read that right!)

Maybe I should explain the deer hunt: Mose Keim told me that about 14 youth would be at a deer hunting seminar on Fred Hershberger's farm in central Ohio. After the seminar, all the youth go hunting, and the parents hang around the tent until dark when they come back. Could I help dispel some of the boredom that descends upon the waiting parents back at the tent? I'll try. Turned out just fine. I sang, the parents listened, and four of the youth got a deer. Mission accomplished. From prisons to deer hunts. Have guitar; will sing.

That's a summary of October. Now fall begins. November reminds us of deer hunting, cool nights, short days, and Thanksgiving. We have so much for which to be thankful...

And that's the news here at the International Worldwide Headquarters of Common Ground Ministries (a barn in the yard). Thank you for your prayers, your presence, your financial support, and your friendship. I want to work while it is day. He is coming soon. Be ready!

November - 2011

Grapevine Faith Academy
VERSUS
Gainesville State Prison

I had the privilege to hear NASCAR chaplain and master storyteller Ken Crosswhite speak at Fairlawn Mennonite Church in November. During his presentation he told this amazing story:

> In Texas, there is a Christian School called Grapevine Faith Academy. Not far away is Gainesville State School, which is a maximum-security youth prison.

Every year the prison coach sends out requests to local (and not so local) schools to ask if they would schedule the prison football team. One of the schools that accepted the request was Grapevine Faith Academy.

Gainesville State School has 14 players. One coach. They play every game on the road. They are always the visiting team. They have never had anyone cheering for them. Their record was 0-8. They've only scored twice. Their 14 players are teenagers who have been convicted of crimes ranging from drugs to assault to robbery. Most had families who had disowned them. Some had no family at all. They wore outdated, used shoes, shoulder pads, and helmets. Faith Academy was 7-2. They had 70 players, 11 coaches, thousands of fans and the latest equipment.

Chris Hogan, the head coach at Faith Academy, knew the Gainesville team would have no fans and it would be no contest, so he thought, "What if half of our fans and half of our cheerleaders, for one night only, cheered for the other team?" He sent out an email to the faithful asking them to do just that. "Here's the message I want you to send," Hogan wrote: "You're just as valuable as any other person on the planet."

Some folks were confused and thought he was nuts. One player said, "Coach, why are we doing this?" Hogan said, "Imagine you don't have a home life, no one to love you, no one pulling for you. Imagine that everyone pretty much had given up on you. Now, imagine what it would feel like and mean to you for hundreds of people to suddenly believe in you."

The idea took root. On the night of the game as the 14 hit the field, they crashed through a banner the cheerleaders had made for them as they ran through a gauntlet of cheering students and parents. The visitors' stands were full. The cheerleaders were leading cheers for them. They had even taken the time to learn their names!

Isaiah, the quarterback/middle linebacker, said, "I never in my life thought I would hear people cheering for us, let alone parents cheering for us to tackle and hit their kid. Most of the time, when we come out, people are afraid of us. You can see it in their eyes; fear, mistrust, disdain... but these people are yelling for us... and they knew our names!"

Grapevine Faith won, and after the game, the teams gathered at the 50-yard line to pray. That's when Isaiah, the teenage convict/quarterback, surprised everybody and asked if he could pray. He prayed, "Lord, I don't know what just happened so I don't know how or who to say thank you to, but I never knew there were so many people in the world who cared about us." On the way back to the bus, under guard, each one of the players was handed a burger, fries, a coke, candy, a Bible, and an encouraging letter from the players from Faith Academy.

This Christmas, maybe we could join Coach Hogan and cheer

for a convict. You never know, it just might change a life. Some people don't know that anyone cares for them.

Thanks, Ken Crosswhite, for a great true story! (Google it!)

MERRY CHRISTMAS!

December - 2011

ENCOUNTERS

2012

I Was in Prison
AND YOU VISITED ME

Let me tell you about one of the most exciting things Common Ground Ministries has done in our 21 years of existence: this December we baked cookies! Well, we coordinated the baking of cookies. For prisoners. Approximately 5,200 prisoners in two prisons, plus the officers, guards, and administration workers.

The Gospel Echoes Prison Team of Goshen, IN, has been taking Christmas cookies into 15 or so prisons for over twenty years. I went with them a couple of times. I often wondered why we don't do that here in Ohio. The Ohio system is more strict, for sure, but last year I asked the chaplain at London Correctional if he would allow us to bring in cookies at Christmas time. He was all for it, but neither he nor us were ready. This year, with the help of Echoes member Glendon Bender, we started asking people, churches, Sunday School classes, anyone who could – to bake cookies. In order for each inmate to get six cookies, we would need 36,000 cookies!

The response was overwhelming! Families, friends, and churches made cookies! 30 dozen, 60 dozen, 100 dozen... One family made 150 dozen! Seventy-some volunteers came together to package them. Eighty-some volunteers came with us to Marysville Women's Reformatory and London Correctional to hand the cookies to the prisoners while we sang Christmas Carols.

How did it go? Let the inmates speak for themselves:

> *"... it means so much to me (and so many other women) that there is actually people out there who care enough to take time out from their lives to come and bless us inmates. The singing, cookies, and the sincere smiles that I received this morning touched me deeply. I walked through that building and was ashamed to hold my head high. But these people reached out to shake my hand and say five words to me: 'God bless you. Merry Christmas.' I looked into the eyes of these wonderful people and couldn't hold back the tears. You guys didn't judge me. You reached out with a handshake to a hand that has caused so much damage and turmoil..." – Julian*

"...it was like a taste of the home where I grew up... For a moment you brought the old days back to me, along with the memories of a better time. Thank you for the precious gift..." – Jeff

"To all the ladies and gentlemen who brought cookies to The Ohio Reformatory for Women: I just would like to thank you for your kindness. I broke down when I heard you singing. That gesture was one of the kindest I have received in the 11 years I have been here... and those cookies were fabulous. I haven't tasted something that delicious in a long time. I don't expect you to understand the impact that you all had on us, but I will try to explain. We are so broken here, and some have no one out there who cares for us at all, and for a stranger to care enough to sing and give us cookies means a lot..." – Rhonda

"I wish I could personally thank the lady who signed my card (Carolyn). I greatly appreciate you all and your (spelling)(forgive me) and your Awlmish, Ulmish, Allmish community. This has touched my heart and I thank you. Keep me in your prayers." – Susan

"God is with me always, but it is nice to have angels appear every so often, too. God bless you." – Caprice

"When I opened the card that came with the cookies and seen that it was a hand written message, it let me know that you actually took time and put a lot of care into doing this for us. A girl named Megan wrote in my card. Please tell her I said thank you and God bless." – Donald

A cookie. Doesn't seem like much, but it touched some broken, hardened people. We let them know each one was made with flour, prayer, and love. We're invited back next Christmas.

January - 2012

The Best Laid Plans
(OR, A GREAT TIME AT WE CARE)

I had it all planned... I would stay overnight at the chaplain's house near Birmingham after our last We Care chapel service at St. Clair Prison on Thursday night. On Friday I would head north to Nashville, where I had an appointment at the Cash Cabin, then I would head home, or maybe even swing east to Harrisonburg to visit Amy and Adam before moseying on home on Saturday... or maybe Sunday.

On Monday I got a phone call. A long time friend and neighbor died. Could I come home to sing at the funeral? In fact, could I preach the funeral? Sorry, I'm out of state. What if we had the funeral on Friday? Sure, I could make it home. I'd be honored. So instead of a good night's sleep and a relaxed trip home, now I would be racing out of the prison on Thursday and driving all night to be home in time for the funeral, with no time for study or preparation. I'm not complaining, just saying that plans can change.

On Thursday evening we were able to leave Birmingham several hours early because the chapel service at St. Clair Prison was canceled. Something happened in the kitchen and supper was late, or some such reason. So, no chapel. I reloaded my sound equipment into the van, entered the prison to get Jeff Miller, who I had talked into going with me to help drive, and we headed for Birmingham to repossess my van. (Oh, yes – a minor detail in this saga – my van broke down on Wednesday afternoon (wheel bearing). Chaplain Steve Stoltzfus came to my rescue, took my van to his friend's garage, loaned me his van, and then picked up my fixed van Thursday afternoon and drove up to Birmingham from Montgomery to meet me and trade vans.) Then Jeff & I drove all night and made it home in plenty of time for the funeral. And it was worth the trip!

WHEN WE'VE BEEN THERE TEN THOUSAND YEARS....

On the way home, Jeff told me an amazing bit of prison trivia. In the St. Clair Prison that we had just left – and he had been a volunteer all week – is the prisoner with the longest prison sentence in America. When he told me how many years this man's sentence was, I couldn't believe it, so I looked it up. Jeff was correct. There is an inmate there who was sentenced to ten thousand (10,000) years! Can you believe that?! Here's an article about him from The Tuscaloosa News, August 30, 2011;

> *According to reports, on Halloween, 1976, Dudley Kyzer went to his estranged wife's mother's house in Tuscaloosa. Police later determined that college student Richard Pyron, a visitor at the house, was shot while on his knees in the den begging for his life. Eunice Barringer, 54, was shot in the forehead*

at point-blank range while on the telephone trying to call police in the bedroom. Barringer's daughter, Emily Dianne Kyzer, was shot in the chest while trying desperately to run away with the Kyzer's six-year-old son. She made it as far as the neighbor's yard before collapsing and urging the boy to keep running for safety. After a four-day manhunt, Kyzer was arrested and brought to trial. The jury deliberated less than an hour, convicted Kyzer of murder, and sentenced him to die in the electric chair.

In 1980, the Alabama Supreme Court declared that Alabama's death penalty was unconstitutional. Kyzer was granted a new trial. In his new trial, Kyzer was found guilty again in 1981, but because the rules regarding death sentences were still unclear, prosecutors did not ask for the death penalty this time. Instead, they sought a sentence that ensured that Kyzer would never go free. Kyzer was sentenced to two life terms plus 10,000 years!

10,000 years! You can't make this stuff up. I read that one reason some juries give multiple life sentences instead of the death penalty is that, in our current system of automatic appeals, a life sentence is cheaper for the state. (I asked if Jeff met this man, but he is in solitary confinement and could not come to chapel.)

Here's another fact that is almost as hard to believe: There is a judge and a system where the wages of sin is death! No plea-bargains, no paying off the judge, no parole, no retrial, no change of administration with new laws... *"...but the gift of God is eternal life through Christ Jesus our Lord."* (Romans 6:23) Can you believe that?

February - 2012

Cruise Control

The first nine days of February were spent at home and were about as relaxing and unplanned for me as any period of time in the past several years. There were no prisons, concerts, or churches. I spent the time at home studying, reading, cleaning up my desk, hanging out with Lydia, and planning for the rest of the year.

Then on February 10 I was back in business: a Valentine Banquet with Steve & Annie Chapman, a variety show in Kidron on the 11th, a Pastors Conference in Apple Creek, and then off to Florida to get ready for our 4th Annual Sarasota Fund Raising Banquet. There were also several Pinecraft concerts, a church service and then...

...off in one of the three Pioneer Trails buses that took 150 Pinecraft residents to Miami to cast off on a five day Gospel Cruise!

And what a wonderful cruise it was! Almost five hundred Amish, Mennonites, Russian Mennonites, Brethren, Baptists, Methodists, and everything in between were part of the group that Ryan Bomgardner got together. He contacted six different Christian artists, including me, to fill the boat (OK, ship) for a short week of relaxation, inspiration, witness, and rejuvenation. There were 1,500 passengers in all. Our group stuck out so much that one man asked Ryan if this was an "Amish Spring Break." That became the joke of the cruise. Several Amish girls went to a shop in Key West and had a tee shirt made for Ryan: **"Amish Spring Break in Key West, 2012."**

In a boat filled with 950 staff from all over the world, we didn't have to think about how we could witness to these kind, hard-working people. Many are Muslin, Hindu, and other eastern religions, and they would ask us, "Who are you?" "You look like 'Little House on The Prairie.' " "What do you believe?" The singing and the general attitude of our group opened the door for many conversations about this Jesus that we claimed to know. Eternity will tell if our presence and our words made a difference in their lives.

Our ship docked back in Miami on Friday morning, and I disembarked and headed for the Miami airport. I was to sing at a wedding the next day in Walnut Creek. Our daughter Katie went back to Pinecraft to her job at Troyer's Restaurant and also to her waiting mother, who opted to skip this cruise.

I'm back in the swing of real life again. A wedding, a rest home, a board meeting, a concert, two funerals, a prison, a youth rally... and guess what? Back to Florida on March 10 at the invitation of The Glen Clark Family to present the gospel to the spring break crowd at Ft. Myers Beach (not to be confused with Amish Spring Break). The college kids that come to Florida need to hear what the real meaning of life is – a life committed to Jesus Christ. Even though you may get this after the fact, pray for this Reach the Beach weekend.

March - 2012

Thoughts About Work

WORK n. 1. physical or mental effort of activity directed toward the production or accomplishment of something: labor. 2. exertion; labor; task; 3. place of employment. work v. to do work; to function; to prove effective...

SCENE I: I was sitting among a group of friends once when one of them pontificated, "Work is a curse." Nobody said a word. Then, one by one they all slowly nodded in agreement.

SCENE II: I stopped in to visit an Amish friend in Indiana. It happened to be his daughter's 16th birthday. In that community, a young person can begin to work outside of the farm at age 16. It was her first day of work in a local mobile home factory. Since she was too young to be around machinery, her job was to clean the homes as they came off the line. She had cleaned 18 full sized units that first day of work! She came home shortly after we had stopped in. Her dress was dirty and her face was red, almost like an athlete after a contest. She obviously had worked. I asked her, "How was your first day of work?" She looked at me with a smile and said, with genuine enthusiasm, "It was *fun!*"

QUIZ: Which of these two people do you suppose is going to have an 'easier' life?

I have lectured my poor children on this subject many times, but here it goes again: If you don't like work, you're in for a hard life, because that's what life is – work. I meet men in prison who are there because they didn't want to work. They took shortcuts. They cheated, they robbed what others had worked for, they bought and sold drugs for easy money... My friend Glen Graber says, "My dad taught me to work, and he almost made me like it." If you enjoy work, no matter how successful you are, you have better odds of enjoying life in general.

When someone asks me, "How do you keep up with such a busy schedule?" I usually answer, tongue in cheek, "It sure beats working!" I thought I was real cute until one man asked, "How would you know?" That got me to thinking. I love what I'm doing, so it's not 'work.' Confucius (among others) said, "Choose a job you love, and you'll never have to work a day in your life." That's me. I'm busy. I have late nights and early mornings. I get tired. But 'work?!'

I've been a plumber, a farmer (sort of), a barn builder; I've built silos, drove school bus... I've loved just about every job I've ever had. The few jobs I didn't like had more to do with the workplace environment or personality clashes.

I've been doing singing and prison ministry now for 22 years. My 'job' makes me tired. But so did football, softball, and all the other sports and activities that I did (and still do) for fun and exercise. My present work is not physical. I sing. I teach. I preach. I travel.

My job provides a living (I Cor. 9:14), it has a purpose, and it is personally fulfilling. I love it! According to the apostle Paul, the type of work I am doing is a high calling.

And whether or not you are in full-time ministry, any work you do for the Lord is not in vain. (I Cor. 15:58)

So, that's my little rampage about work. The Bible says, *"Work while it is day... night is coming, when no man can work."* (John 9:4).

By the way: *"The Lord God took the man and put him in the Garden of Eden to work it (!) and take care of it."* (Gen. 2:15). This was before the curse. Work is a privilege!

April - 2012

The Boundary Lines Have Fallen...

...IN PLEASANT PLACES

At our annual Common Ground Ministries banquet in Greenwood, DE, last night (which went well), Glenn Kanagy, director of The Gator Wilderness Camp in Florida, said something which nowadays is called a 'take-away.' For instance, at our pastor's conference in February, the speaker was talking about church growth and such, and my take-away at that conference was an off-hand comment in the midst of his talk.

He said, "We get saved from alcohol, from drugs, from immorality, from poverty... but the best thing we get saved from is our greatest enemy; God Himself!" Yes, according to Colossians 1:21, 22, we were enemies of God because of our evil behavior, *"...but now He has reconciled you by Christ's physical body through death to present you holy in His sight, without blemish and **free from accusation...**"* (emphasis mine)

That was my take-away from the pastor's conference. I don't remember anything else (except the good meals). And what a message for someone like me who speaks to enemies of God every week! What a privilege to be able to tell men with evil behavior that they can be reconciled, presented holy in God's sight, AND *"free from accusation!"* Many of these men serve their time, get released, and find the police waiting for them at the prison door because of other charges! Wouldn't it be wonderful to be free from accusation? (Answer: Yes, it would!)

Back to Gregg Kanagy. Gregg is a pastor, the grandson of a pastor, and who knows, maybe the father of a pastor or two. His grandfather Erie Renno was a good friend to my father-in-law, Bishop Tobe Byler. Gregg spoke about the troubled boys that come to Gator Camp. Boys from broken homes, drug infested neighborhoods, violent fathers, or no fathers. These boys will test the counselors. They've never been shown love, and they don't trust anyone. They didn't have a pastor grandfather. They act out their hurts, hatred, and aggression until they are 'conquered' by the love and patience of the 'chiefs' who work with them at the camp. Gregg shared the verse his daughter quoted at her baptism:

"The boundary lines have fallen for me in pleasant places; surely I have a delightful inheritance." (Psalm 16:6) This is also Gregg's favorite verse. It was his dad's favorite verse. It was grandfather Renno's favorite verse. Four generations recognizing that *"the boundary lines have fallen for (them) in pleasant places."*

I think that may become one of my favorite verses. My boundary lines fell in pleasant places. Why was I born into such a good family? Why were these boys, or the prisoners I see every week, or my friends in Costa Rica... why were they born where they were born? I had absolutely nothing to do with where, when, or to what family I was born. My boundary lines fell in pleasant places. I have a goodly heritage.

Folks, that's a take-away. I am free from accusation, and my boundary lines have fallen in pleasant places. The one I had nothing to do with, the other, I made a choice. Because of what God did for me, and the choice I made concerning my relationship with Him, I am on the right side of the prison bars. And Gregg is a counselor and not a troubled boy.

One of my goals is to help those with unpleasant boundaries make the right choices so they can break the chain of failure, and their children will be able to quote Psalm 16:6 and smile.

May - 2012

Communication

COMMUNICATE v. 1. a. to make known: disclose b. to manifest: disclose. 2. to transmit to others. 3. to be connected.

When Abraham Lincoln was assassinated in 1865, the news reached London, England, within two weeks. When President McKinley was shot (1901), London heard the news within one day. John Kennedy's death in 1963 reached London within one hour. When President Reagan was shot, London saw it happen!! Communication...

I remember the first time I ever saw a tape recorder. My

uncle came back our long lane and into our farmhouse with a suitcase and a smile. He set the suitcase down on our coffee table, opened it up, and put two tin wheels on the outstretched metal arms. He strung tape between them, pushed a few buttons, then said, "Now, say something into the microphone." Dad said something, I don't remember what, and then my uncle stopped the wheels, reversed them, turned the knob and stepped back. We heard my dad's voice come from the contraption. We must have looked like the dog on the old RCA Victor records. (Remember records – those round plastic discs?) We were amazed!

Now, just 40-some years later, I can take a nap on a Sunday afternoon and discover that so-called 'friends' in London (whom we've never met) are looking at a picture of me sleeping on a chair with my mouth wide open... and I haven't even woke up yet! There was a time when everyone looked on in wonder at a man in a restaurant answering his phone. Today we look at that same man with disgust. Can't he do his talking somewhere else? How rude!

How times have changed! How easy it is to communicate with almost anyone at any time anywhere in the world! My Costa Rican friends, who didn't have cars or telephones when we were there in the '80's, now send pictures and videos of their lives via Facebook or cell phone. Our short (but joyous) phone call from San Jose to inform my parents of Adams birth in 1985 cost us over $50. Now we see ultrasound updates on our cell phones of children still in the womb, sent from all over the world, and it doesn't cost them more than a few cents per transmission.

When I first became a follower of Jesus, I wondered how *"all the nations"* would be able to see the Son of Man appearing in the sky, as implied in Matthew 24:30. I'm still not sure how He's going to do it, but now I realize that if mortal man can do what he has done with speeding up communication around the world, God can probably figure out how to let the whole world know that He is back.

With all the modern means of keeping in touch with each other, getting news out, communicating, do you suppose our generation will be held more responsible to make sure that the Good News (Gospel) is proclaimed? The news that we have to tell is even more sensational than the assassination of a president. Jesus is risen! He is alive! He loves you! There is hope! There is a purpose! (Whew!) Tell someone today. Maybe even someone in London!

June - 2012

Christmas in May?

The last week of May I recorded a Christmas album at The Cash Cabin in Hendersonville, TN. The temperature outside was 90 degrees. A few Christmas decorations in the studio would have helped to get us in the mood, but then again, I sometimes wonder why we only sing Christmas Carols at Christmas time. The message is true all year long.

I had contacted songwriter Steve Chapman a month or so before the recording and told him I am going to do a Christmas CD. Does he have any Christmas songs? He sent me what he claims is the only Christmas song he has written. While I was recording it, the producer asked who wrote it. When I told him it was Steve Chapman, he said, "I've always wanted to meet him!" I contacted Steve, and he came over to The Cabin the next day – right while I was putting finishing touches on his song.

To help you understand what goes on in a recording session, at least for a no-name like me, let me explain what usually happens. The musicians come in the first day and play the music while I sing. They leave. The next day I sing to the music until I get it right. After that, backup singers and possibly another instrument or two are added to give it a full sound.

So while Steve Chapman was in the control room watching the 'vocals' process and shooting the breeze with the engineer, the producer, and my friend Ray Miller who had come with me, I said, "Hey, Steve, would you mind singing backup on this song?" He said, "Sure," and jumped up and came into the studio. He knew the song really well! So, Steve Chapman is singing backup on his own Christmas song that I am singing! That's like having Billy Graham take up the offering while I preach! What a blast! Only in Nashville!

PRISON NEWS

I am leading a six-week seminar at Belmont Correctional called *Not A Fan*. This is a little out of the ordinary for me, because I usually do a concert/chapel service, distribute Gospel Echoes Correspondence Bibles Studies, and then move on to the next prison. To be in one prison six weeks in a row has been refreshing (not that the regular concerts are not).

Not A Fan is a series based on the premise that God wants 'followers' not 'fans.' A fan cheers for the team while they are winning, but when things don't go well, a fan may cheer for someone else. A follower, on the other hand, actually knows the one he is following.

When Johnny Cash was at Alpine Hills in Sugarcreek in 1995, I went. I am a fan. While he was singing, I went down to the front of the stage to get a picture, and he looked right at me. I could tell he didn't recognize me. I remember thinking, "Johnny, it's me! John Schmid! Don't you recognize me?!" In the split second that I was thinking that, I also remember thinking, "Duh! Of course, he doesn't know me! I'm a fan." I knew all about him. I had all of his records. I had been to his concerts, his house, his studio... but I didn't KNOW him. I only knew about him.

I don't want that type of relationship with Jesus. I want to know Him *"...and the power of His resurrection and the fellowship of His sufferings, being conformed to His death..."* (Phil. 3:10) Not a fan. A follower!

July - 2012

A Wasted Life?

We took a stroll through the Mansfield Prison Graveyard last Sunday. I had seen the tombstones many times out in the field as we entered the parking lot. One of the volunteers said, "Let's go see the cemetery." So we went. Here's what we saw.

Every marker was the same size and shape.

I posted this picture of a tombstone on Facebook with the following comment:

> *"We got to Mansfield for a prison service early tonight, so we walked through the prison cemetery. There were no names on the tombstones. No dates. Just prison numbers!"*

INMATE 38148

Here are some of the Facebook comments:

- *"Sad."*

- *"Sad indeed."*

- *"It's beyond sad. It's brutal. And completely unnecessary."*

- *"Numbers here. But God knows their NAMES!"*

- *"I don't care what a person has done. He deserves to have his name on his tombstone."*

- *"Really sad that the families can't do anything about it."*

To that last comment about families, I responded, *"They tell me that the men buried here had no family. Or else the family was so angry or hurt or embarrassed that they wouldn't claim the body. Part of me says you reap what you sow, part of me weeps. So, I keep going to prisons."*

And I guess that sums up my philosophy. Keep sowing seeds of the Gospel. When I hear the sad stories of some of the inmates, part of me thinks, "No wonder you're in prison! I might be here, too, if I had been raised like you were." But another part of me wants to kick them in the rear end and say, "Grow up! Be responsible! Stop being a victim! I know men who had it just as bad as you did, or worse, and they are not just surviving, they are thriving!"

I don't really SAY that to anyone, but sometimes I want to yell it out loud in the chapel. Probably wouldn't do much good. So, I proclaim Christ. In most cases, it has been clinically proven that Jesus knows how to change a man better than I do. If He is lifted up, He draws all men to Himself.

But I still weep when I think of the wasted, lonely (wicked?) life of a man whose total years on planet earth are summed up with a number: 38148. So I continue to go to prisons. There is hope!

August - 2012

Prison Song

About ten years ago I made one of those mistakes that every performer dreads. I don't consider a chapel service a 'performance,' but no matter how you cut it, when a man is singing, even though it is ministering and serving, he is also performing. There are certain unwritten performance rules that a singer does well to follow. One such rule: know your audience.

Have you ever heard the story of the country singer who mistakenly got on the program at a hard rock concert? It didn't go well! Nobody was happy. That's sort of what happened to me at a prison service. For some reason I started singing an old hymn: "I Will Sing of My Redeemer," written by Philip Bliss in 1876. Half way into the first line I thought, "What have I done?! This is not a prison song! It is old, and it uses 'churchy' language that these men won't understand... it is not their style... oh, man!" But like a good carpenter who covers his mistakes, I just kept on singing. Be cool.

> *Sing, oh, sing of my Redeemer, With His blood He purchased me, On the cross, He sealed my pardon. He paid my debt and made me free...*

As I finished singing that last word, "free," all 120 men in the prison chapel stood up and started cheering spontaneously. Loud! The room shook. It sounded like a sporting event! A touchdown! A last second shot! A walk-off home run! I was shocked; I couldn't even act cool because I was so rattled. I forgot the words! I don't remember what I did... I must have finished the song somehow, but what is burned in my memory is the chapel full of clapping, cheering men.

What in the world was in this song that resonated in the hearts of the men who were incarcerated, so much so that they would spontaneously start cheering?

After thinking about it for quite a while, here are my thoughts:

The language of the church is very similar to the language of the judicial system. In a healthy church, we are taught to be a *witness* and give a *testimony*. Witness and testimony are also courtroom terms. Every prisoner would have heard those words as he went through his trial.

Some of the other words that are both in the church and in the courtroom are: *judge, guilt, conviction, condemnation, pardon...* Even *grace* and *mercy* can be found in the system if you look hard. The one word that you will never find in the judicial system is the word, *love*. The system does not love you; it cannot love. The system represents the law, and the law does not love you. The law can only point out where you are wrong. It has no power to help you do right.

God's law is similar. It condemns. It shows where you are wrong. However, if you follow the law, obey the law, the Bible says that eventually you will be led to Jesus Christ.

> *"You will seek me and find me when you seek me with all your heart. "* (Jer. 29:13)

> *"So the law was put in charge to lead us to Christ."* (Galatians 3:24)

> *"The law is holy and righteous and good."* (Rom. 7:12)

I guess a prisoner would understand the churchy words of this

127-year-old hymn better than those of us who have never been incarcerated. *"He set me free..."* Hooray...! (It's hard to print how the noise in that chapel sounded!)

Are you free? If you are, maybe you should cheer. If not, like a prisoner who writes for judicial release, shock probation, pardon, or clemency... anything to try to get out (freedom)... I would suggest that you seek Him **with all your heart**. Jeremiah implies that you will find Him.

P.S. I've changed my mind. "I Will Sing of My Redeemer" is a prison song.

September - 2012

Finish Strong

I received a letter from missionary Floyd McClung. He said;

> *Sally and I are here in the U.S. for a four-month ministry time and break – a mini-furlough. One of the saddest realities we experience when we return to the United States is to learn how many spiritual leaders are not finishing well. Sadly, we hear over and over again of spiritual leaders ending up in divorce, chasing money, and teaching weird doctrines – anything and everything except what really counts, and that is just Jesus. Just loving Jesus and obeying His word.*
>
> *Sally and I are committed to finishing well, by God's grace. It is our passion to focus our lives on what we call the "three loves:" Love Jesus, love the lost and*

love other believers. We believe these three loves are the beautiful basics of our faith. We cannot finish well without friends in our lives. Friends who know us, love us, and who cover us with their love and prayers. We send this note to say thank you for being one of those friends.

I say, Amen! I want to finish well. Several of my friends have stumbled (to put it lightly) in the last half-year, and whenever that happens, I not only feel sad, disappointed, slightly shocked, a little betrayed... I also feel fear! If it can happen to them, it can happen to me. I can name a dozen nationally known Christian leaders who have fallen in the last few years. In fact, I can name five great men in the Bible who did not finish well. Noah saved the world in the ark and then fell into drunkenness. Samson saved Israel and then ended up blind, grinding feed, doing the work of a mule. Saul, Israel's first king, ended up a suicide. Solomon, the wisest king of Israel, is indicted in I Kings 11: *"...as Solomon grew old... his heart was not fully devoted to the Lord his God... he did evil in the eyes of the Lord..."* Hezekiah, with all his reforms and removal of the high places, became proud.

I called an old (ahem, long-time) friend, Rev. Ed Scearce, and asked him about a sermon I heard him preach almost 15 years ago on the subject of finishing strong. "What were your sermon points?" I asked him. He gladly gave them to me. 1. *Maintain personal discipline.* Read God's word and pray every day. 2. *Understand God's calling on your life.* What has God called you to do? Do it! Live with a goal in mind. 3. *Stay in touch with Jesus.* Like Floyd & Sally encouraged us to do.

Ed said a lot more, but it sounds pretty simple, doesn't it? It is! Then why do so many crash & burn?

Dr. John Hong, professor at Asbury Theological Seminary, once asked a small group of us, "How can you be sure you will stay faithful?" We stared at him. We didn't know. If Noah and Solomon and Hezekiah couldn't do it, who did we think we were? His answer: "Surround yourselves with holy men!" Part of what he meant was, be accountable. You can't do it by yourself. We need each other. We need the fellowship of the church. We need to be spurred on to love and good works.

In our bi-weekly Bible study/accountability group, we were discussing the fall of a friend, and one of the men quoted a plaque that hangs in a church office: *"I am just one decision away from disaster."* Everything I have worked for and stood for can be destroyed by one stupid (evil) decision.

But it's not just about avoiding a one-time reputation ruiner (I think that's a word). I want to "work while it is day," to be productive to the end, to not coast to the grave, but loosely quoting Chuck Swindoll;

"I don't want to burn out. I don't want to rust out. I want to wear out. Life should not be a journey to the grave with the intention of arriving safely in an attractive and well-preserved body, but rather to work hard, play hard, and skid into the grave sideways with the Bible in one hand and golf club in the other, body thoroughly used up, totally worn out and screaming, 'Woo-Hoo! What a ride!"

And lo, I am with you always... even to the end... of your life!

FINISH STRONG!

October - 2012

God on the Mountain

I got a call from a friend (I'll call him Dan) on my way home from Florida. "John, you've got to sing this song! It would fit well in a prison service! It's called 'God on the Mountain.' Do you know it?"

I didn't know it. But since I live in the 21st century, I googled the song, and in about a half hour I was singing it as I drove north.

Life Is Easy, When You're Up On The Mountain
And You've Got Peace Of Mind,
Like You've Never Known
But Then Things Change, When You're Down In The Valley
Don't Lose Hope, For You're Never Alone

For The God On The Mountain, Is Still God in The Valley,
When Things Go Wrong, He'll Make Them Right
And The God Of The Good Times, Is Still God Of The Bad Times
And The God Of The Day, Is Still God Of The Night

You Talk Of Faith When You're Up On The Mountain,
Oh, But The Talk Comes So Easy, When Life's At Its Best,
But It's Down In The Valleys Of Trials And Temptations
That's Where Faith is Really Put To The Test!

I agreed it would touch prisoners. It would touch anybody!

One week later I was in Montgomery, AL, at the annual We Care Prison Crusade orientation with almost 400 volunteers from all over the country. I was sitting in an auditorium, being prepared to go into one of the 17 prisons for a week in the southern part of Alabama. As I looked at the list of singing groups in the brochure, I saw the name, Lynda Randle. Lynda Randle! She is the one who sang "God On The Mountain" for the Gaither Homecoming. I had just learned the song! I looked around the auditorium, and sure enough, I saw her. She was recognizable because she has been on Gaither's Homecoming videos. Plus, she was the only African-American in a sea of white Conservative Mennonites. (Yes, I profiled!)

At the break, I went back and asked if she was indeed Lynda Randle. "Yes, I am." "Let me tell you about a phone call I got last week," I said. I told her about my friend encouraging me to sing her song. It would go well in prisons. She smiled and thanked me. Singers love to hear when their songs touch someone. At least I know how it affects me. That's one reason we sing!

On the way to lunch, I called my friend. "Guess who I am having lunch with! Lynda Randle!" "No way!" he said. As we walked to the cafeteria, I noticed that Lynda was walking beside me. "Hey, would you say hello to my friend?" She grabbed the phone, and instead of saying hello, she began to sing "God On The Mountain" as if she were holding a microphone.

"Life is easy, when you're up on the mountain...and you've got peace of mind, like you've never known...."

She sang the first verse and the chorus, said a few words to my friend and then handed the phone back to me. "How about that?!" I asked into the phone. No response. Silence. I thought we had been cut off. Then I heard it. He was holding back tears!

A song can touch the heart. And a series of 'coincidences' like this makes me think that God is trying to say something. If nothing else, He is letting me know that this song is special. He must have a message for me. He really is the God on the mountain AND in the valley. He is with us in our victories and in our down times. He is there during the day and in the night. He is there wherever we are! He is omnipresent! He gives me songs to sing. Thank you, Dan, for your call!

Don't lose hope, for you're never alone...

"GOD ON THE MOUNTAIN" © COPYRIGHT 1988. GAVIOTA MUSIC, INC. / BMI (ADMIN. BY CLEARBOX RIGHTS). ALL RIGHTS RESERVED. USED BY PERMISSION.

November - 2012

Angels We Have Heard on High

Dennis Kinlaw was the president of Asbury College when I was a student there. He tells this Christmas story:

> *I love the story of Joseph of Nazareth. All he wanted to know was the right thing to do. His girlfriend was pregnant, and it was not his baby. She said that an angel had appeared to her and told her that the child was from God. That explanation did not seem plausible, but she had never lied to him before; she had*

always been a model of purity. Now she was telling him that she was pregnant, and he faced a dilemma. If he believed her story, he might be cooperating in her evil. But if he denied her story and it was true, then he would be guilty of evil. What should he do?

At this point, an angel appeared with directions for Joseph. The angel told him to believe Mary and take her to be his wife. Angels do not usually visit people, but at this crucial moment in history, they entered our world in order to help righteous people differentiate the truth from a lie. We must be in communication with the One from outside of our world if we are ever to know what is right and what is wrong. It is no accident that modern America has nothing to say about ethics and truth because true ethics come from outside our space-time universe.

At two other times in Joseph's life, he received supernatural guidance when his only concern was the protection of his wife and her child. Could it be that the purpose of these stories is to let us know that there is no way we can be responsible for our family unless we are in communication with heaven? At crucial points in each family's existence, divine counsel and guidance are needed to protect each member of the family. God provided direction to Joseph. He will do the same for us.

This Day With The Master – Dec. 23

Isn't that interesting? One of the messages of Christmas is that we need Heavenly counsel to have a godly family.

Our children are all out of the house. I think we did seek His counsel while they were growing up, and I discovered that no matter how old your children are, you never stop being a parent. We still pray for them daily.

My Christmas tidings to you: you can't be responsible for your family without counsel from Heaven. God knew that and sent His Son to planet Earth to reach, teach, and save us. We celebrate that event this month. I have often heard it said at this time of the year, "Christmas is for children." That is partly true. Christmas is for families!

May God (Immanuel) bless you and your family this Christmas. May you be in communication with Heaven. May Bing Crosby's song be a reality for you this year... *"I'll (the whole family will) Be Home For Christmas..."*

December - 2012

2013

Another Year...

TIME n. interval between events, 1.a. a nonspatial continuum in which events occur in apparently irreversible succession from the past through the present to the future, b. an interval separating two points on this continuum... – Webster's II Dictionary (The definition goes on and on...)

"If I could save time in a bottle..." - Jim Croce

At this time of the year, we think about time. It's the beginning of a new year. We get a new calendar. We make new plans. We think about New Year's Resolutions. I always promise myself that I'm going to read through the Bible, starting New Year's

Day, and I usually do. The amazingly accurate Mayan Calendar ended on December 21, 2012, and many predicted the end of the world. When our calendar ends (December 31, every year) we just get a new one! As I write this, it looks like the world didn't end, although I sometimes wonder if maybe it really did end and I'm just imagining that I'm writing this letter. But that's another subject.

TIME: what prisoners *do*.

Ex-prisoner Jack Murphy said, "Doing time isn't easy. Oh, anyone can do time; in fact, the only thing some people can do is time... Many of the men around me were sinking, giving up, falling apart. I'd see them sitting in their cells, staring at the floor, doing nothing but time. Time and the weight of incarceration were just caving them in. They had decided to die on the installment plan because life had lost all of its value to them..."

Prisoners think about time all the time. That's the phrase they use for incarceration. I'm "doing time." When I meet someone new on the street, a common question is, "What do you do for a living?" A common question in prison is, "How much time you doin'?"

Little things become magnified in prison. Little bad things become terrible things, and little good things become beautiful. We took cookies into two prisons again this year. A little thing; six cookies for each prisoner. But in a dark place like prison, it became a bright shining light.

Here are some excerpts from a few thank you letters:

> "I want to thank you from my heart for the blessing you gave me and many other inmates here at ORW. Your beautiful shining faces full of love and peace was so touching for me the day you came to sing and hand out cookies. As soon as I entered the room, I was overwhelmed with the Spirit of God and began to cry. I wanted to touch and bless each one of you so much, I almost forgot about getting my cookies. I felt Christmas alive within me again!" – Lora

> "To all the beautiful souls that visit us in ministry: On behalf of all of us at London Correctional, I would like to say thank you. My own personal thanks to sweet young Sierra who signed my card. We cannot thank you enough for all the smiles you bring to us."
> – Jonathon

This man said he made a bad decision to drive home after he had been drinking:

> "I was 50 weeks away from full retirement from Honda (30 yrs.) when I was in an accident that took a life. My plans were to prepare for retirement and chase my 11 grandchildren's activities. That is on a 6-10 year hold. Your group changed my whole weekend! I'm usually depressed on weekends, but not this one. The carolers' harmony was so sweet to the ears. And homemade cookies! Thank you, thank you, thank you!" – Chris

"There is still time." – Ex-con Chuck Wilson, every time he goes past a graveyard.

"If you're not serving Jesus, you're just doing time." – Jack Murphy

HAPPY NEW YEAR! – 365 days of more time!

January - 2013

The Little Girl in the Picture

(A TRUE STORY)
BY: ANNIE CHAPMAN

One day as I was sorting through old photos, I came across a 3x3, black and white photo of a little girl, age five years old. Thankfully, my mother was faithful to write the name, date, and event on the back of her pictures. So as I turned the little-faded snapshot around, I read, "Taken on the way to school, the first day Anne went to school." For some reason, that hand-written memo seemed a little strange to me. Why didn't it say, "Anne's first day of school?" As I looked closer at the date the picture was taken, I understood.

The photo was not taken the first day of school. I had missed the first two weeks of first grade because I was a witness at a trial. A predatory pedophile had raped an innocent five-year-old little girl... me.

As I studied the picture, I began to remember the events of those trying days. I recalled how embarrassed I was. In some ways, the trial felt every bit as traumatic as the crime. I hated that it was so public. The little girl in the picture had been subjected to testifying before a courtroom full of stone-faced strangers. She (I) was required to say words she thought were dirty and she had to describe acts she didn't understand.

The little girl in the picture faced the evil injustice of a judge who seemed to sympathize more with the perpetrator than he did with the victim. "She's young, she'll forget this," he assured the court. Why the dismissive attitude toward such a heinous crime against a child? For years I wondered what the judge might have been doing in his spare time.

The judge told my parents to never talk about what had happened. "Let her forget; don't mention it ever again." The silence added destructive feelings of shame and secrecy to the damage already done.

Now, fifty plus years later, in my upstairs room, I stood face to face with my past as I looked at the little girl in the picture. I put the snapshot in my purse and immediately drove to a photo center to get an enlargement made. They say the eyes are the windows to the soul and I hoped to get a better look at the child's eyes so maybe I could see what was going on in her soul.

Alone that afternoon with the enlarged picture of the little girl, I sat and gazed at her sweet face. I was overcome with emotion, but not the emotions I had grappled with in the past, such as hatred for the offender, resentment against the judge, nor sympathy for the pain my parents suffered for trying to do the right thing by pressing charges. Instead, I had only one overwhelming emotion that day. Compassion. I held the picture of the little girl in my hand... and I talked to her.

"Little girl, I know you. In fact, I used to be you... but I'm not you anymore. Sweet child, you are so young and innocent. There's something you need to understand; none of this was your fault. Little one, I have such deep compassion for you. I am terribly sorry for what happened. But, little girl, you're going to have a beautiful life. You'll see. God has wonderful things planned for you. Don't worry. Jesus is going to heal your wounded soul; He's going to help you forgive what you think is unforgivable."

I dare say, many of us have a '3x3 picture' in a drawer, in an old box, or maybe just in our thoughts. Sadly, it reminds us of hurts as well as failures experienced in our past. The good news is, we don't have to live the rest of our lives as a wounded child. We can grow up, and through Christ, we can grow beyond the hurt.

I can testify that Psalm 103:13, 14 is true. God really does "have compassion on his children... on those who fear him; for He knows how we are formed, He knows we are but dust." It was His compassionate touch that healed me and in turn enabled me to show compassion as an adult to the little girl in the picture, as well as for the perpetrator!

To me, the little girl in the picture no longer represents damage, but instead, redemption. I long for others to know the same lasting recovery. You've suffered long enough. Let the healing begin.

USED WITH PERMISSION. TO READ THE UNEDITED STORY (AND MORE) VISIT:
WWW.STEVEANDANNIECHAPMAN.COM

February - 2013

Of All the Things I've Lost...

...I MISS MY MIND THE MOST

Every month I sit down to write this newsletter for the purpose of keeping you informed, inspired, encouraged, in touch... we don't want you to forget us. We depend on your prayers and gifts to keep us going. This monthly letter is almost like one of those term papers that we used to have to write in school. I need to write something that the teacher (you, in this case) will think is good so that I will get a decent grade. And, by and large, you have given me passing grades. I hear from you folks enough to realize that some of you actually read this monthly missive!

I said all that to say... I can't think of anything to write! My mind is blank, which is pure baloney. I should have plenty to say; it's been an exciting year so far! We're just fifty-some days into AD 2013, and I've already been to Florida (twice), Kentucky (Asbury University Board Meetings), Alabama (six prisons), and Memphis, TN (National Frame Builder's Association – Christians in Construction Banquet). I've held twelve prison services, three church services (Canton Mennonite – Canton, PA, Bartow UM Church – Bartow, FL, and Bay Shore Mennonite – Sarasota), our annual banquet in Sarasota (which was great!), twelve concerts, and have seen numerous commitments to Christ in prisons... whew...!

So, what's my problem? It's almost the opposite of the phenomena that makes people (like me) remember and long for the 'good old days.' Vance Havner says that the good old days are the product of a bad memory and a good imagination. We had no indoor plumbing, no phone, not much money, infant mortality; we walked to school uphill both ways in a foot of snow... you've heard the story. And yet, we want to go back to those days. Well, right now I have a bad memory and a bad imagination. What can I share this month with the folks who partner with us in this ministry?

I wonder if my blank mind is why God told the Israelite children many times to ask, "Why do we observe this celebration?" "What do you mean by this service?" "Why do we celebrate this day...?" And then the child's father would explain the reason. "We celebrate Passover to remember that God delivered our people from slavery in Egypt." "This pile of stones is so we don't forget that God stopped the Jordan River and allowed our people crossed over..." "This holiday is to remember_____."

Nowadays we celebrate Christmas to remember that God became a man. At Easter, we remember that He died on a cross and shed His blood for us. We celebrate birthdays to remind us that God gave us the gift of life. At Thanksgiving, we are reminded of the many blessings we have received...

Holidays and memorial stones and monuments say, "Don't forget!" Newsletters (ahem) say, "Remember us! Don't forget!" Hopefully, in the process, you get blessed.

So, if you remember us this month – mission accomplished. Sorry you weren't inspired or informed this time, but I promise to take notes this month and tell the mighty works of our God next time! Blessings! Have a great March!

March - 2013

Only One Life...

Dad's brother died on March 16. Uncle Syl was a month shy of 91 years old. Born in 1922, he grew up on a farm in Wayne County. When he was five years old, his dad died. Two years later my grandmother married the hired hand. Dad told the story that on Grandpa's deathbed he said, "If John ever asks you to marry him, you'd better do it." Well, he did, and she did, and Dad always said that is what kept them from going to the poorhouse. (Remember poorhouses?) Johann (John) Becker was the man I knew as 'granddaddy.'

Uncle Syl was an innovator. He was on the ground floor of what is now a common sight in America: the 'Drive-Through.' Like Dairy Queen and Kentucky Fried Chicken and almost every other fast food franchise. He built most of the early drive-throughs in this area: Wooster, Holmesville, Apple Creek, Berlin... When I was working construction, I worked on a hotel that his former partner was building. This man had become a millionaire building drive-throughs. Uncle Syl had not followed through. He claims that Ray Kroc had beat him to the patent office, so he quit. His partner seemed to do all right, patent or no patent.

Uncle Syl wasn't a 'finisher.' He was good at starting something, and then he was on to another great idea, so his life was relatively mediocre at best. He was usually a salesman of some sort or another. He often talked of his time in the Air Force during WWII and of his back injury when his plane dropped several hundred feet going through an air pocket. His military highlight was being Vice President Henry Wallace's official chauffeur for several weeks.

Brother Tim and I went to his funeral. It was a small funeral with military honors; a 21-gun salute and a flag presented to a family member. His step-children are my step-cousins. Friendly, but not like the biological cousins that we swam with in our farm pond and threw stones in the creek together when we were little.

I got home from the funeral in time to walk in late to a scheduled meeting. When I got home from that meeting, I noticed a message on my phone from a Fisher cousin in Virginia. "I hate to have to tell you by phone message, but today my dad passed away..." My uncle Fred! Mom's brother. My last uncle died on the day of Uncle Syl's funeral! I had just seen him in January in Birmingham, AL, while I was at the We Care Prison Crusade. He was making plans for his 90th birthday party in July, and I was invited. As it turns out, that is when his memorial service will be, so I'll still be going to his 90th party!

His two sons and I have reconnected in the past ten years after a long time of going our own ways. My cousin Bruce Fisher lives in Virginia and was able to attend Adam's graduation and wedding. I see Brad every January while I'm in prison!

A cousin died last month and now two uncles in one week! I guess I'm at that age when I can expect to see friends and family going 'home.' What a reminder of the brevity of life! When John Wayne died at age 72, he said, "I never dreamed that life would be so short." At ages 90 and 89, my uncles would probably say the same thing. My dad is 89, and he sometimes talks about his childhood like it was yesterday.

Comparatively speaking, it is just yesterday! The Psalmist (90:4) says that a thousand years is like yesterday; like a *watch in the night* (three hours). At that rate, AD 1922 was just a few seconds ago!

Folks, life is short. We've been put here for a reason. In an old comic strip, Lucy asked Charlie Brown, "Why are we here on earth?" Charlie Brown said, "To help other people." Lucy, after thinking about it; "Why are the other people here on earth?" That's a cute child's question, but many older folks have never figured out why they are here. Augustine said we were created to worship God and love Him forever. I think that comes pretty close to the truth, and it is step one in figuring out our specific purpose in life.

Whether it's to build drive-through ice cream stands, drive truck, farm, preach, teach... if you don't find God's purpose for your life, I can guarantee frustration, confusion, boredom, and anger... a life that falls short of what it could be. Paul told the Colossians, *"...whatever you do in word or deed, do all in the name of the Lord Jesus..."* (Col. 3:17) That is what gives your life purpose, even if it's cut short before your three score and ten years.

It's not like I saw my uncles every day. Under the circumstances, we were as close as we could have been. But they're gone. I will miss them. My family is getting smaller. I'm reminded again of the purpose of life and what really counts:

ONLY ONE LIFE AND SOON IT'S PAST:

ONLY WHAT'S DONE FOR CHRIST WILL LAST.

April - 2013

Fame and Greatness

What a week! On Monday I was at a banquet with two Cy Young Award winners; Dean Chance (LA Angels, 1964) and Denny McLain (Detroit Tigers, 1968). Dean coordinates the Roy Bates Student/Athlete Scholarship Award Banquet in Wayne County. He is a local hero for my generation, and now he has become a friend. McLain, the guest speaker for the event, was the last pitcher in the Major Leagues to win 30 games in a season.

On Tuesday I met a rapper (singer?) named Rob who is known as Vanilla Ice. I wasn't sure who he was, but I knew he must be important because his agent, not Rob, called me. I called my daughter in Florida and asked if she's ever heard of Vanilla Ice. "Oh, yes! Why? Is he in trouble?" "No, he's in Berlin." "You're kidding!" When I said that I was going to meet him, she freaked out! She sang me his hit song over the phone. Suddenly Dad was cool.

Rob (Vanilla Ice) is in Amish Country doing construction for several needy families as part of a TV show. He told the local Amish construction crew that he'd like to meet local musicians, so they mentioned me. Turns out he's a great guy, at least from what I sensed in our short meeting. I went online to hear his music, and the sound of it reminded me of the time somebody dropped a pitchfork in the thrashing machine! But he was very friendly and engaging, AND he loves Johnny Cash, so we hit it off real well! I even sang "Ring of Fire" for him, and he & his crew joined in. Yes, I sang with the rapper, Vanilla Ice!

Two days later I got a text from Small Hochstetler; "Want to go to George Beverly Shea's funeral?" I texted back, "Sure!" I had the weekend free, I'm slightly crazy, Bev Shea is a legend... let's go!

We left at 4:30 AM on Sunday and got to Montreat, NC, in plenty of time for the funeral. 1,000 people came from all over to pay tribute to the greatest gospel singer of the 20th century. Bev Shea has sung to more people in person than any man in history. He recorded 70 albums! He worked with Billy Graham for 60 years! He was healthy until the day he died at 104 years old. The day before he died he joked with his wife, "One hundred years ago I was four years old." The funeral was a tribute to a great man, but also to the One he sang about, Jesus. It was worth the 16-hour drive and lost sleep just to be a part of this event.

Baseball players and singers. Fame and greatness. What a thrilling week! I never take for granted that my job has put me in the position to meet some great people!

On Wednesday I took my dad out to eat at Tumbleweed, his favorite restaurant. Dad is in the beginnings of dementia and doesn't drive anymore, so when we entered the restaurant, all the waitresses and even the manager came over to greet him and ask where he's been and how he was. He's not very talkative anymore and he repeats himself, but he is in fair health, still lives by himself, and I could tell he enjoyed the attention and recognition given to him by the restaurant workers who seemed genuinely glad to see him.

As I sat there with Dad wondering what else to say to prompt some sort of conversation, it dawned on me that this was the fourth time this week that I had been with a great man. Two Cy Young winners, a famous rapper, Bev Shea... and, in my opinion, the greatest of them all... my dad! Those other guys are famous and maybe even great, but Dad was my first hero. Outside of Wayne County no one would know him, but he raised our family of three boys, was faithful to Mom for 65 years until death did them part (two years ago), got us boys started in our careers, retired twice, encouraged us in whatever we did... He made almost as many mistakes raising us boys as I did raising our three children, but I always knew that he had my best interests in mind. He was of the generation and bloodline that didn't express love verbally (Mom took care of that), but we knew he loved us and was proud of us. When I needed help financially, he asked, "How much?"

My unfamous dad fits into the category of *great* in my mind. I'm still hoping to be rich and famous someday, but if I can just be great like Dad was, I will consider my life a success. Dean Chance, Denny McLain, Vanilla Ice, Bev Shea... HOMER SCHMID! What a week! I am blessed!

May - 2013

A Song Will Jog a Memory

"When I was young I'd listen to the radio, waitin' for my favorite songs. When they played I'd sing along... it made me *smile..."* – The Carpenters, "Yesterday Once More"

When I hear the first six notes of "I Walk The Line," I think of where I was when I first heard Johnny Cash. I remember where I was standing when I first heard "The Battle Of New Orleans," "The Drummer Boy," and a dozen other songs. "How Great Thou Art" takes me back to 1974 when I happened to be in the same living room as George Beverly Shea and he so graciously sang that song for us. As an eighteen-year-old, I had walking pneumonia when "I Think We're Alone Now" by Tommy James & The Shondells became a hit song. I heard that song every hour for the next three days as I lay sick in bed. About once a year I hear that song on an oldies station. I get sick!

While living in Costa Rica, I happened to find an old long play Christmas record by Evie. At that time there was no Internet, fax, e-mail, computer... We hadn't heard singing in English for several years. I put the record on and as the first notes of "Ring Those Bells" began to play, Lydia looked up in pleasant, surprised shock as if an old friend had just walked through the door. I realize now that that's exactly what had happened. An old friend had just entered the room. "That was one of Dad's favorite songs!" she said. Now, every time I hear the opening notes to that song, I see Lydia's bright, surprised face in our house in La Sabana, San Jose, Costa Rica. *"Everybody Likes To Take A Holiday..."*

"Every sha-la-la-la, every wo-wo-wo still shine..."

A song is powerful. It evokes memories, it evokes emotion, it can make a sad man happy, and it can fire up 40,000 people during the seventh inning stretch at a baseball game! They say that smell is the strongest memory jogger, but a song can jog my memory as much as anything.

I guess I'm thinking these music thoughts because I just read an article, "Why Men Have Stopped Singing In Church," by David Murrow. He says, "...the church has returned to the 14th century where worshippers stand mute as professional-caliber musicians play complex instruments and sing in an obscure language. Martin Luther is turning over in his grave."

In that poignant sentence, he states that it's the 'professionals' who have stunted men's singing. As true as that is, I think the big reason that men (and women) don't sing in church is the 'obscure language.' Unfamiliar songs give birth to nonparticipation and even apathy. Very seldom do I hear *"sha-la-la-la"* in my own church [read: familiar hymn]. When the professionals do strike up an old hymn, the congregation's face lights up in pleasant surprised shock, and the singing suddenly rises a few decibels and becomes congregational, even though federal law prohibits modern worship teams from playing the original tune as written in the hymn book. But when an old friend walks through the door, we light up. Songs = memories.

I'm also thinking of how a song affects us, because about two years ago I started writing a book about how songs have changed attitudes and situations in some of my concerts. That book went into a coma on my shelf, but this month I have made an effort to get back on the wagon and get that thing written. I even talked to an editor! So, even though I have a busy summer (cruise, bicycle tour, prisons, Ireland and Germany trip...) I am going to try to get material to my editor on a regular basis and finish this project. I am predicting a New York Times best seller, but then, I also predicted that tourism would never come to Holmes County! Stay tuned! (And sing in church!)

June - 2013

Biking for Bibles

Well, I did it! I bicycled from Seattle, WA, to Benton, OH!

2,700 miles, 28 days, 12 flat tires, 2 worn out tires, 8 states, 8 concerts, almost $40,000 pledged for correspondence Bible Study courses for Ohio inmates, many towns, many friends... Oh, and a sunburn!

Looking back, I can hardly believe that I did it! It was hard, yet it was easy! Thank you for your prayers, your pledges, and your concern.

WLW

I had blocked off six weeks for the bicycle trip and finished in four weeks, so these two extra weeks are relegated to "WLW" – Whatever Lydia Wants! She stayed home for that whole time and kept the home fires burning, so now we are in Lake Placid, NY, for the next couple of days, visiting our daughter Katie who is working here during July and August. That's what Lydia wanted, and that's what she gets (this is a limited time offer).

It's our first vacation in years with no concerts or speaking engagements. Just Lydia and the girls and me... and beautiful Lake Placid, scene of the greatest athletic contest of the 20th Century. It was The Miracle On Ice – the USA Olympic hockey team (amateurs) beat the 'unbeatable' Russians in 1980! It's also where John Brown is buried. ("John Brown's body lies a-mouldering in the grave..." – that one!)

We got here just 12 hours after the Ironman event – a 2.4-mile swim, 112-mile bike ride, and then a full marathon – a 26.2-mile run! There were 1,200 participants and thousands of volunteers and supporters. The town is still full of very athletic looking people walking around with T-shirts that say "Finisher." Whenever I catch the eye of one of these ironmen, I give him/her the thumbs-up sign. They smile. What an accomplishment! (Even the Harley-Davidson bikers look athletic here!)

Our daughter Amy met us in Belleville, PA, and rode with us the last eight hours (480 miles) to Lake Placid. We will stop back in Belleville on the way home and attend our church conference on Friday & Saturday, and Amy will drive on back to Harrisonburg, VA.

I have been asked several times to speak about my bike trip, and good as it was, right now all I can think to say about it is that I peddled a lot! I'll have to think about how to put some stories together that will keep people's interest and actually have a lesson or two. And I suppose it would be good if some of the stories were true. Whatever platform the Lord gives me to share, I want to use. So, stand by.

THE OHIO STATE FAIR

Saturday, July 27, I had the great privilege to sing at The American Family Insurance Gazebo at The Ohio State Fair.

Paul Marner and Paul Mark Miller joined me as my band for the concert: "A Tribute To Johnny Cash." The two shows were well attended, even in the rain.

Playing at The Ohio State Fair wasn't exactly a lifelong dream, and it wasn't on my bucket list, but it WAS a long time desire. The Ohio State Fair is the king of all fairs in Ohio. It is where I saw Johnny Cash three different times. I even met his guitar player and one of the Statler Brothers on the midway after one of his shows and got their autographs. And although mine was not a gospel concert, it's very easy to sing about Jesus in a Cash tribute simply by telling his story and singing his songs. It was great!

And that's the news for August. Since June 6, I have been home 12 days. Our prayer is that the money raised, the concerts along the bike route that planted seeds of the gospel, the people we met along the way, and the Bible study courses that will be purchased for inmates will have been worth the effort. When I worked construction, I could always look back at the end of the day and see what was accomplished. In ministry, sometimes you don't see results until years later.

As one of Steve Wingfield's professors said, "If you reap, having not sown, someone else planted the seed: be humble. If you sow and don't reap, someone else will harvest: be faithful."

"He who goes out... carrying seeds to sow will return with songs of joy, carrying sheaves with him." – (Psalm 126:6)

August - 2013

God's Timing

Last Wednesday an inmate at Chillicothe asked me, "How is Mary? She graded my Bible Studies." I said she is fine and I will tell her hello. When I told Mary that Jason said hello, she told me the rest of the story.

Two years ago, Jason sent Mary a pair of engraved wood pictures in gratitude for grading his Bible Study Courses and encouraging him with comments on each lesson. One of the engravings showed an angel holding a little girl, and the other had two little girls in the arms of Jesus. What Jason could not have known is that they arrived on April 3, the anniversary of the death of Mary's daughter, Sandra, who was killed in a car accident. She was having a very hard day, as you could imagine, when the Mt. Hope post office called to say there was a package for her.

She picked up the package and when she opened it, she felt the comfort and peace of God come over her. To Mary, these engraved pieces of art represented Gods reassurance that He was with her and was thinking of her. The one picture seemed to be her granddaughter who was protected in the car, and the other picture represented the other two grandchildren who were at Mary's home at the time of the accident. What a comfort! A sign from God!

She wrote to Jason and told him that his gift arrived at exactly the right time. It must have been God's timing, and she explained why. Jason wrote back:

I didn't make those works of art. I had "Angry Joe" do

them. We sent them several weeks ago, but last week we discovered that they were still in the prison post office! I was upset, and Angry Joe was ANGRY. The prison post office finally sent them late, and that's why they arrived right on time.

When I told Angry Joe what had happened and how the 'late' engravings arrived on the anniversary of the death of your daughter, and how they comforted you, for the first time ever I heard him say, 'Well, maybe there is a God.' And even more amazing, for the first time, I saw a tear in his eye!

This Sunday we were at a prison service and Mary's husband was with us. I asked him to tell that story to the men in the prison chapel. After the service, one of the inmates told us he knows Jason and Angry Joe. And, yes, Angry Joe is the angriest man he's ever met.

So God is still working on Angry Joe. He used an incompetent mailroom, a tragic death, and a grieving mother to begin to chip away at his hard, bitter surface. Pray that Angry Joe will turn to God for forgiveness and salvation. His anger probably got him into prison, and if he gets out without changing, it will likely take him back to prison. Only God can set him free.

"In all things God works for the good of those who love Him, who have been called according to His purpose." (Romans 8:28) This verse is not talking about Joe, but it is talking about Jason and Mary who through their obedience will be able to influence Angry Joe.

September - 2013

The Big Ride

I was in South Dakota... or maybe Nebraska... when the thought came to me. "Someday I'm going to ride my bicycle across the United States. Coast to coast, 3,000 miles! Wouldn't that be something?!"

I started riding a bicycle in Costa Rica because we didn't have a car (or money) and it was a good way to get around town. I was 32 years of age, and I hadn't ridden a bike since the day I got my driver's license at age 16. I about died riding this new bicycle home from Ace Hardware in downtown San Jose to San Pedro, a distance of several hilly miles. I was huffing and puffing and wondering, how did I ever peddle a bike all around the dirt roads of Wayne County when I was a young farm boy? Maybe this bicycle thing wasn't such a good idea.

It didn't take long, however – riding from San Pedro language school in San Francisco de dos Rios each morning – until I began to get in shape and ride all around town with no problem. Missionary Dave Miller, who loaned me the money for the bike, started taking me on rides just for the fun of it. We went to neighboring towns and tourist sites, and then we actually rode clear out to the coast – over a hundred miles. And then I got the bright idea to ride from coast to coast! Just over 200 miles from Limon to Puntarenas. At 4:00 AM I dipped my back wheel in the Atlantic Ocean in Limon (that's what the purists do) and at 6:00 PM my front wheel touched the Pacific Ocean in Puntarenas.

Fast-forward 25 years. I'm in South Dakota (or Nebraska?) thinking about 'The Big Ride.' All the way across the United

States! And what am I doing in South Dakota? I'm riding my bicycle from Seattle to Ohio! I was daydreaming and planning and wondering in my mind about this long time dream... and it dawned on me: THIS IS IT! I AM ON THE BIG RIDE! I AM RIDING ACROSS THE UNITED STATES! DUH! Or, WOW!

I guess I had been so busy with prisons and a cruise and an anniversary auction for Weaver Leather and planning a trip to Ireland, and I was so excited (and anxious), that I forgot that this **was** The Big Ride!

As the reality slowly sank in that I was actually in the process of fulfilling a long-time dream and goal, I realized that when I took my daily bike ride at home, always lurking in the back of my mind was the lingering thought; "I'm getting in shape for The Big Ride. Someday I'm going to ride from coast to coast. Be ready." Even now, after it's over and I ride for exercise, there is always a thought way back in the recesses of my mind that I'm getting ready for something bigger.

LESSON: Every day in this pilgrimage of life, in the back of my mind, I am preparing for THE BIG RIDE. It's not always conscious, but it's there. Someday I plan to go from here to Heaven! I'm not sure when it's going to be, but I want to be ready. How do I 'get in shape' for that trip? First, I committed my life to Jesus Christ. That makes me a Christ-ian: a Christ-follower. As in physical events, there are daily exercises. Every day I try to read, pray, study, 'keep in shape.' In physical events, there are contests, races, rides. In the Christian life, there is real life. Living in the community. Helping your neighbor. Getting along with the not-so-easy neighbor. Smiling at the driver who just cut in on you. Giving your resources at church and in the neighborhood. Telling the Story, forgiving, giving, encouraging, living. Every day is a chance to get in shape.

I think you get the picture. There is going to be a BIG RIDE for each one of us someday. I want to be ready. I want my friends to be ready. One of my goals in life and in this ministry is to help people get ready; to convince them of the necessity to be ready. Not everyone will take a long bicycle ride, but every one of us will take the journey of death and beyond. Be ready!

"Therefore, be ye also ready, for in such an hour as ye think not, the Son of Man cometh." (Matt. 24:44)

P.S. I love my daily bike ride. It is not a burden. Our daily walk with Christ is not a burden. It is a joy!

October - 2013

Show Up

"Thank you for helping me forget where I was for an hour."
– Ohio inmate

The chapel service seemed sort of dead. It was an afternoon service on a beautiful day. That's usually a bad combination for a good (full) chapel. The only worse scenario is a beautiful day with a World Series game on TV. There were 50 some men in attendance, not quite half full.

Maybe part of the problem was that I only had one volunteer.

I like to have at least four volunteers with me when I go into a prison, not so much to help with the actual singing or preaching, but there just seems to be some spiritual force (good) that comes along with more 'temples' of the Holy Spirit on the team. Remember, when a Christian walks through the gates of a prison, he is behind enemy lines.

A prison is Satan's turf. I have often said that a church is a taste of Heaven, and a prison is a taste of Hell. Even churches that are squabbling and having problems have the *fruit of the Spirit:* love, joy, peace, patience, kindness, goodness, faithfulness, meekness, self-control (Gal. 5:22, 23). And the nicest prison in the world still manifests the *works of the flesh,* (also found in Galatians): adultery, fornication, uncleanness, lewdness, idolatry, sorcery, hatred, contentions, jealousies, outbursts of wrath, selfish ambitions, dissensions, heresies, envy, murders, drunkenness, revelries, and the like... WHEW! (The "WHEW" was added.)

In war (which this is) a man behind enemy lines can wipe out ten times more of the enemy than the soldiers who are on the front lines. The danger is that a soldier in the enemy camp is so much more vulnerable. He is an easy target. Unprotected. Therefore, while in the enemy camp (prison), I like to have some cover (temples of the Holy Spirit: Christians).

The old Negro Spiritual says, *"I ain't gonna study war no more..."* but I wonder if we ought to realize that we are in a war, and we should study. And in modern war, the tanks shoot missiles over their own men into enemy territory to scatter the enemy so the foot soldiers can go in and 'clean up.' An army chaplain once told me that's what prayer is. Your prayer for this ministry sends 'missiles' into the prison and scatters the enemy so that we can go in with a chapel program and clean up. I believe that when an inmate makes a commitment in one of our chapel services, it may not be so much the singing or the message that was just presented, but the culmination of the prayers of a mother, a grandfather, neighbors, and perfect strangers (Christians) like you, who have prayed for that man.

Where was I...? Oh, yes! The dead chapel service. To my relief, the men did warm up, the Spirit started to move, and even though there were no first time commitments, ten of the men made re-commitments to serve the Lord, and several others prayed to be free from addictions.

The thing that made me realize that God was present in this service was not the recommitments or the smiles that started to form on these hardened men's faces. It wasn't the chaplain's kind remarks and closing prayer. What hit me the hardest was the man who shook hands with us on the way out and with a look of gratitude and peace said, "Thanks for helping me forget where I was for one hour."

I was reminded: Eighty percent of prison ministry (and most ministry) is just showing up. Your presence says volumes. And once you're there, God can do mighty things. Lesson: Show up!

November - 2013

THE YEAR 2013

Merry Christmas!

KATIE, LYDIA, JOHN, AMELIA, AND ADAM & KATIE SCHMID

OUR GREATEST NEED
by: Charles Sell

If our greatest need had been information,
God would have sent us an educator.
If our greatest need had been technology,
God would have sent us a scientist.
If our greatest need had been money,
He would have sent an economist.
But since our greatest need was forgiveness,
God sent us a Savior.

December - 2013

January

TWO THOUSAND FOURTEEN

Well, another year in the books! Another 365 days of life. January is a time to look back and evaluate, but also to look ahead and plan. What could I have done better, differently; what should I adjust in 2014?

A friend told me that he was in the fourth quarter of his life. I mentioned that games are won and lost in the fourth quarter. A football team goes into the locker room at half time to re-evaluate, adjust, get a pep talk, and fix injuries... Most of all, they are encouraged to play hard until the final whistle.

Unlike football, my game could be over before you read this. I need to "play hard" every day, not knowing when my final whistle will blow. My dad's brother died on March 16 and on the day of his funeral, my mom's brother died. My last two uncles in one week! Dad is the last man standing of that generation. He is 89 and in fair health. My first cousin died in January, and his daughter died of pneumonia in August. Life is fragile and "like a vapor." New Year's is a time to remind ourselves to "redeem the time."

I try to live life to the fullest every day. Here's a summary of my year, AD 2013:

JANUARY – Concerts and prisons in Florida, We Care Prison Crusade in Alabama.

FEBRUARY – Church in Pennsylvania, then back to Florida for our Annual CGM banquet.

MARCH – MCC in Pennsylvania, Bristol, VA (NASCAR & The Carter Fold), MCC in Arthur, IL.

APRIL, MAY – Prisons, concerts, churches here at home.

And then – **Summer!** This was my most adventurous summer since I was a boy!

JUNE – A cruise to Alaska.

JULY – A 2,730-mile bicycle trip. (Raised $40,000 for Bible Study courses for Ohio inmates.

AUGUST – A concert tour to Ireland.

SEPTEMBER – A genealogical trip to Germany. (I found dead relatives – in Königsbach – back nine generations!)

In the fall, I was in Chicago, Shipshewana, and Nashville, then home for Christmas concerts, banquets, and prisons... and taking 40,000 cookies to Marysville and London prisons (with 40 volunteers).

This year I sang with well-known singers as diverse as Gaither recording artist Lynda Randel and rap singer Vanilla Ice! I sang to groups of prisoners, Amish, Wesleyans, Baptists, tourists, Nashville stars, recovering alcoholics, Civil War buffs, nursing home residents, and athletes... whew! It seems that singing crosses many boundaries and allows me to be a part of many different venues to plant seeds of the gospel.

As I look into the New Year, I am disappointed about what government and our society is trying to impose, but I'm as excited as ever at what God is planning. I think He must also be disappointed, but He is not shocked or surprised, for... *"He rules the world with truth and grace, and He makes the nations prove the glories of His righteousness, and Heaven and nature sing."* I'm going to keep singing!

May God bless us everyone in the coming year. May He fill your life with meaning, health, abundance, His Spirit, friends, and opportunities to minister... with His love and LIFE! HAPPY (BLESSED) NEW YEAR!

January - 2014

Ice, Ice Baby!

Four hundred volunteers gathered at Abernathy Hall, Alabama State University, on Sunday, Jan. 26, for the annual We Care prison orientation and training session to get us ready to go into 25 different prisons in the state with the good news of Jesus. On Sunday night, after the day of meetings, the volunteers went to their respective areas where they would be based for the week of prison ministry: Birmingham, Montgomery, Troy, Atmore...

On Monday, I went with Ryan & Friends from our base in Birmingham to St. Clair Correctional, about 40 miles northeast of our hotel. On Tuesday, we attended the morning devotional at Grace and Truth Church, then went back to our hotel to relax until it was time to head for our evening chapel service at Kilby Correctional in Montgomery (about 100 miles). It had started to snow in the morning, which is unusual here. Chaplain Jeremy Miller said in the three years he's been in Alabama it had snowed once, so this was sort of a thrill for the local folks. Snow! In Alabama, the snow lasts several hours and then melts.

But this time it didn't melt. It snowed (and iced!) about two or three inches, and the temperature was 18 degrees. All day. And all night. They weren't expecting this! When our teams got to the prisons around 11:00 AM that morning, they were told that everything was canceled. The governor has ordered all non-essential employees (chaplains) to go home. So they turned around and headed back to the hotel.

But it wasn't that simple. The 45-minute trip **to** the prison was now an eight-hour trek **back**. They said the interstates and highways looked like a combination parking lot and junkyard. Cars were bumper-to-bumper and fender-to-fender. Slide, smash, crash... If this snow and ice storm would have been in Ohio it still would have been bad, but add in folks who are not used to winter driving, and you've got 40 miles of "mess" on the highway. And hundreds of dented, smashed cars.

Ryan and I were warm and snug in the hotel (for three days!), and would have felt sorry for ourselves had it not been for realizing what most of the teams were enduring. We walked several hundred yards from our hotel to a hamburger joint for lunch, while many of the volunteers didn't eat until they got back to the hotel at 8 or 9 PM. Chick-fil-A closed their restaurant, but since the employees couldn't get home, they came back and cooked up several hundred chicken sandwiches and walked out to the interstate and gave them to hungry, stranded motorists. Free! One doctor walked six miles to his hospital to perform an urgent surgery. My nephew and his wife, who live in Alabama, each walked several miles to get their children from school. Many students stayed at their school all night.

There's more, but you get the picture. A mess. I made it to two of the six prisons where I was scheduled. Four hundred volunteers were stranded in hotels (after they got back from the prisons) for several days. I'm wondering what God is up to. This is one mess you can't blame on Satan. God controls the weather (and everything), so we're stepping back and trying to see the silver lining behind this cloud. Thousands of hours & dollars, talents and time, seemingly wasted.

But since I know that God is in absolute, total control, I trust that He had a plan. From our viewpoint, it didn't look smart. But for my part, I got to know many of the volunteers better. Even though we see each other year after year, this year we really got to know each other. And who knows what God might have spared us from: a prison riot, a tragic accident, or some other unknown disaster.

So, that's the report of the 2014 annual prison crusade. We plant, chaplains water, but God gives the increase.

It will be interesting to see what reports may come out of "The Year of The Ice." I know this: *"...always give yourself fully to the work of the Lord, because you know that your labor in the Lord is not in vain."* (I Cor. 15:58) And, *"All hard work brings profit..."* (Prov. 14:23)

February - 2014

Timothy's Gift

I had a full ride academic scholarship to Duke University when our family just 'fell apart.' My sister committed suicide, which put my mother into deep depression. She got hooked on prescription drugs and lost her job as a pharmacist. My Dad divorced her. Then someone shot my brother! I was so filled with rage that I went after the shooter and shot him. So, here I am with a 25-year sentence that has been reduced to 15 years because of a new law in the state of Florida concerning juveniles' sentences. I was 16 when all this happened. I'll be 32 when I get out.

That was Joe's story as we had a visit with five inmates at the Timothy's Gift Hope Tour Concert at Sumter Correctional in Bushnell, FL, in February. Ron Miller, the founder of Timothy's Gift, invited 46 of us to observe their high-powered, love-filled chapel program put on by volunteers from Gracepoint Church in Nashville. There are quite a few musicians at Gracepoint, including six Grammy Award winners, so this was not your average chapel service.

Ron arranged for five inmates, including Timothy Kane (for whom Timothy's Gift is named), to have a visit in the morning before the 1:00 PM concert. We heard their stories. I learned as much about what goes on in a prisoner's life that morning as I had in 25 years of prison ministry! We had about 20 minutes with each inmate as they rotated from each table of volunteers in the visitor's room and told their stories and answered our questions. They even had some questions for us.

Here are some of the common threads of their stories:

- They all became Christians while incarcerated.

- None of them blame anyone but themselves.

- Each one of them was angry or bitter (even hateful) towards his father.

- Each one forgave his Dad and now has a relationship with him. (It took "Bill" twenty years, but he eventually wrote that letter and made that phone call.)

- They all hope to get out of prison someday (not all of them will).

- They all hope to come back to prison as ministers.

- They were all excited that Timothy's Gift was back (4th time) at Sumter.

Then came the chapel service. Grammy Award Winner Melissa Greene, who sang with the well-known Christian groups Truth and Avalon, headed up the Nashville quality singing and speaking team that sang, shared, laughed, and loved for two hours. Their pastor, Stan Mitchell, preached a short, powerful sermon and then washed Timothy's feet as a symbol of the love and communion that God wants to have with all the inmates. Then everyone took communion! Together. Prisoner, officer, distinguished guests... all stood in line together to partake of the body and blood of Christ. The bread was given to me by a congressman and the "wine" by an inmate! I even said something to the visiting congressman about it. He said, "I was afraid you were going to make a comparison." I said, "No, the inmate wasn't that bad." :-) It served as a reminder that at the cross we're all on the same level. The Spirit of God was in that place!

Ron Miller started Timothy's Gift after seeing Tim's case on Dateline NBC. Thirteen-year-old Timmy went with a seventeen-year-old and a nineteen-year-old to rob a house at halftime of the Super Bowl. When he saw what they were going to do, he wanted to leave, but his "friends" threatened to shoot him if he left. While Tim cowered under the kitchen table, the other boys shot and killed a woman and her son in their own home. Under Florida law, Tim Kane is a murderer because he didn't leave or try to stop them. He was sentenced to life in prison at age 14. He is now 32 years old. Ron has been trying to get clemency or pardon for Tim for over 15 years! It's a slow, frustrating process, but Ron doesn't give up.

Pray for Ron, Timothy, and the thousands of inmates with similar stories. And pray for the ones who are flat-out evil. Eighty-some percent of them will be released into our communities someday. If they come out with changed hearts, all of society will benefit.

VISIT: WWW.TIMOTHYSGIFT.COM FOR MORE INFORMATION.

March - 2014

Pavoncito Prison, Guatemala

Jose Chaves (not his real name) was just starting a 35-year prison sentence at the Pavoncito Prison in Guatemala City when a riot broke out. Twenty-four inmates were murdered, decapitated, and burned in a horrible pile in the prison yard. He showed us where the slaughter took place, where the bodies were burned, and the trough-sized sink where they threw the heads.

He got permission to start a church in that very area of the prison yard if he would clean up the blood and bodies. He and his fellow Christian inmates did the gruesome work of undertakers, sanitizers, interior decorators, and painters; they cleaned up the area, which now houses a prison church of 200 inmates (out of 800 total prisoners).

That was about ten years ago. Jose is out of prison now (he miraculously got out in just under eight years!), but he comes back in every Monday to help pastor the church he started, which has changed the atmosphere of the prison. This prison used to average more than one murder a week; there has not been a killing now in over a year. Pastor Chaves pointed to the sink/trough that was full of heads after the riot and said with a slight victory grin, "This is where we baptize our members!"

And what a service we had when evangelist David Harriman and I were at this prison chapel in March! These men were hungry for the word, yet satisfied with Christ. The chapel area was crowded with over 200 men. They had deacons, ushers, assistant pastors... they even took up an offering! Unlike U.S. prisons, Guatemalan inmates can have currency. Unlike U.S. prisons, there is not much food. If you don't have a family to bring food in, you will be hungry. The prison serves food, but it's equivalent to a concentration camp diet. As we walked through the prison on a mini-tour, we saw wives, children, girlfriends, parents... What a place! One of the inside pastors has been in prison for three and a half years and has not gone to trial yet. We even met an American there. And a Costa Rican – whose family I knew! Small world.

Chaplain Jose is a convicted felon. He cannot get work in Guatemala because of his prison record. But every week he rides a bus for the three-hour trip to the prison to be there for the church. I asked some local pastors about him. Is he real? Is he faithful? Is he worthy of help from outside? How could we help? How does he make it without a job?

His wife is a secretary and makes enough to keep them alive. Our friend Pastor Elias said that Jose could use help; any financial aid could be sent to Vida Abundante, the mission we were with for the two weeks we were there. They would see that it is distributed correctly.

I just got a book entitled, *When Charity Destroys Dignity: Overcoming Unhealthy Dependency in the Christian Movement.* How can we give without creating a spirit of dependency? There is a balance, but we are considering taking the risk and helping Jose on a monthly basis for a year. If his story has touched your heart and you would like to join us in helping change the culture of a Guatemalan prison, let me know.

Speaking of funds; I was in Guatemala because of your prayers and financial support.

April - 2014

The Power of a Cookie
(AND A HUG)

My name is Susan Wilson (not her real name). How I came to know you is that you came to Marysville Prison around Christmas time of 2013 and sang Christmas carols and also passed out cookies for the girls. The day that you came, I remember like it was yesterday because I was planning on committing suicide. You see, I had just arrived at prison Nov. 21 and I was very depressed.

Six months prior to being sent to prison, my whole life fell apart. On March 22 I had a baby boy named Daniel James. Me and my two little girls and brand new baby lived with my father whom I was very very close to. You could say I was a Daddy's girl!! :-) Anyhow, three weeks after I gave birth, my dad got very sick. He was rushed to the hospital with meningitis. He began to get better from that when an aneurysm burst in his stomach. The doctors said he would not make it, that he was the sickest man in the hospital. Long story short, my dad's health went back and forth from him getting better to worse. This went on for six weeks, and my father ended up passing away on Aug. 13, 2013.

When that happened, his social security check stopped, and I had no means of supporting my three children. We lost our home and everything in it. I had to give up my children, which broke my heart, but I had no choice.

I have no more family, so when all this happened, I decided to give up. I stopped checking into probation, stopped eating and sleeping. I had nowhere to go at this point. I prayed for God to take my life, to not let me wake up the next day – but I kept waking up. Finally, I was arrested. I still don't know why God spared my life. The only conclusion I can come up with is that He really does love me!!

When I ended up in prison in November, I was done, tired, lonely, broken, sad, depressed, and definitely broken-hearted and spiritually dead inside. I just wanted to die. But then all of you came singing and caroling and as you passed out the cookies, one of you hugged me and put my hand in yours to let me know it was OK to cry, and boy, did I cry!! When those tears started coming, it was like a breakthrough to my soul. It let me know there was still a little bit of emotion left in me. The devil didn't take all of me and destroy me.

So what I wanted you to know was thank you, thank you, thank you so very much for saving my life and letting me know that someone still cares and loves me. What you do for inmates is beautiful, and I wanted you to know how grateful I am. I would love to have a pen pal/friend to write to from Common Ground Ministries. I don't have any family that writes me, and it gets lonely here. I hope to hear back from you soon."

Sincerely with love,
Susan

This letter, which has been slightly edited (spelling and punctuation), was sent in Feb. '14. I often say that 85% of prison ministry (give or take a few percentage points) is simply showing up. We didn't preach or give an invitation as we do in a chapel service. We simply showed up.

May - 2014

Generosity

GENEROUS adj. 1. characterized by a noble or kindly spirit; showing kindness to others. magnanimous 2. liberal in giving, more than is necessary or expected.

I come from a relatively generous family. I live among generous people in a generous community. That's one reason I am able to do what I do in this singing/prison ministry. It's also why the following conversation has taken place more than once after a weekend concert with other groups while we're packing up to leave:

Him: "What is your full-time work?"

Me: "I'm in full-time singing and prison ministry. This IS my full-time work!"

Him: "How can you be full-time?! You're not THAT good!"

OK, he didn't say that, but that's what his face said.

Why am I so fortunate to be able to concentrate full time on singing and ministry, when other groups who are much more talented and more effective than I am need to hurry home so they can be at work the next morning?

My conclusion: The grace of God – AND the generosity of His people.

I was talking to one such (generous) friend yesterday, and he mentioned how giving to others has blessed him. (Yes, being generous is beneficial to your health.) It reminded me of the story of how a greedy, sick, miserable, and hated man was transformed into a happy, healthy, beloved man because he became generous.

*His name was John D. Rockefeller. Because of his obsession with more and more profits, the world's first billionaire had alopecia, a condition in which all the hair falls out. He was sick, lonely, and miserable. His biographer said he looked like a mummy. His digestion was so bad that he could eat only crackers and milk. He was so hated in the Pennsylvania oil fields that he was hung in effigy by the men he had impoverished as he climbed the ladder to become the wealthiest man in the world. He had bodyguards day and night. His wealth brought him neither peace nor happiness. At age 53 he was

"... the oldest man I had ever seen," according to one journalist. He was skinny and frail, and it was generally agreed that he would not live to see his 54th birthday. He couldn't sleep.

In one of his many sleepless nights, this dying man was struck with the realization that he would not be able to take one dime of his wealth with him to the next world. He was dumbstruck. He became a changed man! In the morning he immediately started the plans that eventually developed into The Rockefeller Foundation. It was to help him distribute his money before he died. He began to help worthy causes. He gave hundreds of millions of dollars to universities, hospitals, and mission organizations... He was the one who helped rid the South of its greatest economic and physical scourge – hookworm. His contributions aided in the discovery of penicillin and in the research that saved millions from malaria, tuberculosis, diphtheria, and many other diseases.

As he began to *give* instead of *get* and as he was transformed from *greedy* to *generous*, a miracle occurred. He started to feel better. He began to sleep, to eat, and to enjoy life in general. The bitterness, rancor, and the deadness of self-centeredness fled, and refreshing streams of love and gratitude began to flow to John D. from those who used to hate him. He was changed from a repulsive and lifeless man to a vibrant and happily active person. As he unwittingly began to practice one of God's eternal laws, he reaped the benefits: *"Give, and it shall be given unto you; a good measure, pressed down, shaken together, running over, will be poured into your lap..."*

This 53-year-old dying, bitter, sick, hated, "mummy" who could only digest crackers and milk lived to be one of the most beloved and happy men in America. He died at the age of 98!

He experienced God's principle: *"...For with the measure you use, it will be measured to you."* (Luke 6:38)

Thank you for your generosity. What a blessing!

Quoted from None of These Diseases, S.I. McMillen pp.126ff

June - 2014

Bicycle Tour!

I left Benton, OH, on Sunday afternoon, June 1, and stuck my front bicycle wheel in the Atlantic Ocean on Friday evening, June 6. I had challenged you folks to pledge per mile, and I estimated that the trip would be 500 miles. The pledges added up to $27.00 per mile ($13,500) to be used for our transportation needs. When I went to perform the symbolic "wheel in the ocean" ceremony, I noticed that my odometer read 499 1/2 miles, so I rode a half-mile farther down the beach and held the ceremony there! Yes, folks, it was 500 miles! And it wouldn't have been 500 if I hadn't got lost a couple of times on the way.

I was sore every mile of the way. My arm hurt because of a rotator cuff that I finally got fixed by surgery the end of June. As I write this, I have to rest every other sentence or so because my arm is still sore and tired from surgery. I can take the sling off now and then, but I'm tender.

I didn't miss any concerts or prisons, however. The first weekend I formed a new group called "The Wounded Man Band, "

and they played three concerts while I sang with my arm in a sling. By the second week I was able to play guitar, even though I grimaced a little until about halfway through the first song. At Southeastern Prison yesterday, the inmates would not have known I was hurting if I hadn't told them.

LET ME TELL YOU A (BICYCLE) STORY...

When I was in 8th grade, we played basketball against Mt. Eaton, the school with the Ohio High School basketball record that may never be broken: 99 losses in a row! When we played them, they only had 5 players. No one on the bench. One of their players was an Amish boy, with his long denim pants and work shoes, clumping up and down the floor. No uniform. Looking back, I'm guessing that they only had four players and the coach probably grabbed this big Amish boy and asked him to stay after school and play. Who knows?

Since he was the tallest boy on the floor, he jumped center. When the ref held the ball between the two centers, he slapped the ball out of his hand into the gut of one of his surprised teammates. The kind referee blew his whistle and explained the rules to this novice.

We Franklin Township boys have laughed about that scene for lo, these many years. But about six years ago it dawned on me that I would probably know this boy. I've been around the block a few times since my isolated Franklin days, and I know a lot of people in the Mt. Eaton area. He would be my age.

I asked my Kidron buddy, Ray J. Miller, who that would be. What Amish boy was in my grade in Mt. Eaton? He didn't even hesitate. "Oh, that would be Freeman Miller, my cousin."

"Would I know him?"

"Probably not. He left the area, got his GED, went to med school, and is now an orthopedic surgeon in Wilmington, DE."

I called him up. "This is John Schmid. Have you heard of me?"

"No."

"Do you remember playing basketball in eighth grade?"

"Oh, my!" (I think maybe he was trying to forget.)

I refreshed his memory, and we laughed. I sent him a couple of my CDs, and we have exchanged a few phone calls over the last six years.

Ray J. Miller drove out to Greenwood, DE, to haul me and my bike back to Ohio after my bike tour. On Saturday we decided to call Freeman Miller, 100 miles north of Greenwood, and try to get together. He said he was having a cookout with some friends, but come on up.

We got there in time to meet his 14 guests, all orthopedic surgeons, all students of his. Two were from Jordan, one from Georgia (the country), two from China, and several from various states. This ex-Amish basketball player's influence in medicine is worldwide! I met him (again) because of a bicycle trip. (And he barbecues a mean steak.)

July - 2014

More on Dr. Freeman Miller

Since I wrote about meeting the Amish boy that I had met in eighth grade who is now an orthopedic surgeon ('met?'... we played in the same basketball game – we didn't even talk to each other...), I have heard several more interesting and even heartwarming stories about him from neighbors, relatives, and friends.

Betty Miller (Milan's Betty) came running over to me on a trail ride at Salt Fork State Park (OK, she wasn't running, but she was walking toward me with purpose) and told me that she had read my newsletter. She then shared this Freeman Miller story:

> *I was in first grade at Mt. Eaton School when Freeman would have been in 6th or 7th grade. I got picked on quite a bit. I was small for my age and I wore thick glasses, and I was very backward and bashful. The older boys would hit me on the head with their books and trip me on the school bus. They called me 'frog eyes.' I soon learned, however, that if I would just always stay within earshot of Freeman Miller, he would stick up for me. "Knock it off!" he would yell. "Pick on somebody your own size!" Freeman was big for his age, popular, and the smartest boy in the class. He was a leader, and he watched out for 'nobodies' like me. I'm sure he doesn't even remember me, but I sure remember him. He helped me survive my first couple of years in school.*

I received a letter from Mt. Eaton resident Abe A. Yoder:

> *99 losses in a row! YES! I remember that very well. It was the 1953-54 school year. (This was the last year that Mt. Eaton was a high school. They became a part of Waynedale the next year.) I was in the 6th grade at Mt. Eaton School. We had a real celebration after the losing streak was broken. BUT, when I was in the 8th grade we LOST only ONE game! In the game against Apple Creek, I stepped to the foul line with a one & one. I sank the first shot, and the team came running out on the floor, shaking my hand and slapping me on the back – even the CHEERLEADERS! I didn't realize the score was tied, and my shot gave us the victory. We had to practice foul shots until we were blue in the face and it paid off. We had three team members who shot over 80% at the foul line. I was number 12, and I believe that jersey is in the school museum now. And I sure remember Freeman Miller. We were neighbors growing up. His dad operated the neighborhood thrashing rig. Freeman's brother, John, and I were school friends and still are. He can preach a lot faster than I can talk!*

At the Rainbow of Hope Auction in Mt. Hope (July 26), I spoke about my 2013 bicycle trip from Seattle to Holmes County, and then this summer (2014) to the east coast. In the course of the evening, I mentioned the grade school ball game and meeting Dr. Freeman Miller at his home in Wilmington, DE. Among the dozen or so people who came to me afterward to tell Freeman Miller stories was Glen Shoup. He was a freshman on that Mt. Eaton team, and he played in the game when they beat Fredericksburg to avoid 100 losses in a row. He said reporters from The Wooster Daily Record, The Cleveland Plain Dealer, and The Akron Beacon Journal were all at that game. He claims that even Sports Illustrated was there. (I haven't been able to verify that one!) They celebrated as if they had won the State Championship!

Since my last newsletter, while attending various events and consuming coffee in Berlin and at the Town & County Restaurant in Kidron, I have met three of Freeman's brothers, several cousins, a neighbor or two, and numerous friends. It seems as though everybody has a Freeman Miller story and my mention of him has opened the floodgates of fond memories of a boy who had sense enough to give up a doomed basketball career to pursue an almost equally unreachable goal of becoming an orthopedic surgeon. (Remember, Freeman did not go to High School.) Obviously, he is a very intelligent, hard-working, goal oriented, and moral man. Betty Miller's story makes me think that it would be a blessing to be one of his patients.

And I finally got to meet him because of a bicycle ride!

August - 2014

Every Day is a Gift

On Tuesday, August 12, we got the tragic news that our friend Orley Miller was killed in a freak horse and wagon accident while driving some of his family through an animal park near Berlin. A week later, I was having breakfast at the Mt. Hope

Auction when the phone rang. It was Lydia.

"Jerry's wife, Mary Ann, died this morning!"

Jerry Schlabach had been sick and nauseated with Hepatitis C medication for close to a year, so I realized that Lydia was so distraught that she got it mixed up.

"You mean Jerry?"

"No! Mary Ann!"

"Mary Ann!! How can that be?! She was the strong and healthy one!"

Since that fateful August 12 Tuesday notice, at least six people from this area that I knew well have passed into eternity. Thankfully, every one of them was ready to go. But we weren't ready to let them go. Especially Orley and Mary Ann. Orley left a young wife and six children, ages 1-14. He was an excellent teacher in an open enrollment school, which is very unusual among Amish schools. Amish schools are purposely regional so that the students can walk to school. If someone lives more than a couple of miles away, another school is built. But Apple Valley had a waiting list, and some students lived too far away to walk, so they came by horse & buggy, bicycle, or hired a driver. To give you a glimpse of how special Orley was as a teacher, one student was heard to lament, "Now we're just going to be like every other normal school."

Mary Ann and Jerry often went to prison services with us. She had nursed Jerry through a year of medication that made him sick and discouraged. This procedure wasn't guaranteed to cure him of the Hepatitis C that he contracted from a blood transfusion, but just a month ago the doctor declared Jerry healed, and now they could resume life as normal again. Then on August 20, Mary Ann died very unexpectedly of a heart attack.

In 2011 I went to the hospital to visit my good friend, Jr. Miller (Josie's), who had been hit by a car while riding his bicycle. Tubes were coming out all over the place, and he was breathing with the help of a machine. As I looked at his struggling body (we know now that he had already departed), I made a vow: I will never take another day of life for granted. I had made that promise before, but this time I think it stuck. More than 4,800 days have passed since that sad hospital visit, and I'm sure that on more than 95% of those days I have thanked the Lord for another day of life. I'm more and more aware that I am not guaranteed tomorrow. Or tonight. I woke up to a 'normal' day today. Just like Orley did on August 12. Just like Mary Ann did on August 20. But God called them home on those normal days. We didn't know it, but their work on earth was done.

I don't know when my work on earth will be done. I hope it is not today. I've got plans. I still haven't seen any grandchildren. Maybe I'll still get a chance to sing on the Grand 'Ole Opry. There are prison services scheduled. We're reminded to live each day *"...very carefully... not as unwise but as wise, making the most of every opportunity (King James: 'redeem the time'), because the days are evil. Therefore... understand what the Lord's will is."* (Eph. 5:15-17)

I want to live my life so that I can say what D.L. Moody said:

"Some day you will read in the papers, 'D. L. Moody of East Northfield is dead.' Don't you believe a word of it! At that moment I shall be more alive than I am now; I shall have gone up higher, that is all, out of this old clay tenement into a house that is immortal; a body that death cannot touch, that sin cannot taint; a body fashioned like unto His glorious body. I was born of the flesh in 1837. I was born of the Spirit in 1856. That which is born of the flesh may die. That which is born of the Spirit will live forever."

Dwight Lyman Moody (1837-1899)

September - 2014

A Song Can (begin to) Change a Heart

"You sang that song two years ago when you were here, and it really got me to thinking."

I had just come off stage from my half hour slot at the London Correctional Freedom Rally, which is put on jointly every two years by Common Ground Ministries and The Gospel Echoes Team from Goshen, IN. The bearded inmate with no upper teeth, lots of tattoos, and bright eyes, was smiling as he thanked us for coming.

"That song you sang about turning the wine into water [by T. Graham Brown] really spoke to me two years ago when you were here. I was angry, bitter, an alcoholic... I was out of control. That's why I'm here. I beat someone unconscious in a drunken rage. I'm labeled as a violent offender. My nickname is so vulgar, it's not spoken in polite company [think: proctologist]. When I heard that song, I decided I needed to change my ways."

This man (let's call him Mike) went on to tell how he started to look for answers, and although I don't remember all the details, he ended up talking to the chaplain, committing his life to Christ and... "Now I attend chapel every time the doors are open. I am no longer angry. For the first time in my life, I have peace. And for the first time in many years, my son and I have a good relationship. We didn't like each other, but now he calls me Dad, and he calls me his best friend."

Then Mike did something that slightly shocked me. He pointed to a man sitting in the front row of the crowd and said, "That's him right there!"

His son was also in prison! I didn't ask too many questions, but it is not uncommon for several family members to be in prison at the same time. Mike had his judicial release papers all ready to send in – meaning he could have been released last year – but he heard that his son was being sentenced, so he elected to stay in prison (!) and "welcome" his son in!

"I was the first person my son saw as he entered the prison gates! I was able to be right there at the entrance to meet him and help him understand the prison culture and protect him. He was as angry and bitter as I was, but we have mended our relationship, and he has become a Christian. We'll both be released within the next year, and we will be able to start afresh in the free world."

Two weeks after this prison encounter I was singing at the Nappanee Apple Festival, IN, and a man came up to me and said, "Boy, you hit the nail on the head." He got all teary eyed and choked up as he went on, "When you sang "Branded Man" [Merle Haggard] I couldn't keep from crying. You're absolutely right – once you've been in prison, you're a branded man. I spent time in prison for being stupid when I was young, and the people here don't ever let me forget it. I'm a branded man."

He went on to tell his story, but here's the point; songs touch the heart. I am ordained to preach, which I love to do. And when I preach, I feel that people listen. But when I sing – there is power. A song can bypass the resistance, the resentment, the anger towards the church or parents or whatever, and it can speak to the inner soul in a way that a frontal confrontation, such as preaching, isn't always able to do. These stories convince me to keep singing.

"Singing seems to help the troubled soul..." – Johnny Cash

October - 2014

My Word... Shall Not Return to Me Void
ISAIAH 55:11

In the last year, we spent over $20,000 sending correspondence Bible Study Courses to Ohio Prisons.

Question: Do they do any good?

Last week, our area grading coordinator, Mary Mast, forwarded this note that was attached to a Bible Study that she graded:

> In Nov. 2013 we had a family gathering – my mom got into an argument with my brother, and it got out of control to the point that I saw my brother commit suicide right in front of me. My brother (who was my best friend) is gone. My mom never liked me, and I couldn't cope – so I went for alcohol – then I shot my mother because she "killed" my brother with words that hurt too bad for him to cope.
>
> Since my mother never liked me anyway, I shot her. My 15 and 17-year-old daughters begged me not to do it, but with all the alcohol in my system, I did it in a flash. Now my life is changed forever.
>
> While in this prison, I found the Lord through this [Gospel Echoes] Bible course. Now I have Christ, and I have peace.
>
> Please pray that my two daughters and my husband are protected and will find Christ as well.
>
> I'm in for 15 years to life. But I have Christ.

Well, a little bit late, but at least this woman now has an Anchor: a Governor, something besides her own will and out-of-control anger to help guide her life. And if she continues her studies in the Bible and develops into a mature Christian, when (if) she gets out, she will be a productive citizen instead of a threat or a burden to society.

Forty years ago, Marv Beachy saw prisoners handing old cigarette packages with handwritten Bible verses on them through the bars, from cell to cell, because they had no other paper to write on. He vowed right there in that prison cellblock to see what he could do to provide Bible Study material for inmates. Over the next 40 years, he provided the "Home Bible Study Course" that was offered on the old radio program, The Mennonite Hour. After that program no longer aired, he obtained the copyright for the studies, adapted them for prisons, and last year alone, over 130,000 studies were printed at the Gospel Echoes print shop in Goshen, IN! I called the Echoes office to ask how many courses may have been sent out since that day forty years ago. The conservative estimate: over three million!

Common Ground Ministries (me) conducts 50-70 prison chapel services a year. We also go to churches, camps, banquets, and secular events, but I'm starting to think that the most productive and effective thing we do may be sending Gods word behind prison walls through these Correspondence Bible Study Courses!

"His word is living and active, sharper than a two-edged sword, able to divide soul and spirit, bone and marrow; it judges the thought and intentions of the heart." (Heb. 4:12)

"Thy word is a lamp to my feet and a light to my path." (Ps. 119:105)

"All scripture is given by inspiration of God, and is profitable for doctrine, for reproof, for correction, for instruction in righteousness: That the man of God may be complete, thoroughly equipped for every good work." (2 Tim. 3:16, 17)

November - 2014

Seeds That Grow

My word... will not return to Me void. (Is. 55:11)

From 1980 to 1987, Lydia and I lived in Costa Rica where we taught school at Colegio Metodista and then worked with several different groups. These included an English speaking Youth Group, El Grupo PAS (University Students), La Vida (a high school Young Life group), and La Comunidad PAS (a church that grew out of El Grupo PAS).

This November I went to Costa Rica for a reunion of the Young Life group. Those students are now in their 40's. I went a week early so I would have time to look up friends and former students and I am happy to report that many of our 'disciples' are doing well. I thought of 3 John 4: *"I have no greater joy than to hear that my children are walking in truth."* Here is a report on some of our former students and friends:

MAURICIO was a high school student at Colegio Tecnico (Vocational High School) and came to our Young Life Club, where he became a Christian. After high school, he went to John Brown University on a Sam Walton Scholarship. He returned to Costa Rica (a requirement of the scholarship), worked for several international companies, and just last year took a position with The National Bank of Costa Rica as their Corporate Director of Marketing. He is head of a department with 60 workers. He invited me to sing for his team on the 14th floor of Banco Nacional and share the real meaning of Christmas. In all my years of singing, I had never sung to a bunch of bankers (that I can remember). One of the men came up to me afterward and said he had worked at Banco Nacional for 30 years and "I have never seen anything like this." He was referring to my singing, but also to a boss who thought enough of his team to allow them to leave their cubicles for 45 minutes for an entertaining sermon in song and word. Mauricio is doing well, financially and spiritually.

BENJAMIN is a Costa Rican who was part of our English-speaking youth group and is now married to one of our 'missionary kids.' He has a ministry called Theo's Place. There are three main groups: University Students, High School students, and Professionals. I visited his Professional Bible Study. Two hundred people came on Wednesday night to hear one of their own teach from God's word. This teacher had been a skeptic just one year ago, but the love and persistence of Theo's Place friends convinced him to go on one of their outreaches to an indigenous Indian tribe, and he saw that not all Christians are hypocrites as he had thought. He became a Christian. Out of Benjamin's three groups, there are 40-some home Bible Studies happening! Benjamin and his wife Debbie are working in the kingdom, reaching thousands!

ELIEZER, JOSE ALFREDO, RONALD: all from the La Vida group. **Eliezer,** who came from poverty, is now the head of one of the branch banks of Banco Nacional (Mauricio's bank) and is a leader in La Vida. **Jose Alfredo** is an electrician and is on the board of La Vida. **Ronald** was wiped out on drugs when we left Costa Rica in 1987. He came to the Bible Study clubs but was never real faithful. When I saw him at the hotel where the reunion was, I thought he was the hotel manager. He greeted me and called me by name, and I gave him a blank stare. "No me concoces?!" (Don't you know me?!). "MACACO!" (his nickname) No, I didn't recognize him. He is now a pastor, husband, and father, and he no longer has long hair and ragged clothes: he's drug-free! God finally became real to Ronald sometime in the years after we left. He said he always knew the Truth; he just couldn't surrender. The seeds that were planted grew without us. Ronald is doing well.

LUIS GUILLERMO is the wildest story. He graduated from Colegio Metodista the year I got there. He was a part of La Comunidad PAS. He is now The President of Costa Rica! He wanted to see me while I was there, but I was just too busy. (Just kidding! I'm not sure he even remembers me.)

There were so many more great stories and memories told, and I'm sure there are some sad ones. I suppose the folks who were not doing well didn't feel like coming to the reunion, but I was encouraged and challenged by those who were there. God is working. His Word will not return void.

"If you sow and don't reap, someone else will reap. Be faithful. If you reap, having not sown, someone else planted the seed. Be humble." – Steve Wingfield, quoting one of his professors

December - 2014

2014 Summary
(2015 VISION)

JANUARY – Florida concerts and We Care Prison Crusade

FEBRUARY – Guatemala, singing and preaching

MARCH – Belize, concerts, meetings, and prisons

APRIL – Concert tour in Alabama with Lynda Randle

MAY – Virginia concerts; Pennsylvania *(a croquet tournament)*

JUNE – Bicycle trip (500 miles) to east coast; Concert in Manitoba; shoulder surgery

JULY – Prisons, local concerts

AUGUST – Illinois concerts; Little Eden Camp in Michigan

SEPTEMBER – Oregon, my 50th state to visit!

OCTOBER – Nashville, new recording

NOVEMBER – Reunion in Costa Rica

DECEMBER – Banquets, cookies to prisons, family, dad to a nursing home

For me, it was a good year. This is always a time to reflect, evaluate, plan, regroup, and make resolutions... I wonder, what could I have done better; more of, less of? I think of the prophet's lament in Jeremiah 8:20; *"The harvest is past, the summer has ended, and we are not saved."* Have I neglected something? How many chances have I missed?

2015 VISION:

The Hebrew culture thinks differently than the Western Culture (us). We look into the future. The Hebrew backs into the future; he looks into the past. We each think the other is wrong, but the Hebrew rightly claims that he can see the past. We do too... "Hindsight is 20/20." You can't see into the future. So as we walk straight into the future that we cannot see, we bump our noses and plunge into the unknown. The Hebrew backs into the future, and as it goes past, then he can see it. That's us, too, if we think about it.

All that to say, we still need to plan. And trust. *"Trust in the Lord with all your heart and lean not on your own understanding. In all your ways acknowledge Him and He will make your paths straight."* (Prov. 3:5, 6) And work. *"Go to the ant, you sluggard: consider its ways and be wise... It stores its provisions in summer and gathers its food at harvest."* (Prov. 6:6, 8) And live! *"...I came to give you life..."* (John 10:10)

I have plans for 2015. I have goals. Who knows if they will come to fruition? But some things are pretty steady: get up, eat, go to work, plan, study, pray, deal with problems...

If you feed on a steady diet of our news media, you will be discouraged and frightened. If you feed on a steady diet of The Good News (God's word), you have reason to be confident, positive, and excited about what the future holds. Every Christmas I am reminded that no matter how bleak things look in our country and in our future, God is in absolute, total control, and as we sing "Joy To The World" we remember that –

"...He rules the world with truth and grace..."

HAPPY (AND JOYFUL) NEW YEAR!

January - 2015

The Acts of an Apostle

(OR...MY JANUARY SCHEDULE)

Every January for the last 15 years we have gone to Sarasota to sing at the Christian Fellowship Mission Haiti Fund-Raiser Concert with The Inspirations of Bryson City, NC. It is an honor and a pleasure to be a part of this vital ministry and to become friends with such a well-known and 'real' quartet.

(Not all well-known groups are 'real.') This concert blew my theory of how to book a concert. I never liked going to the same place two years in a row because I thought the people would get tired of me. For the last 15 years, we have gone to the same church with the same singing group, singing the same songs to the same people. And every year the same people pack the place out! (Where in the world do I get my theories?!) The concert raises much-needed funds for the CFM orphanage in Haiti.

It takes me about ten days to get restless and want to come back to snowy Ohio (the real world) before I turn around and head to Alabama for the We Care Prison Crusade (now called "ReNew Hope"). Four hundred volunteers, 29 prisons, thousands of prisoners... It's an intense, glorious week of singing, preaching, fellowship, and not much sleep. The chaplains tell us how much the inmates look forward to this week, which has been going on for 39 years! And this year was extra glorious (at least for me) since Ohio State won the National Football Championship. OSU fans have taken some verbal abuse the last six years from these former National Champs (three times since 2009... give 'em credit!). Because I am so humble, I never brought it up to my Alabama friends until they criticized my beautiful OSU Sugarbowl hat (reminder: OSU 42, Alabama 35 – in the Sugarbowl). When the Crimson Tide loses, not many folks in Alabama maintain a sense of humor.

THEN back to Ohio so we can get ready to go back to Florida for our Annual Sarasota CGM Fund Raiser Banquet; this year, it's on Feb. 17. I know, this schedule is not the most efficient use of vehicles, but it just seems to have worked out that way. When we are old enough, we may just stay in Florida the month of January until it's time to go to Alabama.

This March I will have the privilege of traveling with the We Care Fund-Raiser Banquet Tour (see schedule). What a worthy cause! We Care is the granddaddy of most of the prison ministries that I deal with. When Martin Weber wanted to bring 'civilians' into the prisons to minister, the officials thought he was crazy. Now they come from ten different states to blitz almost 30 Alabama prisons for a week with the love of Christ!

Think of it... When a prisoner gets saved and turns his life around, not only does he become a responsible citizen, but as ex-inmate Arcella said, "Just think how many robberies won't occur now that I'm following Christ. I used to pull off two or three robberies a day to get enough money to support my drug habit!" Hmmm... between 750 and 1000 thefts will not occur this year because this lady is now a Christian!

92% of all inmates currently incarcerated will be released someday. How would you like them to return? More bitter and angry then when they went in? More cunning and 'professional' in their pursuit of crime? Or changed; wanting to serve God and man and be productive citizens in society? Fact: they will be in our communities. Let's reach them with the Gospel before they get there.

February - 2015

Homer Schmid
1924 - 2015

"Another member of the Greatest Generation drops out of formation..." – Brad Fisher. (My cousin)

Dad passed into eternity in the early hours of Feb. 4, 2015. He was 90 years old and relatively healthy until December. He lived by himself until last summer when he took in a boarder who needed a place to rent, but who also helped Dad fill the lonely hours. He suffered a hard stroke in December, rallied for a while, but then started to fail in February. The professionals and family called in Hospice, which made him comfortable in his last days and hours.

He grew up on a farm in Wayne County. He was two years old when his dad died. Grandma later married the hired hand, John Becker, and that's who we called granddaddy. Dad always referred to his parents as "Mom & John." I figured when a person gets older, he calls his dad by his first name (?). I was named after Granddaddy John Becker.

Those of you who knew Dad may have figured out that he wasn't perfect, but I sure didn't know it until I was around ten years old. He was my hero. Gradually, I began to see a few chinks in his armor, but he was a good dad, a good provider, a good husband and a friend to all (with maybe one or two exceptions).

I don't think I really understood how much he loved us (he never said the words) until I got involved in prison ministry and heard, over and over, the heartbreaking, tragic stories of abandonment, neglect, and abuse by the fathers of the average prisoner. I realized that Dad, as imperfect as he may have been, only wanted the best for us three boys. I began to understand that his strict discipline (well, I thought it was strict) was not because he was mean, but it was for our good. His belt *(the fastest belt in the east!)* was one of the reasons that I am singing and preaching in front of prisoners in the prison chapel, rather than sitting in the audience with them.

He grew up working on the family farm in the Shreve area. His graduation trip was to the Philippines on the USS Inch with The US Navy. He married Mom in 1945 just before he was discharged, and they were together until death did them part, 65 years later (2011). We three boys grew up in the Moreland community and then Mom & Dad moved to Wooster. Dad was a businessman, having started several businesses: Schmid & Miller Plumbing & Heating, Homer Schmid Plumbing, Gumm & Schmid, Hofacker Drilling, and The Battery House... (I'm sure I missed one).

He was not a churchgoer, but at age 88 our friend Jerry Durham visited him and asked two simple questions; "Homer, do you know where you're going when you die?" and "Would you like to know?" Dad said, no, he didn't know and, yes, he would like to know. Jerry then led him in the "Sinner's Prayer," a prayer of commitment. He was in the beginnings of dementia, but he knew what he wanted and what he didn't want (ask the caretaker who came in daily), so we have that blessed hope that Dad knew what he was praying and is with Mom (and Jesus) right now.

I think it's ironic that the great reformer, Martin Luther, had trouble praying the Lord's Prayer because it begins, "Our Father..." His father was so harsh and strict that He felt God must be the same, but when I say the word, "Father," I think of a person who only wants the best for me.

Thanks, Dad, for an idyllic upbringing. We were (are) blessed. **See you soon.**

March - 2015

April News

March came in like a lion, and it went out about the same! I'm talking about the weather, of course. But ministry-wise, it also came in like a lion. Eleven events in eight days on the We Care Prison Ministry Banquet Tour:

    Seven banquets,

        two prisons,

            one coffee house,

                and one church service!

Virginia, Pennsylvania, and Ohio. It was a blast... and it was profitable. Much-needed funds were raised for the chaplains that We Care supports in Alabama.

As I write this, **Lydia** is in Sarasota where all of our children are right now. **Katie** is working for The Amish Baking Co., making donuts at Florida festivals. **Adam** is there with The

Walking Roots Band for the 50th anniversary of The Lakeland Christian Retreat Center in Bradenton, as well as two Sunday church services and Birky Square on Monday night. **Amelia** went down to support Adam and the band.

NOTE: I couldn't go because I preached at Light In The Valley Church on Sunday morning, March 29. But I flew down Sunday after church and surprised them as I walked into their after-concert party. I was able to be at their Birky Square Concert on Monday night. It went well.

WRONG PRISON

Last Sunday we did a very unusual thing... we went to the wrong prison! And they let us in! Unheard of! I have been turned away because my name was spelled wrong on the gate pass ("Schmidt" instead of "Schmid"). I had the wrong kind of pants one time and got sent packing (the same black denims I always wear, but wrong on that particular day with that particular guard). So to show up unannounced and be let in... the Lord must have wanted us there for some reason. It was a good service, by the way.

As we checked in, the officer inspected my guitar. He pulled my capo out of the case (used to change keys on a guitar) and looked at it real close, turned it around a few times and then said, "I used to make these." The capo has the brand name, Kyser stamped on it. I had never paid attention to it. This officer was a neighbor and a friend of Mr. Kyser, and an employee at his capo factory! He told us how and where they were made and a bunch of trivia about the capo. We wonder if that is what distracted the front gate enough to allow us to enter.

RIGHT PRISON

Another first; The Abe Hochstetler family went with me to Marion Correctional. Nine of his eleven children and their spouses plus four married grandchildren went in. Twenty-six total volunteers, and all from one family! The chaplain got permission for them to bring cookies in, so after I had sung two songs, I introduced Abe, and he and the family sang three songs. I then sang and preached about the crucifixion and resurrection of Jesus, and the Hochstetlers closed with a slow Amish church song, "Lebt Friedsam." And then cookies! A great, unusual Easter prison chapel service. They loved it! HE IS RISEN!

April - 2015

Here I Stand, I Can do no Other

I saw the Cathedral of Worms in Germany last week, where Martin Luther was put on trial in 1521 for standing against the heresy of the church. He stood alone against the whole world as he was asked, "Did you write these books?" "Yes." "Do you recant?" Luther must have swallowed hard, but history says that he looked at the authorities and said, "Unless I am convinced by the testimony of the Scriptures or by clear reason (for I do not trust either in the pope or in councils alone...), I am bound by the Scriptures I have quoted, and my conscience is captive to the Word of God. I cannot and will not recant anything since it is neither safe nor right to go against conscience. Here I stand. I can do no other. May God help me. Amen."

This speech is considered a world classic of epoch-making oratory. I don't think we can imagine the courage it took for Luther to stand for the Truth. In our culture, the case would be, "The State vs. Martin Luther," but really it was, "The Whole World vs. Martin Luther."

I've always wondered if I would have the courage to stand for what I believed, no matter what the circumstances. I read the story of Columbine student Cassie Bernall, who was asked, with a gun in her face (by a deranged Dylan Klebold), "Are you a Christian?" Knowing that an affirmative answer would mean death, she looked him in the eye and said, "Yes." He shot her in the face.

When the authorities come into our church with guns and tell everyone who isn't serious about Jesus to leave (like happened in the former Soviet Union), will I stay? Will I leave? Would my name have been in Martyr's Mirror as one of the faithful who was tortured but never denied Christ?

Thirty years ago some Russian Christians visited Holmes County. One of their questions was, "Are you persecuted here for your faith?" "Oh, no," was the answer. "We have perfect freedom." The lady's next question has haunted me for 30 years; "Then... how do you know that you are faithful?"

Who would have thought that in my lifetime, in the free-est country in the history of the world, I would have a chance to find out? We live in such anti-God, anti-Christian times that I am bracing myself for the test. Just last week a statement was made by over 200 Christian leaders as the US Supreme Court stands ready to redefine the four-thousand-year-old definition of marriage.

MARRIAGE REDEFINITION: "A LINE WE WILL NOT CROSS"

"We respectfully warn the Supreme Court not to cross that line," read a document titled, *Pledge in Solidarity to Defend Marriage.* "We stand united together in defense of marriage. Make no mistake about our resolve."

The men and women who courageously signed this pledge did so knowing the hell-storm that is about to be unleashed on them – and their families.

"We have no choice," said Mathew Staver (Chairman, Liberty Counsel Action). "We cannot compromise our clear biblical convictions, our religious convictions."

That sure sounds like Martin Luther to me.

Friends, we live in perilous times. We need revival. We can blame the political parties and the powers that be, but in the end, the church needs to be the church. *"For it is time for judgment [revival?] to begin with the family of God; and if it begins with us, what will the outcome be for those who do not obey the gospel of God?"* (I Peter 4:17)

When push comes to shove, will I be like Martin Luther, Jan Huss, John Wycliffe, or Cassie Bernall? Will I say, "I am bound by the Scriptures I have quoted, and my conscience is captive to the Word of God. I cannot and will not recant anything since it is neither safe nor right to go against conscience.

Here I stand. I can do no other. May God help me. Amen?" I pray that I will be faithful.

"... *Stand firm. Let nothing move you. Always give yourselves fully to the work of the Lord...*" (I Cor. 15:58)

Let us pray for each other that we will stand firm, be faithful, and believe that God will be with us to the end!

May - 2015

Spring Gleaning

The month of May started out with a Bill Glass Weekend Of Champions prison program at Belmont Correctional Institution near St. Clairsville, OH. There I met Scott Caraboolad of the motorcycle stunt team, StarBoyz. He amazed the inmates and the volunteers (us) with wheelies, tricks, speed, and crazy motorcycle stunts – including blowing up his back tire in a cloud of smoke as the finale! The inmates cheered. Then Scott and I were together again on Memorial Day in Harrisonburg, VA, where he performed at the Victory Weekend with Steve Wingfield Ministries at the Rockingham County Fair Grounds. Same thing: wheelies, speed, crazy stunts, and smoke. He gave his testimony of how God brought him from a life of drugs, thoughts of suicide, and bitterness towards God after his dad died, to this ministry where he can use his amazing talent and daring (with which he formerly terrorized motorists and outran the police on interstate highways) to now proclaim Christ!

God also miraculously brought Scott and his wife back together, after they were on the brink of divorce. He is still crazy... but now crazy for Christ.

BELIZE

On May 7 I left for a long weekend in Belize, where I teamed up with evangelist David Harriman for six programs in four days. We were at a prison in Hattieville and did a concert and sermon in the coastal town of Dangriga. On Saturday night we had a concert in the Old Colony Mennonite community of Shipyard, on Sunday morning a church service, and then a Sunday evening concert/sermon at the park in Spanish Lookout. There was a men's breakfast on Monday morning before we left. David and I have teamed up together in Guatemala a couple of times, but this was quite different for Dave because the official language in Belize is English; David's first language is Spanish (he grew up a missionary kid in the jungles of Bolivia). English is my first language, so I was able to sing and minister with a little more freedom of expression than I had in Guatemala. In Spanish, I talk like a foreigner. But it went well in Belize, and they want us to return next year.

GO WEST, YOUNG MAN...

On the 20th of this month (June), we plan to leave for a family reunion in Idaho. We want to go to British Columbia to meet Iranian friends that we got to know in Costa Rica, where they were trapped for seven years in a political mess. They have been trying to understand the Christian faith and may have even embraced it by now, but it is so hard for a Muslim to understand the Trinity. Come to think of it, it is hard for a Christian to understand the Trinity. I accept it by faith, but Muslims and Jews have had it drilled into their heads and hearts that God is One, which is true, and that is why they (and we) have a hard time grasping that God is Three in One... Anyway, that is our friends' stumbling block, but they are great people and since the family reunion is in Bonner's Ferry, ID, we decided to go a few days early and visit them. Amelia and Katie stayed with them on their way to Alaska last summer, as they used "Mennonite Your Way" as their lodging choice. Our Iranian friends were honored to have them for the night, and our girls were grateful for a roof, bed, and food. (Can you Mennonite Your Way in a Muslim house?)

MISCELLANEOUS (MINI MINISTRY REPORT)

The month of May saw us in five prison services, four banquets, two retirement homes, three church services... twenty singing events total. The crowds for which I had the privilege to sing vary from inmates to retired folks to festival attendees to customers at a store concert. Oh, and church folks. No matter what background a person comes from, the needs of the human heart are the same, and the only real answer is Jesus. The punks, inmates, and gang members are looking for the same thing that the high school valedictorian and the retirement home resident is looking for: acceptance, hope, love, security, and a future... Only Jesus can fulfill that order permanently. That's why I sing about Jesus amidst all the truck driving, farm, and cowboy country songs. It's rewarding to win the attention of a crowd with country songs and then watch as they willingly listen to songs about Jesus.

June - 2015

Story of a Faithful Chaplain

I don't remember all the details. I just remember that the chaplain was in trouble. He had preached a sermon on comparative religions, and an inmate filed a complaint. "The chaplain is criticizing my religion!" The amoral, politically correct prison office let out an institutional gasp and immediately put the chaplain on unpaid administrative leave.

Again, I have forgotten some details, but it was a six-month inquisition while the chaplain sat at home with no income and pretty soon, apparently, no job. The reason I even remember this story is that six weeks ago I was at the chaplain's office and I happened to ask about this case that happened 20 years ago.

"Let me tell the rest of the story," he answered with a smile.

> *My release papers (read: dismissal, fired...) were signed and on the desk of the assistant warden when he got a call from our local senator. A friend who goes to the same church as this senator had alerted him to my situation. The senator then called the prison and asked to speak to the warden. When a senator calls, the warden listens.*
>
> *"I'm curious about the case against the chaplain. Could you please fill me in on the details?" The warden referred him to the assistant warden who informed him that the papers were right here on his desk and*

he had just signed them this morning. The chaplain would be fired as soon as the papers reached the state office.

"Could you explain the charges?"

"He violated prison policy about criticizing another religion."

"What exactly did he say?"

Well, the assistant warden didn't really know. He was simply going on the recommendation given to him by someone down the chain who had received the complaint from an inmate who had joined the religion called 'Wicca.'

"Could you please give the exact wording of the offensive language to make sure that this chaplain did indeed violate your policy?"

That put the dismissal of the chaplain on hold while they actually investigated the 'offensive' remarks. I don't remember if the sermon was taped or if several witnesses were interviewed, but when the actual words of the offense came to light, it was nothing more than a description of each religion as found in the encyclopedia.

"Reading the encyclopedia description of a religion is grounds for dismissal?!" asked the Senator.

The warden was a little embarrassed, the case was dismissed, and the chaplain was reinstated and is "back in the saddle."

But... the rest of the story...

The inmate who filed the charges did not back off. He continued to attend chapel just to taunt the chaplain, knowing that he had caused him so much grief and could probably do so again. For *18 years(!)* this inmate was a thorn in the chaplain's side.

Then, after 18 years, this evil, vile Wiccan (Wiccan: witch, wizard) fell under the spell of 18 years of the faithful chaplain's proclamation of the gospel, and he gave his heart to Jesus! In old Asbury Methodist terms, he got "gloriously saved." He confessed, repented, rejoiced... and he became the Chaplain's right-hand man until his release from prison!

He is out of prison now, involved in a good church somewhere in Ohio, and he keeps in touch with some of his inmate buddies who report his progress to the chaplain. (The chaplain is not allowed to have contact with former inmates.)

Six months of anguish and no pay. Eighteen years of grief by a mixed up, evil, Satan worshipper. Eighteen years of love, faithfulness, patience, and endurance by the chaplain. Result? A convert. A man who can say with Paul, *"I was the chief of sinners."* (I Tim. 1:15) With John Newton, he says, *"I once was lost, but now I'm found, was blind, but now I see."*

I wonder how many others were influenced by the chaplain's faithfulness and this inmate's conversion? I was. As I write this, I can think of some "thorns" in my side. May God give me (and us) the love, faithfulness, and patience of this chaplain to love people into the Kingdom.

I can just imagine my conversation with God.

Me: "I have patience, Lord, *but 18 years?!*"

God: "Not 18 years, but 18 X 18 years."

July - 2015

A Firm Foundation
...AND SOME GENEALOGY

Near Grantsville, MD, is a pioneer village of log homes built by early white settlers. One of the houses was built by Benedict Miller, Lydia's great-great-great grandfather. Here is how the house is described in The Spruce Forest Artisan Village brochure:

> Built by Benedict Miller, Amish Bishop, and his son Joel B. in 1835 near what is now Springs, PA, the Miller House was moved to this campus in 1986 and restored in 1987.
>
> The home, furnished with Miller family treasures, provides a context for the accounts of Benedict's benevolence, as well as the story of the spiritual and social foundations of this mountain community known as Brothers' Valley. The Amish way of peace allowed the white settlers to build communities alongside the Shawnee and other Indian nations. The Miller House served a triple purpose: a home, a place of worship, and the first school in the area. Always open to the needy and to the traveler, Miller's homestead stood for charity, good works, and faith.
>
> The Miller House is one of the finest examples of early

craftsmanship in the area. A close look reveals carved beading and joinery common to the finely crafted log homes of the mid-19th century.

What the brochure doesn't mention is that the log houses were moved to the village by taking them apart log by log, numbering each log, loading them on semis, and then rebuilding them as close to original as possible at the village. But not Benedict's house. His house was so solidly built and so well preserved that they were able to lift the structure in its entirety onto a flatbed trailer and haul it in one piece to the village. The only changes were to replace the main oak beam under the second floor, and also the roof.

My sermon at Little Eden Camp yesterday was "Foundations." From I Cor. 3:10-13 *"...I laid a foundation as an expert builder, and others are building on it. But each one should be careful how he builds. For no one can lay any foundation other than the one already laid, which is Jesus Christ... [a man's] work will be shown for what it is because the Day will bring it to light... the fire will test the quality of each man's work."*

Benedict's work was shown for what is was by the test of time. His work was obviously high quality. After raising several generations of his family in this house, it was able to withstand the earthquake of a four-mile semi ride 151 years after it was built.

He built not only solid buildings; Benedict also built a solid life. He was a builder, a preacher, a teacher, a 'mayor' of sorts, a leader in the community, and a friend to all. When he learned in 1830 that an Amish boy, Wilhelm Bender, was an indentured servant [that is, slave] near Baltimore, he rode his horse the 190 miles and paid the farmer the remaining several year's wages to redeem him. As they rode together back into Springs, PA, Benedict's daughter was heard to say, "Maybe he will be a husband for one of us." She was right. He later married her! Wilhelm is Lydia's great-great-grandfather.

Benedict once noticed that his corn was being stolen, so he set up a trap. One morning he heard someone calling for help. A man was caught in his trap. "Can you help me out?" "Are you caught?" was Benedict's innocent question. "Yes." "I'll help you out on one condition," was Benedict's reply. "You must eat breakfast with us." "But I'm not hungry!" "Well, that's the only way I'll help you out." The man ate breakfast with the Millers, and no one mentioned a word about the incident. As he left, Benedict gave him a bag of corn.

Story after story reveals that this ancestor built solid buildings, solid relationships, and a solid life. A huge percentage of his descendants are 'solid.' My wife is exhibit A. There's more, but here's my point; Make sure you have a good foundation. Live a life for Christ. Will your 'house' be in good shape in 151 years? In 1,000 years? In a million years?

"No other foundation can anyone lay than that which is already laid, which is Jesus Christ." (I Cor. 3:11)

Your ancestors are rooting for you.

August - 2015

God's Timing is Perfect

Mike Swiger got a frantic call from his brother. "I got into a fight with my best friend, and I killed him!" Mike jumped in his car and drove the several hours to the college where his brother was attending. "What are we going to do?!" Mike knew what the right thing to do was, but his love for his brother clouded his sense of right and wrong. He helped his brother cover up the crime. They lied to the police.

For a year and a half, Michael lived with the guilt and secrecy of what he was covering up. Then one day the police knocked on his door. He was arrested for complicity to aggravated murder. He pled guilty. He was sentenced to 50 years in prison for involuntary manslaughter.

I met Michael at Lorain Correctional shortly after he was sentenced (1990?). We got to be good friends over the 16 years he was incarcerated. He was released from prison in 2006, and not long after that, he spoke at our Common Ground Ministries annual banquet in Walnut Creek. He eventually became the pastor of Gospel House Church in Walton Hills, OH, and is now executive director of a prison ministry called True Freedom Ministries (Cleveland) with fellow ex-convict minister Gary Koly.

Several weeks ago I was singing at an event in Middlefield, OH, and Mike was in the audience. I had called to let him know that I would be in his neck of the woods. When I was done singing, we talked over coffee and ribs, and he told me the following story:

You came to Lorain Correctional sometime around 1999, and you preached about Barabbas. Remember? I took notes in the margin of my Bible. The next Easter as I read the story I saw the notes. I couldn't remember where they came from, but I wrote an article about Barabbas and sent it to several magazines and church publications. I got no reply. Not a thank you, no acknowledgment, not even a rejection notice.

When I got out of prison in 2006, I applied for a job in many places, but as you know, it's not easy for an ex-convict to get hired. One of the places I applied was The Salvation Army in Cleveland. As I was filling out the application, I was chatting with the guard in the lobby. He was very friendly. He noticed that I checked the box, "Were you ever convicted of a felony?" All of a sudden the atmosphere changed. His demeanor was no longer friendly. I could feel the tension, and a spirit of depression began to come over me.

I completed the application and slid it under the window to the lady on the other side and sat down in the lobby. To calm my shaky nerves, I picked up the Salvation Army publication War Cry *and there on the front cover was my name! The lead story this month was "Barabbas" by Mike Swiger! I couldn't believe it!*

I went into the interview, and the lady had obviously noticed that I was a felon. She was professional and cold.

"How can you get a college degree while in prison...?"

"It says here that you are a writer…"

"Do you have any examples of your writing…?"

I held up the magazine and showed her the lead article in the current issue of War Cry.

The lady's face showed amazement mixed with disbelief. She took the magazine from me and looked at it and looked back at me and then back at the magazine. I got the job!

Mike went on to thank me for coming to prison and for the story of Barabbas that God used to not only give him a job, but give him hope and encouragement right when he needed it most. God's timing is perfect. Mike sent that article six years ago. He never heard a word. Right when he was being questioned about his ability (and his integrity), the article showed up in the very place it needed to be for him!

To know more about this amazingly redeemed inmate, visit: www.MichaelSwiger.com.

To know more about our amazing God, read the Bible. ;-)

September - 2015

We'll Understand it All By and By

I had the privilege to be on the Sing & Sail Cruise to New England, Nova Scotia, and New Brunswick last week. One of the musicians was Eduard Klassen, who grew up in a Russian Mennonite Colony in the jungles of Paraguay. He is now an internationally known harpist, traveling all over the world, playing his harp (not a harmonica – a real harp) and telling his story.

Here are two of the many amazing stories he told this week:

> One day a man from Canada came into our village and preached the gospel of Jesus Christ in our own language. Although we were very religious and went to church three times a week, he made us aware that religion won't save you. Only the blood of Jesus can save a man. We had never heard that before. We were taught that if we follow the rules and dress a certain way and do certain things, we would go to Heaven. And only our church would go! But this man said Jesus came for the whole world!

Eduard then told how he was eventually converted from religion to Christ as a result of the seeds planted during this man's visit. He tells this story every time he has a concert. Several years ago, thirty-some years after he first heard this man, Eduard was telling this story at a concert in Canada. After the concert, a man came up and said, "Eduard, I can't believe you told that story of the preacher." With tears in his eyes, the man said, "I was that man. I never knew, until tonight, that my visit to your village made any difference in the Kingdom! You are traveling all over the world telling many more people than I ever did about Jesus. You have fulfilled the longing in my heart to know if my life counted. Thank you!"

When Eduard was ten or twelve years old, there was a commotion in his village. "Come! Look!" Everyone ran out to the edge of the village and there in the field was a plow. Not a one-horse walk-behind plow, which is the only kind he had ever seen, but a plow with a seat! You could plow sitting down. He couldn't believe it; sit and plow at the same time!

Someone from the US had sent this plow for the whole village, to help the people. Everyone wanted to plow.

When Eduard told this story several years ago in Northwest Ohio (he couldn't remember where – near Archbold) a man came up to talk to him after the concert. "Eduard, I can't believe you told that story! That was my plow! One day many years ago we got a request from MCC; 'Does anyone have a horse-drawn plow that could be sent to the Mennonites in El Chaco, Paraguay?' We had sold our horses years before, so I found our old rusty riding plow half buried, dismantled it and cleaned it and painted it and boxed it up and sent it to MCC, who shipped it to Paraguay. That's the last I heard of it. I had forgotten about it – until tonight. I never thought that someday I would meet one of the Paraguayan men who used our old plow. And was even blessed by it! Blessed by our old plow! And it took so little for us to send it to you."

When I worked construction, it was easy to measure what had been accomplished each day. You could see the difference that eight hours made when you looked back at your work at quitting time. Not so in ministry. Sometimes you wonder if anything happened. Is what I'm doing making a difference? There is no "measuring stick." And then I hear the stories of Eduard Klassen.

His enthusiastic testimony and stories in his German accent (English is his sixth (!) language) kept us captivated. We laughed and cried and were encouraged by his life and music. He reminded us to be thankful for the little things: shoes, food, electricity, good houses, family... And he reminded us to not take our salvation in Christ for granted. There are people like Eduard who will never hear the gospel unless someone goes. Unless someone gives. Unless someone prays.

"...how shall they believe in Him of whom they have not heard? And how shall they hear without a preacher? And how shall they preach unless they are sent?" (Romans 10:14,15)

"If you reap having not sown, someone else did the sowing. Be humble. If you sow and do not reap, someone else will reap. Be faithful." – Steve Wingfield (quoting his professor)

Get to know Eduard Klassen: *www.eduardklassen.com*

October - 2015

Old Friends

Three days ago I was at an Amish wedding in Lancaster, PA. An 'old' man shook my hand and called me by name. "Have we met?" I asked. He told me his name, but I didn't recognize it. Knowing that most of the Lancaster boys had nicknames, I asked if he had one. He hesitated and grinned. "Ketchup," he said. "Ketchup! Yes, I remember you! Florida!" We ran with the same bunch of youth in Pinecraft forty-some years ago! I had never heard his real name. We reminisced until the wedding started.

This morning I saw an 'old' man paying his bill at the local coffee shop. I happened to catch his eye from where I was sitting, and he nodded a friendly greeting. I nodded back. On his way to the door, he swerved over to my table and said, "Hello, John. Do you remember me?"

Oh, man... I looked him in the eye as I went through my mental Rolodex, trying to think of some polite way to let him know that I have "old-timers" disease. He does not look familiar. But as we looked at each other and he stood there waiting for recognition, a strange transformation occurred. Instead of staring into the eyes of a sixty-year-old Amish bishop with a beard and straw hat, I was looking into the eyes of a 20-year-old second baseman wearing white pants and a green Kidron Auction jersey. I *saw* him scoop up a ground ball and fire it to first! "Joe!" I blurted out. (Not his real name). "Is that you?!" It was. We caught up on old times for a few minutes.

Last week, Lydia and I had a meal with a couple of friends – our 20th year in a row. Once a month my high school class gets together at a restaurant in Wooster. Several times a week I go to the coffee shop – not necessarily for coffee. There is just something about friends, especially old (long-time) friends.

MAKE NEW FRIENDS, BUT KEEP THE OLD;
THOSE ARE SILVER, THESE ARE GOLD.

NEW-MADE FRIENDSHIPS, LIKE NEW WINE,
AGE WILL MELLOW AND REFINE.
FRIENDSHIPS THAT HAVE STOOD THE TEST,
TIME AND CHANGE ARE SURELY BEST;
BROW MAY WRINKLE, HAIR GROW GRAY,
FRIENDSHIP NEVER KNOWS DECAY.
FOR 'MID OLD FRIENDS TRIED AND TRUE,
ONCE MORE WE OUR YOUTH RENEW.
BUT OLD FRIENDS, ALAS MAY DIE,
NEW FRIENDS MUST THEIR PLACE SUPPLY.
CHERISH FRIENDSHIP IN YOUR BREAST.
NEW IS GOOD, BUT OLD IS BEST,
MAKE NEW FRIENDS, BUT KEEP THE OLD;
THOSE ARE SILVER, THESE ARE GOLD.

- Joseph Parry

Who is my oldest friend? Well, outside of family, I have friends that I met in first grade and some that I knew before I started school. (I didn't get out much before that.) I keep in touch with high school friends, college friends, barn building friends, missionary friends; friends I met plumbing, singing, silo building, traveling... oh, and ball-playing and Florida friends.

But there is a Friend who sticks closer than a brother (Prov. 18:24). Joseph Scriven wrote about Him in a poem that became a song entitled: "What a Friend We Have in Jesus." *"Can we find, a friend so faithful...?"* (Answer: No) *"Do thy friends despise, forsake thee?"*

"You are my friends... No longer do I call you servants, for a servant does not know what his master is doing: but I have

called you friends, for everything that I have learned from the Father I have made known to you." (John 15:14, 15)

Old friends. The Bible writes about them. Singers sing about them:

"Bless my life and grant me one old friend, at least one old friend." – Willie Nelson singing Roger Miller's song.

"What A Friend We (I) Have In Jesus" – Joseph Scriven

I cherish old (and new) friends. Especially my most faithful Friend, Jesus. Do you know Him? I would be glad to introduce you to Him.

November - 2015

Christmas 2015

"And it came to pass in those days, that there went out a decree from Caesar Augustus, that all the world should be taxed." (Luke 2:1)

The Christmas Story! It is told in Luke 2, which I memorized in fourth grade. With a little practice, I can still recite the first 20 verses.

Some things have changed since God came to earth as a man. In fact, some things have changed since I came on the scene. Devotions in public school, for instance. At Franklin Twp. School in Wayne Co., we had devotions every morning. My first Bible memory was the 23rd Psalm, which our 2nd-grade teacher challenged us to memorize. Our fourth-grade teacher helped us memorize Luke chapter 2 – The Christmas Story. The first time I ever read the Bible in front of people was in eighth grade morning devotions – in public school!

I'm not sure if devotions in school had anything to do with the fact that during my 12 years of school, I never heard of a school shooting, a teacher's strike, talking back to teachers (well, I did hear of it, but it was punishable by paddling – yes, they "touched" students back then), or even assaulting teachers, which has happened several times in the U.S. this year. I know "things were different back then," but I wonder if our freedom to worship and speak of Jesus Christ publicly was one reason that things were different?

On the other hand, some things have not changed. Man is still sinful; people still need attention, self-worth, fellowship, and recognition. Sin still causes men to lie, steal, murder, and deceive... Man still needs a Savior. And Christmas time is the easiest time of the year to talk about Jesus, even in this anti-Christian culture. Especially for someone like me, who uses concerts as a platform. Church, banquet, or secular format, Christmas carols tell the Gospel story in an "inoffensive" way.

So, this Christmas season, I want to wish you a MERRY CHRISTMAS! May the Little Child who grew up and became our Savior be more real to you this year than ever before. May His peace that passes understanding be yours (ours). May you talk about Him this Christmas season.

December - 2015

2016

Happy New Year!

A look at AD 2015 in my rear view mirror:

JANUARY – The year started out with my 90-year-old dad in a rest home after suffering a stroke in December while on a fishing trip to Florida with brother Steve. He rallied a couple of times but passed into God's presence on Feb. 4. A good dad. He gave us a great childhood. I miss him every day.

- A Haiti fundraiser concert in Sarasota with The Inspirations the second Friday of January.

- A week-long prison crusade in Alabama the last week of January.

FEBRUARY – Prisons and concerts at home (and Dad's funeral). Back to Sarasota for our annual Common Ground Ministries Banquet in February.

MARCH – A ten-day banquet tour with We Care Prison Ministry.

APRIL – To Germany for a Dialect Festival in Bockenheim.

MAY – A concert tour to Belize.

JUNE – A family reunion in Idaho in June.

JULY – An annual trip to Little Eden Camp (Michigan) as the Resource Person.

AUGUST – An exciting opportunity to sing at The Ohio State Fair, set up by Dean Chance (who passed away in Oct). A prison fundraiser in Hutchinson, KS.

SEPTEMBER – A cruise to New England in September! The year finished up with various prisons, concerts, weddings, and THEN...

NOVEMBER / DECEMBER – Seventeen(!) company Christmas banquets in Wayne and Holmes Counties, and eleven Christmas concerts at the Amish Country Theater in Walnut Creek, OH – all of them sell outs! The whole family was home for Christmas. On the 28th Lydia and I headed to Florida so I could fly to Peru on New Year's Day for five prison chapel services here in Lima, where I am writing this letter.

2016 – I am looking forward to another year of life! There are some exciting things already on the 2016 calendar, even though our country and the world is in trouble. I read an interesting combination of verses this morning;

"You will hear of wars and rumors of wars, but see that you are not alarmed..." Three verses later: *"...you will be handed over to be persecuted and put to death..."* (Matthew 24)

Don't be alarmed... you will be put to death...

They will put me to death, but I shouldn't be alarmed?! That is the peace that passes understanding.

We are not promised one more breath of life, but we are promised life eternal if we follow Christ. My prayer is that this year will be lived for Christ to the fullest of my potential.

Only one life and soon 'tis past, only what's done for Christ will last.

"Be very careful how you live – not as unwise, but as wise, making the most of every opportunity, because the days are evil." (Ephesians 5:15, 16)

HAVE A BLESSED 2016!

January - 2016

A Letter of...
HOPE, REDEMPTION, FORGIVENESS, AND NEW LIFE

I went to school with Bob and Cheryl Moeller, who now live in Chicago. Cheryl showed me this letter she received from a Native American friend. I asked permission to reprint it here.

From Shirley Duncan, National Church Representative, Hephzibah Children's Home Ministries:

Hello Cheryl,

I called my mother early Sunday morning to check on her. My stepbrother answered the phone. He is younger than I am. He has been in the hospital with pneumonia but is doing better. He was visiting my mother. Carl has lived a rough, violent life using drugs. He was an alcoholic and has been in prison a number of times. He has been living like his father lived, the stepfather who was so abusive to me and the entire family growing up.

After his last prison sentence, Carl started thinking that he needed to change his life. He did not want to go back to prison. He has two sons in prison who are serving life sentences for murder. Carl has burned many bridges and ended up homeless. He could not get a public job because of his prison background. He has worked odd jobs, doing whatever he could here and there. He rakes leaves and mows yards. He started working with a cousin in lawn care and was able to buy a small camper to move into. He is an excellent flower gardener and has a reputation for being a hard worker. He walks, rides his bicycle, or he depends on others for transportation.

A businessman was told by a friend what a hard worker Carl was, so he said, "I'd like to hire him to do some yard work." When the friend and Carl arrived at the 'businessman's' home, Carl saw the man and said, "I know that man! He's the District Attorney who sent me to prison three times! Get me out of here!" The friend talked him into staying. When the businessman (District Attorney) saw Carl, he couldn't believe his eyes.

"Mr. Scott!" he said.

My brother said, "Sir, I ain't the same Scott you saw in the courts years ago and sent to prison! I know you were just doing your job and I ain't up to bad stuff anymore!"

The DA let him stay and work, and my brother became his regular lawn care man. He was impressed with his skills and the quality of his work. During November and December Carl had to work in the cold and rain. He got very ill and ended up in the hospital.

Carl said, "Sis, you won't believe the call I got two days ago! This District Attorney told me to take care of myself and get better and not try to work in this bad rainy weather. 'Whatever you need, my wife and I will take care of it! If you need food or money, you call me!' Sis, do you know who this man was?

"He's the man that sent me to prison three times! Well, he didn't send me to prison, I sent myself; he was just doing his job! I can't believe how bad I was and this District Attorney that sent me off to prison has called and told me to stay inside and not work, just to get *better, and he will take care me! I have been so bad in my life, and this is humbling me!"*

My response, "Carl, that's just like our Heavenly Father; it doesn't matter what we have done. He's always there with open arms waiting for us to come home!"

Carl's sister is right; that's just like our Heavenly Father. He's waiting for us to repent (turn around) and come home. It's also a lesson in forgiveness. Billy Graham once said that half of the hospital beds in America are filled with people whose sickness can be directly or indirectly related to unforgiveness. I don't know how accurate his percentage is, but the point is well taken; unforgiveness affects every aspect of our lives. It is an acid that eats up everything it touches, including the container. There is also a terrifying statement at the end of the Lord's Prayer: *"...if you forgive men when they sin against you, your heavenly Father will also forgive you. But if you do not forgive men their sins,* **your Father will not forgive your sins.***"* (Matt. 6:14, 15) (emphasis mine)

I hope to meet Carl someday. He is a modern prodigal son. And I hope to meet the DA: He represents our Heavenly Father who waits for us at 'home' and longs to forgive us.

February - 2016

Thoughts on Community

On Wednesday, February 24, 2016, a tornado hit Lancaster County, PA. Fifty buildings were damaged or destroyed. One of the completely destroyed buildings was a schoolhouse, the Whitehall Amish School. On Monday, February 29, classes were held in the new building! Yes, folks, it took three days to clean up the destruction and build the new building! The students missed two days of school! The news reported that more than 1,000 volunteers showed up around Lancaster County on Thursday to help where they could. That is community!

I feel fortunate to have been born in a community where something like what I just described is not unusual. I worked for Josie Miller, the man who would be called on when a barn burned or a tornado hit. He would be on site while the embers were still smoking and neighbors were cleaning up the debris, drawing up plans on a paper bag or a cardboard box or a piece of paper. The next day, the portable sawmill would be brought in and trees from the owner's farm or a neighbor's woods would be cut and dragged in. Within a day or two, the beams and boards and braces would be cut and milled to Josie's specifications. In the meantime, a crew was laying up block and setting the floor joists and laying temporary (un-nailed) flooring, so the bents could be assembled and laid on the floor, ready for the barn raising in a day or two. I have been on a dozen or so barn raisings (frolics, 'uffstellings') and it's one of those things that always amazes, even though I've seen it many times. From a pile of lumber at 7:00 AM to a completely built barn, sometimes with hay and straw in the mow, by dark. I was at barn raisings where the cows could have been milked by milking time if they hadn't been at a neighbor's farm. 98% of this happened with volunteer labor.

In my lifetime, I have seen the community come together in a way that astounds the world. The 1969 flood showed Fredericksburg, OH, (among other towns) that community can clean up mud and destruction and rebuild in a very short time.

Before the waters had totally receded, neighbors were in town with shovels, brooms, and chain saws, cleaning, shoveling, helping in any way they could.

The same summer that Hurricane Katrina hit Louisiana and Mississippi, a tornado destroyed or damaged 50 homes and buildings in Daviess County, IN. While we heard the victims of Katrina point fingers and blame the government (while they sat and did nothing), the victims of the Daviess Co. tornado started cleaning up the same day, while busloads of 'neighbors' from similar communities came to help. A helicopter took the governor up two days after the storm to observe and take photos of some of the homes and businesses that were hit. In EVERY photo, there are people working on the roofs, people on the ground, vehicles in the driveways... In one instance the governor was touring the damage, and at one home he asked, "Why did you bring me here? This house sustained no damage." He was informed that the house had been totally destroyed and this was the NEW house. Built in one week! He didn't believe it until someone produced photos of the destruction. "But, the insurance adjusters could not have had time to get here!"

"We don't have insurance. We have each other."

If you and I could sit down with coffee, I could probably cite 20 more examples of community coming together to help in time of need. My neighbor Roy Yoder and a friend, Bob Bender from Indiana, are two of my many acquaintances that work with Mennonite Disaster Service, an organization formed for the express purpose of helping in time of need. They are like minutemen. Ready to go when disaster strikes.

Interestingly, the examples I mentioned here, as well as all that I can think of, come from a 'faith based' (read: Christian) community. There is something about real Christianity that encourages us to love our neighbor. The government or the insurance company may help, but the Christian brother is there NOW, helping to clean up, helping to rebuild, helping you to cope with the emotional loss, not questioning how much insurance you have...

"Love your neighbor as yourself." (Lev. 19:18)

"Better a neighbor nearby than a brother far away." (Proverbs 27:10)

One last thought: Would you rather depend on the government? Or your Christian community?

March - 2016

Thoughts on Education

"Any fool can know. The point is to understand." – Albert Einstein

> *Si Hoc Legere Scis Nimium Eruditionis Habes*
> *(Per contra, Scientia est Potentia)*

TRANSLATION:
If you can read this, you have too much education.
(On the other hand, knowledge is power)

I'm reminded of the story of the Harvard professor who informed his class that he spoke five languages. "For example," he said, "the word horse in Spanish is *caballo*, in German it's *pferd*, in French it's *cheval*, in Italian it's *cavallo*, ... and of course, in English it's *horse*." Just then the bell rang and class was over. As the professor walked out into the courtyard among his students, a loose horse galloped by. "Oh my goodness!" cried the professor. "What sort of beast is THAT?!"

Maybe I'm thinking of this because I have coffee in the mornings with very successful businessmen who didn't go to high school. I live in a community where education is looked on with a degree of suspicion. For instance, my board is made up of very successful businessmen who love the Lord. None of them went to high school. If I would sit here and think, I could name 20 successful businesses in this county started and run by men with only an eighth-grade education. Hundreds, maybe thousands of local people are given employment by men who can't even be labeled dropouts, because they didn't go to high school to drop out of! I often ask, "If not for the folks who didn't go to high school in Holmes Co., who would hire the college graduates?"

Don't get me wrong; I think education is very important. I've got a bunch of it. When we lived in Central America, education was about the only way out of a life of poverty. A lack of education – and especially the inability to read – is directly proportional to a person's chances of ending up in prison. "Readers are leaders." And by inference, non-readers seem to be losers. I always encourage an inmate to study for his GED. An ex-con has two strikes against him. An ex-con with no high school is almost an automatic 'out.'

So... is education the answer? I guess it depends what the question is.

There is in this country today an educated class who wouldn't know what common sense was if it came in wearing a name tag. You know the type. They've never had a real job. They've never lived in the real world. They don't know the challenges of everyday living that you and I face. But they have a diploma. They are the plumbing inspectors who never really 'plumbed.' They are the milk inspectors who never farmed. They are the lawmakers who don't have to follow their own laws. They are in government and tell us how to live our lives. They teach in the colleges that our children attend.

I guess I'm also thinking of education because college debt (school loans) has passed credit cards as the number one debt in America. Young people are graduating with six-figure debt, and they discover that their degree is not useful in the real world. They are prisoners of debt.

That young person who flipped your Big Mac may have a degree in history or English or philosophy and a debt of $90,000. He's been tricked!

So... what are my thoughts on education (learning)? I agree with the farm wisdom I heard at the Moreland Feed Mill when I was a boy; "It's what you learn after you know everything that counts." Or Edwards Deming; "Learning is not compulsory... neither is survival!" Or eighth-grade graduate Ray J. Miller; "When you don't have any education, you have to use your brains."

So, every morning I... *"Study to show yourself (myself) approved, a workman who does not need to be ashamed, rightly dividing the word of truth."* (II Tim. 2:15) Now and then I take continuing education classes in the form of seminars, correspondence courses, classes on CD... I want to be the best I can be. But, I am aware that *"...knowledge puffs up (makes arrogant). Love builds up."* (I Cor. 8:1)

"When you quit learning, you're old, no matter what your age." – Henry Ford

April - 2016

A Redeemed Life

Every now and then I hear a story that encourages me to keep going. I plan to keep going, no matter what, but encouragement always helps. I received this letter recently:

Hello John and Lydia,

When I saw you last week, I really wanted to tell you about my ex-daughter-in-law. She was sentenced to 18 months in prison for theft of doctor prescription pads and impersonating a doctor.

She became an opiate addict because of health problems she had at age 17. The addiction destroyed her marriage to our son, but God has been so very good to her in prison, and a miraculous new person emerged!! She is now working with our local judge for the past year in a program directed for persons being released from prison. She is leading this group called Half-Way Home, which the judge is mandating they attend before they get the final release by him.

God has answered so many prayers I prayed. I am in contact with her regularly, even though she is my ex-daughter-in-law.

I stand amazed in the presence of God, how he works in His mysterious ways. I thank you both for the ministry you do.

The Kairos group in prison is a much-needed ministry, and we continue to support them.

God IS in the prisons, but these persons really have to work hard to change their lives, and many of them do not have the people like my daughter-in-law had to help them during and after their release. Most of her roommates have been re-admitted to prison due to the difficulty of making it on the outside. Most of them are from families with many problems, and they try to find love and acceptance from all the wrong groups of people.

Thank you again and may God bless you as you continue your ministry. Joe and Mary

After talking with this couple, I remembered that we had visited their ex-daughter-in-law in prison. We saw her during a chapel service – we knew she was there, but we didn't know her, although she knew who we were. I hope to meet her now that she is out. It sounds like God did a great work in her life.

May - 2016

The Power of Prayer

In 1986 our son, Adam, was in Millersburg Hospital. It was just a few days shy of his first birthday, and since he didn't talk yet, he couldn't tell us where it hurt or what was wrong. He just writhed in pain and threw up.

He wasn't sick when he and Lydia came home to the states. I had stayed behind in Costa Rica to help run the annual beach campout for the Young Life Club. I would come home when it was over, about ten days later.

When I called home (via ham radio in those days), Lydia said Adam didn't feel good. The next day, just before I left for the beach, I made one more call, and Lydia said Adam was in the hospital and they didn't know what was wrong. Since he had just come from a tropical country, they thought it might be malaria.

And since it was Adam's first birthday, I got calls from all over:

"Hey! How's Adam? Happy birthday!"

"He's in the hospital in the states, and they don't know what's wrong."

"We'll pray."

Our friend Jim Scionka called. He was now a student in Dallas at Christ for the Nations School. He requested prayer in their chapel. Galen Stutzman, fellow language student and a Wycliffe worker in Columbia, alerted the Wycliffe prayer chain. Jon Showalter called, he told Rosedale Bible School. Marv Asfahl told the Young Life Headquarters about Adam. LAM missionaries all over the globe were praying. Our home church, Berlin Mennonite, got the message and Mennonites all over the county and country were praying. I can't remember who called from Wilmore, KY, but they heard our plea and Asbury College and Seminary students were praying. Folks, only eternity will tell, but I wonder if the people praying for our little boy didn't number in the thousands – in many different states and countries!

About two days into our campout on the coast, my boss Marv Asfahl came in from San Jose and said, "Adam is going to have exploratory surgery, and I got you a ticket to go home. Let's go."

The trip home is a story in itself, but I got to Akron/Canton Airport and they had lost my luggage. "Sign these papers." "Keep the luggage!" I yelled, and we ran for the hospital. When I got to Akron Children's hospital, I learned that Adam was in exploratory surgery with a Dr. Bachman, one of the best surgeons in the US.

Long story short: Adam had Meckle's Diverticulum: a 'kinked' intestine. When Dr. Bachman opened him up, he unkinked the hose and the blood started flowing into the pale intestine. If the surgery had been several hours later, the chance of gangrene would have been high, as well as infection, sickness and...

God heard the prayers of His people. Adam still has a foot-long scar across his stomach as a reminder of God's faithfulness and the power of prayer. Some of you reading this were among the prayer warriors.

Why do I bring this up now? This April, our daughter Amelia was diagnosed with thyroid cancer. Although that's the most treatable kind, it's still cancer. We trusted God, but we were still a little stressed. It's 30 years after Adam's event, and now we have Facebook. When Amelia went to surgery on Friday, May 20, I put a prayer request on FB. Within an hour there were over 100 'likes,' meaning at least that many people saw the request. There were over 50 'comments;' encouraging words and promises to pray. They were from many states and probably a dozen countries: Costa Rica, Hong Kong, Germany, Switzerland, Canada, Honduras, Guatemala...

Long story short: God heard your prayers. He healed our

daughter. Maybe He would have been gracious and merciful and healed Amelia without the prayers of His people, but why not obey Him? *"Is any among you sick? Let him call... for prayer... And the prayer of faith will save the sick, and the Lord will raise him up..."* (James 5:14, 15)

God answers prayer. He is an awesome God. Would I be this happy if God had chosen not to heal Amelia (or Adam)? No. Would I still think He is awesome? Yes. Would I still praise Him? *"Though He slay me, yet will I praise Him."* (Job 13:15)

(Oh, I did go back for my luggage 30 years ago.)

June - 2016

Howard Gray
1948 - 2016

I heard of Howard Gray at a Ramblin' Jack Elliot concert in the fatigued basement of one of the stately College of Wooster buildings in 1990. Neighbor Ed Schrock had tickets to hear this legendary folk singer and invited me to go along. We sat at tables with random folks and one of the 'randoms' at our table was Gary Hall, a singer. "You're the man who sings 'Howard Gray!'" Ed exclaimed. "Yes, that would be me," answered Gary.

And the story was told. Gary sang Howard's song. And I bought Gary's record (yes, that's how long ago it was – a record). And I began to sing the story of Howard Gray, a boy who got picked on in school and another boy who joined the mockers and then got a glimpse of Howard's tear-stained eyes looking right back at him.

The writer was Lee Domann, singing about his shame at joining the ones making fun of Howard. And he regrets that he never had the chance to ask forgiveness because Howard's family moved away soon after the incident.

I called Lee Domann soon after learning the song (1991?) to get permission to record it and to find out where to send the royalties. "Is that a true story?" I asked him on the phone. "Yes. I'm ashamed to say that it is." "Anything come of it?" I asked. "Interesting that you would ask," Lee said. "My father passed away last summer, and I went home to the funeral. As they lowered my dad's casket into the ground, I looked into the crowd through my tears... and right into the eyes of Howard Gray! He had come to my dad's funeral! I went over and stood beside him. He was looking down at the ground. I put my arm on his shoulder, and he said, 'I heard the song.' After an awkward pause, I said, 'Will you forgive me?' 'Yeah,' was his one-word answer.

"Twenty years of shame and guilt was lifted off of my shoulders that day. I consider myself fortunate that I was able to find Howard and make things right," said Lee. "Many folks never get the chance."

Several years later I called Howard and introduced myself. I told him that I sing the song about him. He sort of chuckled. He wasn't much of a conversationalist. Several years later, Lydia and I stopped in to visit him in Topeka, KS. We took his wife and him out for a meal. I saw that he would be easy to pick on. Unassuming, bashful, no self-image...

Howard and Lee Domann and I kept in touch by phone and a visit or two over the years. Several times I called Howard right during a concert to have him say hello to the crowd. He never said much. "Hi," was about all I could get him say. But it showed the people that he was a real person, just like the ones they were thinking of while I sang the song. Many of us can relate to Howard's experience.

Howard was not a roaring success by worldly standards. He was retired and on disability by the time I met him. I began to send him 'royalty checks.' I told him that every time I sang his song, I would pay him a royalty of $25.00. About once a month I sent him $100.00. If I didn't, he would call me.

On June 1 we put a royalty check in the mail for him. That night I got a call from his son. "Dad passed away today. He laid down to take a nap and died in his sleep."

Howard did not live an easy life. He didn't have a lot of victories. Lee Domann's song may have given him a little satisfaction that his life made a difference in other's lives. (It sure did!)

RIP, Howard Gray. Your story will live on.

"You've got to try a little kindness, show a little kindness, shine your light for everyone to see." – Glen Campbell

"Be kind, for everyone you meet is fighting a harder battle."
– Plato

"Kindness is a language which the deaf can hear, and the blind can see." – Mark Twain

"Do unto others as you would have them do unto you." – Jesus

July - 2016

A Totally Committed Life
IN CRAB ORCHARD PIKE, KY

Henry Clay Morrison was a Methodist preacher before he became president of Asbury College and founded Asbury Theological Seminary in 1923. This is his story of a remarkable woman in his first parish in Stanford, KY, around 1887.

> *When I got to Stanford, KY, as the new pastor, I stayed at a boarding house with a most delightful family. The Baptist pastor, Rev. John Bruce, a single man, was also boarding with the same family.*
>
> *When I inquired about the spiritual state of the community, Rev. Bruce said, "Well, it's none too good. We need a revival. But there is a wonderful woman down at the toll gate on the Crab Orchard Pike about a half mile out of town. Her name is Mary McAfee. She is a most remarkable Christian; a little peculiar in her views, but wonderfully filled with the Spirit. If we had more like her, the churches would be in much better condition. By the way, she is a member of your church."*

Rev. Mallory pastored the Presbyterian Church. He called to see me a few days after my arrival, a most delightful gentleman. He talked earnestly about the need of a revival in our town. By and by, he said, "Have you met Mary McAfee? She is a member of your church. She keeps the toll gate down on the Crab Orchard Pike, about a half a mile out of town. She has some queer notions, but she lives very close to her Lord."

Well, you may be sure I was becoming deeply interested in Sister McAfee, so I went down to see her. I found a very modest, little maiden woman who must have been past forty years of age. She told me a remarkable story of how she had received the baptism with the Holy Spirit in sanctifying power. How that after being bedridden for seven years she was miraculously healed, and that the Lord was graciously using her in the salvation of souls. I had never met anyone to whom Jesus seemed a more real, gracious, and present Savior. Tears trickled down my cheeks while she talked. I asked for an interest in her prayers and went away profoundly impressed.

We had a skeptic in the town; you always find one in a County Seat. I went up to his office and had a talk with him. He was a bit sour; he criticized the religious life of some of the men in the churches and was disposed to find fault. I was a bit embarrassed. But then he said, "There is a little woman, though, by the name of McAfee, who keeps the toll gate down on the Crab Orchard Pike about a half mile out of town. If I could get the kind of religion she has, I would like to have it."

I remembered that my Master had likened a consecrated, holy life to a "city set on a hill that could not be hid." When ministers visited me, I would take them down to the tollgate and ask Sister McAfee to tell her experience. Each one was deeply moved. She was never excited, never afraid. She was resting in the calm of full redemption and perfect love. Her education was limited, but her comprehension of scriptural truth was most remarkable and her thinking wonderfully clear. She prayed earnestly that I might be wholly consecrated, entirely saved from sin, and filled with the Holy Spirit. She was a power in our revivals. Everybody believed in her. Her testimonies were quiet and convincing. She walked with God. She breathed the spirit of prayer, forgiveness, and love, and people who came in contact with her longed to know more about Jesus.

A newspaper reporter went down and had a talk with her and published her testimony in the Louisville Courier-Journal. Rev. W. W. Hooper, down in Mississippi, read her testimony and traveled 600 miles(!) to Stanford to ask her about her experience and ask for her prayers. While there, he received the baptism with the Holy Spirit in sanctifying power. He returned to Mississippi to preach a full salvation in Christ received by faith.

It would take a case full of books to tell how the fire spread. Sinners were converted, preachers were sanctified, missionaries went out across the seas. Years passed. Little Mary's health failed, and she faded gradually. Then her saintly spirit, on wings of love and faith, rose to meet and dwell with her blessed Savior forevermore.

The good people of Stanford sent for me to say some words at her funeral. As I stood by the plain coffin and looked at her quiet, saintly face that seemed to tell of a soul that had entered into eternal rest, I hadn't a doubt but directly and indirectly 100,000 souls had been touched for good through the holy life and the testimony of a little maiden woman who kept the toll gate on the Crab Orchard Pike about a half mile out of town near Stanford, KY.

THIS ARTICLE FROM THE PENTECOSTAL HERALD, NOV/DEC 1988

August - 2016

Little Boy Blue
OR...TRY A LITTLE KINDNESS

I sang a few songs, including "Howard Gray," at the Belmont Prison Chapel service on Sunday, and then I invited the volunteers who came with me to introduce themselves and share whatever God laid on their hearts. Here is what Atlee Mast shared:

That song, "Howard Gray," sparked a memory. I remember a boy in my third-grade class who was very timid; even backward. He was a new kid. He didn't know any of us. His name was Jr. He got picked on unmercifully by the students. I remember kids kicking and punching him and laughing.

One day Jr. came to school with his shirt inside out. The teacher asked about his shirt. He didn't answer. (It was probably dirty.) She came back to his desk and asked, and again Jr. didn't answer. He just sat there. She slapped him on the right cheek. Then with her other hand, she slapped him on his left cheek. Then, back and forth in rapid fire, she slapped him with her left hand and then her right hand (a third grader!). Left, right, left, right... His cheeks were bright red from the abuse. Jr. didn't cry. He didn't say a word. Just sat there.

One day in the boy's restroom, Jr. got kicked and punched and shoved up against the wall as the boys pulled his long hair and banged his head against the wall. I saw all of this, and like the song, "Howard Gray," I did nothing. I just stood there and watched. Out in the hallway, I remember asking Jr., "Do you like school?" (I don't know why I asked that.) "Not much," he mumbled. I guess that was my meager attempt to befriend him.

Jr. was only at my school for one year. I guess he went back to the Amish school. I never saw him again. Then in 1987, I read a story in Reader's Digest en-

titled, "Little Boy Blue." The frozen body of a little boy in blue pajamas was found in a ditch near Chester, NE on Christmas Eve, 1985. No one knew who he was or where he came from or what had happened to him. The community came together and gave the boy a funeral. They buried him under the name Matthew, which means "gift of God," and referred to him as "Little Boy Blue," because of his blue pajamas. "The church was completely packed, and nobody had any idea who this child was," said Thayer Co. Attorney Daniel Werner.

Two years after the article, it was discovered that Little Boy Blue was nine-year-old Daniel, son of Eli Stutzman, Jr., my third-grade classmate! Jr. (Eli) grew up to live a life of deception, crime, homosexuality, and eventually murder. He died a suicide after 13 years in prison.

What if I would have befriended Jr.? What if I would have stuck up for him? What if I have done something to defend this poor little backward Amish boy? I wonder how different his life and the lives of his wife and child and others might have been? If...

I sang this song after singing "Howard Gray" (and before Atlee's story of Jr.):

You've got to try a little kindness, show a little kindness, and shine your light for everyone to see.

And if you try a little kindness, then you'll overlook the blindness

Of the narrow-minded people on the narrow-minded street."

I believe that we are all responsible for our actions, no matter what our background is. Grow up! Be responsible! We make our own choices. BUT, I have to wonder if God will hold that third-grade teacher partly responsible for the death of an innocent nine-year-old boy, abandoned in a ditch.

"Be ye kind to one another, tenderhearted, forgiving one another, even as God for Christ's sake has forgiven you." (Eph. 4:32)

"Kindness is a language that the blind can see, and the deaf can hear." – Mark Twain

October - 2016

I Come From a Long Line of Dead People
I KNOW WHO I AM

Genealogy is not fatal... but it is a grave disease.

Several miles from where I grew up, and about the same distance from where I now live, there is a flow of water beside State Route 83 known as Butler's Spring. It's a couple of miles north of Holmesville and most of my life, if you looked real close (and quick) as you drove by, you could notice a small white cross a few feet up the hill from the spring. Today, you'll see a plaque.

On May 30, 1782, a group of soldiers from Crawford's Expedition Against Sandusky camped there. One of them became ill and died. Twenty-one year old Philip Smith helped dig the grave with his tomahawk. The other soldiers used their tomahawks to build a coffin from barrel staves [puncheons].

Four days later they fought in the ill-fated Battle of Sandusky, where they were routed by the Indians when the British showed up from Detroit to reinforce them. Philip Smith ran for his life. He was shot in the elbow in a shootout with an Indian and was lost without food, horse, or weapon for over a week while he tried to find his way back home. He made it safely to Mingo Bottom (Steubenville) ten days later. Colonel Crawford was captured and tortured to death as revenge for the massacre of the innocent Moravian Indians, which had taken place just two months before in the village of Gnadenhutten.

The reason I mention this bit of local history is that in my recent genealogy search I discovered that Philip, the gravedigger, is my fourth great-grandfather! He fought with Colonel Crawford! He knew Simon Girty! He was a pioneer settler of Ohio!* I have known about that spring and the legend of a soldier buried there since I was a boy, and now I learn that I have a family connection to the soldier who died there 234 years ago, five miles from where I was born. A connection to history!

My family doesn't seem to care about family history. When I visited the village of Königsbach in Baden, Germany, where great-great-grandfather Adam Schmid was born, I brought home a book of the village and Schmid relatives to show my Dad. He yawned. The rest of the family showed similar excitement. I'm guessing that a good percentage of you who are reading this are asking the same question my family seems to ask about genealogy: "So what?!"

I ask that myself: Why am I so anxious to find out who my ancestors were? Who cares? What difference does it make? I can answer you in three words: "I don't know." But I remember the feeling I got the first time I gazed at the gravestone of my great-great grandparents. "I am somebody. I came from somewhere. I belong." Did those feelings have validity? I just know that's what I felt.

Rev. Alvin Kanagy once preached on genealogy and made this statement: "The people who **know** who they are, **where** they came from, and **where** they belong are usually the most stable citizens in any given community." Right now I'm feeling real stable.

Of course, the important thing is not **who** you are and **where** you came from, but **Whose** you are and **where** you are going. I plan to stop at the battle memorial the next time I go through Upper Sandusky, where great-grandpa got routed by the Delaware, Wyandot, and Shawnee. I have been to great-great-grandpa Adam's hometown in Germany. I will continue to be curious about my ancestors and see what I can learn. But more than that; I am a child of the King. And if you want to check out my genealogy there, look at Matthew 1:1-16. Verse 16 doesn't say it, but that's where I fit in: *"...Jacob the father of Joseph, the husband of Mary, of whom was born Jesus,* *who is the Christ." [and is a brother (and Savior) of John Schmid.]* That's my Brother! (and Savior). God is my Father. I am somebody! Talk about stable!

"...command certain men not to... devote themselves to... endless genealogies..." (I Tim. 1:4) (Mine aren't endless.)

* FROM *A HISTORICAL ACCOUNT OF THE EXPEDITION AGAINST SANDUSKY IN 1782* BY C.W. BUTTERFIELD, 1873 PP. 86,126,166,168

November - 2016

Good Tidings of Great Joy...

No matter where you stand politically, you may have noticed in the last few months that the mainstream media has not been very accurate in their attempt at prophecy. They haven't even done a very good job of simply reporting the news. In the recent presidential election, they reported that Donald Trump would not run. Then they reported that he would not last two weeks. Then they gave him two months. Then they reported that he was a fraud. He's a decoy, just in the race to help his old friend Hillary. He would not win the Republican primary. When he did become the Republican nominee, they said he had no chance to win the presidency. "You watch; he's going to drop out." And up to the last hour, rather than *report* news, they continued to *prophesy* the outcome of the election. They had a perfect record: They didn't get one thing right! The news was wrong. The polls were wrong. The politicians were wrong. The man who 'had no chance' won in a landslide.

So.... now that I have lost all trust in the news media, what can I believe? Who can I believe? Where can I go for accurate news? At least I think I can believe the sports page. I actually listened to the Ohio State/Michigan game, so I can testify that they got that news report right. But what about anything political? What about editorial opinion? What about the front page?

"When the foundations are destroyed, what can the righteous do?" (Psalm 11:3)

WHAT CAN WE BELIEVE?

Friends, I have good news for you! You can believe the Bible. It is profitable for doctrine, for reproof, for correction, for instruction in righteousness. And it contains Good News:

"Fear not! I bring you good tidings [news] of great joy... For there is born to you this day in the city of David a Savior, who is Christ the Lord." (Luke 2:10)

Not only is the announcement of the birth of Christ real news that you can believe, but it is also the best news that has ever been reported on planet Earth! It's 2,000 years old, to be sure, but it is also the latest, freshest news today! And it wasn't the usual Israeli mainstream media who reported this amazing event... it was angels, sent by God! And it is recorded in the most reliable, best selling book in history: the Bible.

"With the angelic host proclaim, Christ is born in Bethlehem... Hark! The herald angels sing!"

Christmas is a reminder of the wonderful news that God came to us. "Immanuel" – God with us. Christmas reminds us to trust not in horses and chariots (government; politicians) but to trust in the Baby who was born in a lowly stable just a few miles from the palace of the most powerful, ruthless, wealthy, influential politician in the region, Herod the Great. Who would have thought at the time that 2,000 years later the little Baby would still be known and worshiped, but the only memory we have of the politician Herod is that he killed the babies?

Who can you believe? Jesus. What can you believe? His book. It's reliable. It's good news.

He rules the world with truth and grace, and He makes the nations prove the glories of His righteousness and wonders of His love... Joy to the world!

What good news! You can believe it!

B.I.B.L.E.
Basic Instructions Before Leaving Earth

December - 2016

ORDER MORE COPIES OF THIS BOOK AT:

www.jpvpress.com